AMERICAN INDIANS AND
THE AMERICAN DREAM

AMERICAN
Policies, Place,
INDIANS AND
and Property
THE AMERICAN
in Minnesota
DREAM

KASEY R. KEELER

University of Minnesota Press | Minneapolis | London

Support for this book was provided by the University of Wisconsin–Madison Office of the Vice Chancellor for Research and Graduate Education with funding from the Wisconsin Alumni Research Foundation.

Portions of chapter 3 are adapted from "Putting People Where They Belong: American Indian Housing Policy in the Mid-Twentieth Century," *NAIS: Journal of the Native American and Indigenous Studies Association* 3, no. 2 (2016): 70–104, https://doi.org/10.5749/natiindistudj.3.2.0070.

Published by the University of Minnesota Press
111 Third Avenue South, Suite 290
Minneapolis, MN 55401–2520
http://www.upress.umn.edu

ISBN 978-1-5179-0924-6 (hc)
ISBN 978-1-5179-0925-3 (pb)

A Cataloging-in-Publication record for this book is available from the Library of Congress.

Printed in the United States of America on acid-free paper

The University of Minnesota is an equal-opportunity educator and employer.

For Violet
In memory of Kyle

CONTENTS

ABBREVIATIONS

AIM	American Indian Movement
BIA	Bureau of Indian Affairs
FDIC	Federal Deposit Insurance Corporation
FHA	Federal Housing Administration
FSLIC	Federal Savings and Loan Insurance Corporation
HIP	Housing Improvement Program
HOLC	Home Owners' Loan Corporation
HUD	Department of Housing and Urban Development
ICA	Indian Citizenship Act
IHLGP	Indian Home Loan Guarantee Program
IHS	Indian Health Service
IPUMS	Integrated Public Use Microdata Series
IRA	Indian Reorganization Act
JOM	Johnson-O'Malley Act
MCTFC	Minnesota Chippewa Tribe Finance Corporation
MPC	Minnesota Population Center
NAHASDA	Native American Housing Assistance and Self-Determination Act
NAIS	Native American and Indigenous studies
ONAP	Office of Native American Programs
OYOH	Own Your Own Home
PUMA	Public Use Microdata Area
SEC	Securities and Exchange Commission
VA	Veterans Affairs

Introduction

SUBURBAN INDIANS
FAMILY, IDENTITY, AND HOMEOWNERSHIP

> We lived in the suburbs, but we visited Oklahoma at least once and often twice a year, and I sometimes spent the whole summer in Lawton, where my grandparents lived, or on the farm where my white grandparents lived.
>
> —PAUL CHAAT SMITH, *Everything You Know about Indians Is Wrong*

> When Americans discuss the good life, they still speak about their hopes and fears in terms of buying houses. Homeownership has symbolized a family's social status ever since developers promoted it as an alternative to wasting money on rent.
>
> —DOLORES HAYDEN, *Redesigning the American Dream: Gender, Housing, and Family Life*

GROWING UP IN THE 1980s, I have vivid memories of my family driving to Minneapolis to see the doctor and the dentist at the Indian Health Board clinic, located only a few blocks off Bloomington Avenue in South Minneapolis. Just as today, I can still see the Native people on sidewalks and at the park, perhaps on their way to the Indian Center just around the corner, as we took the Hiawatha Avenue exit and passed the Little Earth housing complex. I can still remember the name of the kindly older woman who worked at the front desk of the Indian clinic, the woman who always cheerfully greeted us as we stepped off the elevator—Ramona. During my childhood, I assumed everyone who lived in our

1

suburban community, a twenty-five-minute drive north of Minneapolis, had to travel to the city to see the doctor or dentist. I do not think I realized it at the time, but we were going to the "Indian clinic," and this, in fact, was a marker of identity—both race and class.

Another fond memory of my childhood is visiting my maternal grandmother, who lived in the small southeastern Oklahoma town of Hugo, every summer. These visits occasionally coincided with family reunions near Shawnee, Oklahoma—where the Citizen Potawatomi Nation is headquartered. Each visit to my grandma's entailed learning bits and pieces of my family history, including why all my mother's family lived in California or Oklahoma, not Minnesota, and why my grandmother and most of her siblings had lived in California and Oklahoma. When I was young, I also assumed most people's grandparents, and aunts and uncles, lived far away and were only visited in the summer, much like mine. It was not until the summer after my freshman year of high school that I remember first visiting the reservation community in east-central California where my mother was born and raised, along with her two siblings, and where they each reside today, my reservation community too. The Tuolumne Band of Me-Wuk Indians is a small, federally recognized tribal nation located in the foothills of the Sierra Nevadas; their rancheria (or reservation) is not far from Yosemite, a site of gold-rush era violence. Through old photographs and stories, I know I had visited long before, as a toddler, over a decade prior. But this was a life I did not know. I was raised in suburban Minneapolis, a suburban Indian.

During the mid-1980s, Coon Rapids, Minnesota, remained a predominately white community. Immediately adjacent to the Mississippi River, it was still a developing and rapidly changing suburban community, with an increasing amount of single-family new home construction. In 1987, only a few years after I was born, my family moved to Coon Rapids, just twenty minutes north of Minneapolis, chosen for its convenience to the city, where my father worked for the railroad, and for its affordability. Before I was born, my parents, neither of whom is from Minnesota, had lived a short time in Minnesota but made the difficult decision to move to Oklahoma, near my maternal grandmother, when my dad was laid off during the Reagan years and the economic downturn of the early 1980s. After several years in Oklahoma—where we had family ties, the cost of living was significantly cheaper, and my parents

Figure 1. Photograph of the author, her mother, cousin, grandmother, cousin, and sister [*left to right*] at their family's reservation, Tuolumne Me-Wuk Rancheria, in the mid-1980s. Courtesy of author.

were able to secure employment—we briefly moved to Aberdeen, South Dakota. Here my dad was able to secure a better-paying job before we eventually returned to Minnesota when he was finally called back to his employment with the railroad in Minneapolis. As a young, working-class family, with both of my parents working blue-collar jobs, we lived in an apartment complex for a brief time before my parents were able to purchase a lot in a new subdivision and build a home. My sister and I, both in the early years of elementary school, were simultaneously enrolled in the local school district as well as the district's Indian Education Program. As I grew from toddler to teen and learned over the years, this program, exclusively for American Indian students in the suburban district, would be influential in my perceptions of self, how others perceived me, and how I eventually found my way to both college and graduate school. It would be through this institution, the Anoka-Hennepin Indian Education Program, that I would begin to interrogate, historicize, and analyze the complexity of what it means to be a suburban Indian and how access to the suburbs, based on centuries of federal Indian policy and housing policy, remains guarded and off-limits for many American Indian people.

I spent the bulk of my childhood and adolescence in Coon Rapids. As a first-generation college student, I returned home to Coon Rapids after completing my bachelor's degree, when I began the process to land my first real job. In the fall of 2005, I was hired by the Anoka-Hennepin Indian Education Program to serve as an academic adviser. As a liaison between Native students, their parents, and schools, I worked with approximately 150 American Indian youths in kindergarten through grade twelve. With nearly forty thousand students, Anoka-Hennepin remains Minnesota's largest school district. At the time of my employment, the district served over five hundred Native students across all grades. Notably, this was the exact same Indian Education Program I had participated in as I made my way from kindergarten through twelfth grade when I was enrolled as a student in the district. The Anoka-Hennepin Indian Education Program, which first began serving students during the 1973–1974 academic year, works to "encourage and inspire the academic achievement, social and emotional development, and cultural awareness of [the district's] American Indian students."[1] To be eligible for services, each student must be an enrolled member of a federally recognized tribe or have a parent or grandparent who is an enrolled member of a federally recognized tribe.[2] As a federally funded program, with additional state and local support, the Indian Education Program also relies on the Johnson-O'Malley Act, passed in 1934, for supplementary funding, which is contingent on the number of Native students enrolled in the program who meet specific blood quantum criteria.[3]

My experience, as a Native woman who was raised in a predominately white suburb and as an educator working with Native youth in a predominately white suburban school district, forced me to reconcile what it means to be a Native person who lives in a suburb, as well as ask additional questions about who has access to suburban living. As a school district employee, I regularly faced difficult questions, both from the general public and from district staff, about the Indian Education Program. These inquiries, at times accusations, were almost always about the program's purposes, the "missed learning time" when Native students left their regular classes to participate in cultural programs and receive academic support, how and why the program was funded, how it was perceived as an "entitlement" program, and why only certain students were eligible. I was forced to defend the very students I worked with, and in many ways I had to defend myself. I regularly faced seemingly ignorant and hurtful comments based on the students' (assumed) blood quantum and Native identity, (assumed) need for services or lack thereof, and (assumed) entitlement. In time, I too began to question what it means to be a suburban Indian. Specifically, I wondered where the suburban Indians I worked with and interacted with every day were from, both regionally and tribally. How long have Indian people lived in the suburbs, and why did they come here—as if we are somehow so different from everyone else who lives in a suburb? Why does there seem to be such a disconnect between *Indian* and *suburb*? Eventually I began to grapple with my own history—as a suburban Indian, distanced from my home reservation and having never lived there—and the struggles I saw many of the students I worked with face, many with few ties to a reservation community and most under pressure to identify in certain ways. I wondered what the students' connection to a larger (i.e., more visible) Indian community was, if any. After all, I lived in Minnesota, an Ojibwe and Dakota place, but I am an enrolled member of the Tuolumne Me-Wuk (California) and a direct descendant of the Citizen Potawatomi Nation (Oklahoma). Why are we seemingly invisible? What types of racism and discrimination do Indians face as suburbanites? What is the relationship between suburban Indians and those on reservations or those who live in urban centers? Finally, I began to think more broadly about suburban Indians and place. Though these places have become increasingly recognized as contemporary suburbs, certainly Indian people lived in these areas before the extensive development and suburbanization of the twentieth century. What role did Indian people play in mid- to late twentieth-century suburbanization? How many Indians actually live(d) in suburbs? How are suburban Indians different from urban or reservation Indians and why? I thought about these and other questions on a nearly daily basis as I advised and learned from over 150 suburban Indians in the Indian Education Program for the Anoka-Hennepin School District. My experiences in suburban Minneapolis gave way to the scholarship set forth in this book. This story, my family story, is not unlike so many other Native peoples, as we have long worked to navigate housing, access to space, identity, and belonging.

Suburban Indians

American Indian suburbanization is not new; indeed, suburbs are historically Indian places. As suburbanization and mass home development have expanded, so has the number of American Indian people who call these distinct residential places home. In fact, today the majority of all American Indian people live outside of rural, reservation environments and instead reside in metropolitan areas. Increasingly, these American Indian people live in suburbs, outside the urban core. Yet few scholars or community members recognize this growing population, nor has attention been paid to the entanglement of federal Indian policy and federal housing policy that has led to the creation of such a racialized residential demographic.[4] Indeed, American Indian suburbanization must be observed as a direct result of federal housing policies that have limited and dictated where American Indians can live since at least the early nineteenth century when American Indians were actively removed and confined to reservations. This notion is expounded on by Canadian geographer Owen Toews; he reminds us of the immense role "that state power has consistently played in relation to capitalist development and settlement on Turtle Island."[5]

According to the 2010 U.S. Census, 20 percent of all individuals who identified as single-race American Indian in the state of Minnesota lived in a suburb of the Twin Cities; of those who identified as American Indian in conjunction with one or more races, 38 percent lived in a suburb of Minneapolis or Saint Paul. Despite federal Indian policies and housing policies that sought first to confine Indian people to reservations and eventually to relocate them to urban areas, today's growing suburban American Indian population underscores the resiliency and survivance of American Indian people.[6] In this way, I emphasize the many American Indian people, though largely ignored in processes of suburbanization and left out of policies that promoted homeownership, who played an active role in the growth and development of suburbs. Through this work, I recognize and establish a new and important category of American Indian identity: the suburban Indian. This is something no other scholarship in Native American and Indigenous studies (NAIS) does. Suburban Indians challenge conceptions about place-based identities and more accurately represent the diversity of American Indian people across the United States, signaling a move beyond dated reservation and urban Indian binaries.

American Indians and the American Dream: Policies, Place, and Property in Minnesota is an interdisciplinary, historical study that answers key questions about American Indian suburbanization and, more specifically, the codependent relationship that exists between federal Indian policies and federal housing policies that shaped suburbanization and access (or lack thereof) to suburbs for American Indian people. Federal Indian policy is at the very center of suburbanization, as suburbanization by necessity requires American Indian dispossession, both historic and contemporary. Throughout this book I critically think about the histories of place, what placemaking has looked like and can look like, and the movement of Indian people. I offer a critique of both federal Indian and federal housing policies as I build a framework that requires and advances a rethinking of access to suburban spaces. The processes of suburbanization offer a method, for scholars in NAIS and beyond, to examine land use, complicated by entanglements of family and state, and how identity is embedded in place and property. Suburbs offer a lens to view housing and homeownership for American Indian people that is markedly different from on-reservation housing. By historicizing suburbanization in Minnesota, I bring a new and unique perspective to the legacy of federal Indian and federal housing policies that have rendered today's suburban Indians largely invisible. I consider the following policies and temporal moments as key to my analysis: the U.S.–Dakota War and the Homestead Act; New Deal–era housing programs and the Indian Reorganization Act; the GI Bill and the Indian Relocation Program; the establishment of Indian housing programs under the Department of Housing and Urban Development and the creation of the Little Earth housing complex; and the limits to federal funding for American Indian homeownership through the Section 184 Indian Home Loan Guarantee Program during the home construction boom of the early 2000s.

These broad policy areas, American Indians and housing, are not mutually exclusive. Rather, the former is, by design, intent, and execution, inclusive of American Indians while the latter is deliberately and intentionally exclusive of American Indians. By examining federal Indian policy alongside federal housing policy, I highlight tensions that exist between and across federal agencies, specifically in terms of who policies are designed and intended for, the ways in which federal money is allocated and spent on differing (racialized) groups, and how space and place (for example, suburbs and reservations) have become racialized through policy. Federal housing policy has not been about American Indians and federal Indian policy has not been about access to housing. Therefore, by juxtaposing federal Indian and federal housing policy, I draw attention to the frictions that exist between federal, state, local, and tribal governments. It is precisely this focus that allows me to counter common narratives of suburbia and U.S. suburbanization that originated almost exclusively in the World War II era and that regularly ignore the Indian places and the American Indian people who have long called these (suburban) spaces home—and continue to do so, despite efforts to remove, contain, and regulate. Therefore, I resist and push back on urban histories that center mid-twentieth-century housing and racialization, as these processes have long been at play, and instead link nineteenth-century treaty-making to this longer legacy.[7] Indeed, the land on which suburbs have been built has long been contested land—land that was violently taken from tribal nations and Native communities through treaties and the long history of settler colonialism. This recentering and historicizing allows us to think more critically about larger federal policies over time.

Throughout the book, I consider the ways American Indian people in suburbs have been rendered invisible through the application of federal housing policies that uphold settler colonialism.[8] To counter this, I point to the active role American Indian people play and have played in the development and growth of suburbs despite a long history of policies that often worked against them. Here I build on J. Kēhaulani Kauanui's use of the term *enduring indigeneity*, recognizing that American Indian people did not simply move out of the way of settler development, rather they engaged with, adapted to, and resisted continuous displacement.[9] The assumed absence, or invisibility, of American Indians from suburbs is only made legible when we consider both the formal and informal actions of American Indian individuals, families, communities, and organizations that have worked to (re)claim, (re)create, and (re)make space in suburbs.[10] In this way, we must frame American Indians as agents of placemaking, as agents of homemaking and homeownership, and as agents of change, not as bystanders to it. Much like Paige Raibmon demonstrates, American Indians of the Pacific Northwest engaged with colonialism and settler colonialism on their own terms, which is reflected in their identity and agency; the same holds true for suburban Indians.[11]

American Indians and the American Dream pays particular attention to the migration and movements of suburban Indians who returned to and arrived in metropolitan areas during the twentieth and twenty-first centuries. As historians Chantal Norrgard and Brenda Child demonstrate, though the historical migrations of Indian people, based on seasonal rounds, have been well documented, changes in the labor market during the twentieth century forced American Indian people to adapt.[12] I build on the work of Norrgard and Child to focus on more recent twentieth-century migration patterns of Indian people that continued to hinge on economic livelihood and sustainability. Though migrations and movements of Indian people are often self-propelled, it was often powerful federal Indian policies that spurred Indian peoples' movements during the late nineteenth century and into the twentieth century. In fact, as historian of American Indian urbanization Douglas K. Miller argues, Native people worked to take advantage of federal Indian policies in ways that would benefit them.[13]

Yet in many ways federal housing policy has continued to dictate where Indian people live into the twenty-first century. While federal housing policies stimulated the growth and development of contemporary suburbs as we recognize them today, shifts in federal Indian policies provided an incentive for Indian people to leave reservations for metropolitan areas. Once in cities, American Indian people faced limited housing options and were often excluded from housing programs and residential areas due to racism and bureaucratic red tape.[14] As federal Indian and federal housing policies coalesced in the mid-twentieth century, suburbs became white and the opportunity for envisioning suburban Indians was rapidly closed. Despite this public memory and erasure, today's suburban Indians are remarkable, as they overcame significant barriers to get where they are now, further emphasizing the resiliency of Native people who have remained and returned to Indigenous places—places policy has long excluded them from.

By reframing American Indians as active agents of change, we are better able to challenge long-engrained narratives that presume suburbs are non-Indigenous places where Native people do not belong, as well as the fallacy of white, heteronormative, middle-class suburbs. Suburban Indians allow us to interrogate the ways whiteness, assimilation, and belonging unfold in suburbs. Thus, when proper attention is given, we can see the many ways American Indian people challenge the multiple modes of Native erasure that have occurred over time through processes of non-Native placemaking: specifically, the settler colonial (re)naming of cities and towns, the (re)naming of lakes, rivers, and streams, and the establishment and naming of parks and streets during the twentieth century across suburbs. It is precisely these visible and declarative inscriptions, inherent to the processes of settler colonialism, that continue to render American Indians as invisible and as not belonging in suburbs, something that has occurred for far too long. As this book demonstrates, Native people have worked to affirm their presence in suburban spaces, places that have long Indigenous histories, as suburbs are inherently Indian places. In this way, Native people challenge and disrupt who the American Dream is for, what it can look like, and what it means.

The American Dream

American Indian peoples' access to suburbs and homeownership, the heart of this book, highlights the contradictions and limits of the American Dream. Popularized during the Great Depression in James Truslow Adams's 1931 *The Epic of America,* the concept of the American Dream has long guided Americans' preoccupation with land and property ownership. However, in revisiting Adams's words, perhaps we have lost sight of what the American Dream can be. Adams writes, "[The] very foundation of the American dream of a better and richer life for all is that all, in varying degrees, shall be capable of wanting to share in it. It can never be wrought into a reality by cheap people or by 'keeping up with the Joneses.' . . . If we are to make the dream come true, we must all work together, no longer to build bigger, but to build better."[15]

The American Dream has become deeply ingrained in the American psyche, and its pervasiveness spans genres and generations. The American Dream, often synonymous with suburbanization, has been bolstered by various levels of government and the real estate industry as it "is continually (re)produced and reconstituted to maintain consumer demand and support the profitable investment of capital in the built environment."[16] Today, the American Dream has become a constant goal, ever-present, and seemingly attainable if you simply work hard enough. Yet there exists a paradox in the American Dream. The American Dream, understood as land- and homeownership, by necessity, and much like suburbanization, requires the dispossession of American Indian people, past and present.

It is this last component of the American Dream—land—that deserves additional attention. Kenneth Jackson, the seminal scholar on American suburbanization, describes the presumed inherent desirability of the American Dream as follows: "[Whether] well-born or an indentured servant, practically everyone set himself quickly to the task of organizing the landscape into private parcels and somehow procuring a share of the division. The American dream was in large part land. . . . Large land holdings became a prerequisite for social acceptance."[17] Yet the American Dream, commonly thought of as a yard to call your own, simply does not and cannot exist without the dispossession, removal, and relocation of American Indian people away from their homelands. Land and property, as the backbone of the American Dream, have come to signify what it means to be an American. Yet, virtually absent from discussions and narratives of the American Dream are American Indian people and American Indian history. In Jackson's widely read and path-breaking *Crabgrass Frontier,* he makes only a brief (yet problematic) mention of American Indians.

> The original Americans—called Indians by the Europeans—did not join the rush. Unfamiliar with the concept of permanent land ownership, they believed instead that the soil, like the wind, the rain, and the sun, would be used, but not possessed. The typical Indian assumption was that each human was as much a passer-by on the land as the wild creatures were passers-by to him, and that no person had any more right to a particular habitat than any other person or any other living thing. This notion of land as social

resource was swept aside, however, partly because Indian ways were held in contempt, partly because of the vastness of the national domain, and partly because the harmful effects of individual ownership were not apparent for generations.

Although the European immigrants appropriated Indian lands without any moral or financial niceties, the colonists did agree with the original Americans that meadows and fields should serve a useful rather than an ornamental purpose. In rural areas, this meant that the value of a parcel was a function of the amount of corn or potatoes it would yield or the number and size of farm animals it would nourish. In cities, value was determined by the number and importance of the shops and houses that could be fitted on the lot. In both scenarios, land was thought of primarily as economically productive.[18]

Not only does Jackson dangerously diminish the capacity of Native people to understand land and property rights, thereby equating them to animals, he naturalizes settler colonialism. The American Dream can only exist through our failure to recognize and account for the violent dispossession, theft, and erasure of Native bodies from these geographies. In fact, as other scholars point out, today's American Dream relies on the maintenance of the fear of a racialized other.[19] In this way, the American Dream has become increasingly exclusionary, available and attainable for some, but certainly not for all.[20]

Importantly, and beyond discussions of land, the American Dream has become inherently linked to homeownership. As scholars argue, and as I discuss throughout the ensuing text, though the linkages between homeownership and the American Dream have grown increasingly clear, we must not diminish the role of the federal government and business and industry in promoting homeownership.[21] Despite recent economic setbacks (the Great Recession and job loss due to Covid-19), homeownership has remained a goal of most Americans. As recently as 2014 and 2017, surveys conducted by the National Association of Realtors and Fannie Mae have demonstrated that 90 percent and 86 percent (respectively) of those surveyed found homeownership desirable in the future.[22] A careful look at these numbers reveals the ways capitalism, as articulated and measured through the housing industry (including developers, builders, and realtors, etc.), largely influences the way many think about homeownership, and the American Dream, despite economic downturns and the increasing financial costs of homeownership. In fact, capitalism and suburban consumption cannot be separated.[23] As Dolores Hayden shows, homeownership has become a seemingly natural evolution of capitalism linked to such other American ideals as freedom, industriousness, individualism, and religion, much of which can be traced to early nineteenth-century Jefferson-era virtues of land, individual property, and gender roles.[24]

Over time, homeownership has come to be reflected in citizenship —what it means to be a good citizen and who has access to citizenship (read as land, property, and homeownership). As a result of colonization and settler colonialism, American Indian peoples' access to land, property, and homeownership, and thus the American Dream, has always been regulated, managed, and contained. The limited ability of Native people to access suburban homeownership requires us to consider the ways in which the American Dream differs for American Indians and the ways American Indians have carved a sort of paradox out of the American Dream and all that it entails. Throughout this text, I seek to push readers to consider the colonial, dispossessive, and exclusionary nature the fulfillment of the American Dream requires and the ways Indigeneity can unsettle the American Dream. It is this messiness and discomfort with the American Dream that so few members of our society, including scholars, engage with. It is important that we consider the limits of the American Dream and what the American Dream means for American Indian people—to own property, to own land, and to hold power through property.

Centering Suburbs

This book, with an important and new focus on American Indian suburbanization, housing, and homeownership, makes significant contributions to Native American and Indigenous studies scholarship. While there has been growth in critical scholarship on alternative and more nuanced narratives of American Indian urbanization by such scholars as Nicholas Rosenthal and James B. LaGrand, who center Indian people in Los Angeles and Chicago (respectively), my research builds out from a geographic urban core.[25] In particular, this book complicates histories of American Indian urbanization by pushing against geographic boundaries to be inclusive of a substantial suburban American Indian population. Simultaneously, I look to Coll Thrush's *Native Seattle* to emphasize the long, complex, interwoven Indigenous histories, and presence, across suburban places that predate settler arrival.[26] Indeed, suburbs are inherently Indian places. By focusing on geographic locations outside the urban core, in this case Minneapolis and Saint Paul, my work accounts for the lived realities of geographically diverse Native people, past and present. In this way, I examine not only the ways federal Indian and federal housing policies have shaped suburbs but also the ways American Indian peoples have accessed suburbs. In doing so, I rescript those very suburbs as "home" to Native people in a more historic sense that accounts for settler colonial dispossession. Thus, rather than focus on the Twin Cities as a settler colonial space remade by non-Native bodies, I emphasize the power of Indigenous place and renewed potential for Indigenous placemaking.

By centering suburbs and American Indian peoples' experiences accessing housing and homeownership, I rely on the work of scholars who have increasingly sought to theorize and examine homeownership for people of color. In particular, the work of Jody Agius Vallejo, Leonard S. Rubinowitz and James E. Rosenbaum, Keeanga-Yamahtta Taylor, and Wendy Cheng has contributed to the rich body of knowledge that has begun to break down whitewashed narratives of suburbanization and homeownership by bringing Black, Brown, and immigrant voices to the table.[27] While suburbanization and homeownership are distinct categories of analysis, the work of these scholars, and others, is crucial to telling a critical and more accurate version of history while also highlighting the contemporary barriers to accessing homeownership for Black, Brown, and immigrant families today. As we know, homeownership is a very direct corollary to improved educational outcomes, employment opportunities, and eventually, the ability to generate generational wealth, as I discuss in chapter 5.

From the beginning of this book to the end, I continuously grapple with the structure of settler colonialism. By recognizing the ever-present waves of settler colonialism, as Owen Toews describes in his analysis of Winnipeg, I seek to remind readers that dispossession is constantly occurring around us, in policy and in action, and that suburbanization was a well-crafted and deliberate set of processes meant to exclude.[28] Similarly, it is important to link contemporary policies to a longer history of settler colonialism, recognizing the scaffolding that occurs over time, making it difficult for many to recognize the direct consequences of land theft that are felt today as a result of actions that occurred during nineteenth-century treaty-making. In linking this interdisciplinary work, I am indebted to those, like J. Kēhaulani Kauanui, who have provided a theoretical framework for understanding American Indians in suburbs.[29] It is also my responsibility to call on others who write about suburbs and housing to include the voices and histories of Native people.

Throughout *American Indians and the American Dream,* I maintain a focus specifically on the suburbs of Minneapolis and Saint Paul—or, rather, the larger Twin Cities region—as a microcosm to examine American Indian peoples' access to suburbs and homeownership. While there is a long history of suburbanization across the United States and across the globe (specifically Europe), my focus remains on the development and evolution of suburbs since the second half of the nineteenth century, with particular attention given to the second half of the twentieth century. Suburbs have largely been imagined as places outside the urban core, places of open green space, available land, personal property, and single-family dwellings. Increasingly, suburbs have come to be places of respite for those who travel to the city for work or leisure, as places of marked economic distinction (as opposed to urban rentals and older and cheaper rural homes), and as sites of gendered domesticity.[30] By centering my analysis on suburbs, I move beyond multiple binaries, including the reservation/urban binary that continues to limit other possibilities for American Indian peoples.

Methods and Structure

All the way through *American Indians and the American Dream,* I maintain a focus on Minnesota. The suburbs that surround Minneapolis and Saint Paul provide an interesting and important site of analysis for suburban Indians and the multiple processes of suburbanization. First, Minnesota is the traditional homelands of Dakota and Ojibwe people with eleven federally recognized tribal nations across the state, each with a designated reservation land base held in trust by the federal government.

These reservations are located throughout the state, with the seven Ojibwe reservation communities located in the northern half of the state and the four Dakota reservation communities located in the southern third of the state.[31] Second, and crucial to my examination of suburban space and placemaking, is the Shakopee Mdewakanton Sioux Community, located within Scott County (thus within the seven-county metro area) and the Prairie Island Indian Community (located just outside the seven-county metro area in Goodhue County). Third, the urban cores of Minneapolis and Saint Paul are home to a large, well-established, recognizable, and relatively visible urban Indian population. This urban Indian community garnered national attention during the 1950s Indian Relocation Program and later during the 1970s when the American Indian Movement was engaged in visible public activism. Finally, the Twin Cities area is a sort of hub where American Indians and Indigenous peoples throughout the region remind us of the diversity of Native peoples who call today's suburbs home.[32] These Native and Indigenous people represent tribal nations from across the country and beyond—from the Taíno of Puerto Rico to Alaska Natives and CHamoru of Guam. These Native and Indigenous people open the door to rethinking not only what it means to be a suburban Indian but what it means to be Indigenous in the suburbs, often while living on someone else's homelands.

While existing NAIS scholarship on urban Indians has examined such geographies as Chicago, Los Angeles, Albuquerque, Seattle, and the Bay Area (in addition to places like Winnipeg and Toronto in the Canadian context), the Twin Cities of Minnesota, despite having a substantial urban Indian population and being a de facto Relocation destination during the 1950s and 1960s, has not been considered in such studies.[33] My research opens the door to engagement with Native peoples across the entire Twin Cities metropolitan area—urban and suburban. With a focus on Minnesota and the Twin Cities, I recognize the unique relationships that exist across time and space—from traditional homelands to the establishment of reservations across the state, to the growth of settler cities and suburbs, and now, as Native people work to reclaim place in the face of settler colonialism. In this way, the Twin Cities are unique, as they offer an opportunity to examine American Indian suburbanization as an outgrowth of Indian urbanization and as a return to Indian places, with nearby reservation communities. This is different from Chicago, for example, as there are no reservations within the state of Illinois, and distinct from urban areas of California, as tribal communities throughout the state are significantly smaller and less visible than the reservations across Minnesota. By centering Twin Cities suburban Indians and suburban places, alongside reservation and urban communities, this research complicates settler geographies that do not neatly fit into an urban (or reservation) context.

The areas I consider suburban throughout this book include places within the seven-county metropolitan area, excluding the urban centers of Minneapolis and Saint Paul. The seven-county metro area I refer to throughout this book to delineate suburban areas differs from the metropolitan and micropolitan statistical areas delineated by the U.S. Office of Management and Budget that are applied to U.S. Census data.[34] These counties include Anoka, Hennepin, Carver, Scott, Dakota, Washington, and Ramsey. I keep my attention on this seven-county metro area because, over time, these counties have remained most consistently suburban (apart from the urban cores of Minneapolis in Hennepin County and Saint Paul in Ramsey County) and have been viewed as places located near the urban centers. Within this geography, the areas today that are widely accepted as suburban are those with higher rates of single-family homes in relative proximity, with neighborhoods connected to each other by paved roads, and that are linked to the urban core by local streets, highways, and interstates. However, I recognize suburbs do not begin and end at county or city lines and that the places we consider suburban today would not fit the same definitions of *suburban* fifty or one hundred years ago. I have chosen to refer to the seven-county metro area throughout this book for matters of consistency. However, I do acknowledge when places are not quite suburban by today's standards, and I point this out and offer a description of place. In addition to the clearly demarcated geographic boundaries and borders I use and refer to throughout, I also refer to other concepts of place. This includes my use of the term *Twin Cities*. When I use the term *Twin Cities,* I do not mean Minneapolis and Saint Paul exclusively, but I use the term to refer to the larger, encompassing region, inclusive of suburbs and urban areas that span the seven-county metro area.

In early chapters, I often use the term *Indian place*. By *Indian place* I mean a geographic land area or geographic feature for which the tribal

Map 1. The seven-county metropolitan area of the Twin Cities region. Map by Katherine Koehler.

nations have traditional and cultural claims and connections, which are primarily based on historical ties to specific place. I use *Indian place* to describe such things as contemporary suburbs, cities, lakes, confluences of riverways, and Indian mounds to underscore the lengthy Indigenous claims to space across the Twin Cities and the state of Minnesota. When I identify a place as an Indian place, I make clear the historic Dakota or Ojibwe connections to the place and use census data and historical archives to support my claims. These Indian places, often located along riverways, became the first places non-Native explorers, settlers, and travelers arrived on their journey to and through what became the state of Minnesota.[35] Much like Abenaki scholar Lisa Brooks demonstrates of New England in her book *The Common Pot,* and as Mishuana Goeman argues in *Mark My Words,* I contend that all of present-day Minnesota was and has remained an Indian space despite the dispossession of Native people, Euro-American settlement, development, and the renaming of place. My use of census data and personal and family narratives demonstrates that the many places we think of today as suburbs have much longer and more complex histories as Indian places. This juxtaposition should also be acknowledged rather than overlooked and, in many cases, erased. I also build on the work of geographer Yi-Fu Tuan, who describes how place becomes such as it becomes increasingly familiar and is less abstract than space. *Place* can demarcate a sense of home, permanence, or homeland.[36]

Throughout this book I use several terms to refer to Indigenous people at a local level and more expansively. Most commonly, I use the term *Indian.* I chose to use this term for its simplicity in writing and conversation, and I take this to mean "people Indigenous to the United States"; this includes Dakota and Ojibwe people but also American Indian peoples from outside of Minnesota. I use *Native* interchangeably with *Indian* to also mean "American Indian." In addition, I use the term *Indigenous* several times throughout this text. This term is generally viewed as more inclusive of peoples outside the United States, and I use it in reference to American Indian and other Native people when I want to be inclusive of globally Indigenous peoples as well. At times I use tribally specific terms like *Dakota* and *Ojibwe* when I refer to or focus on individual tribal groups and Native people of Minnesota specifically and exclusively. Importantly, each of these designations relies primarily on self-identification, how individuals perceive themselves and identify at specific points in time.

American Indians and the American Dream aims to speak to a wide audience, including scholars from such diverse fields as human and cultural geography to public policy and housing studies. Importantly, this text is also meant for American Indian community members, specifically those who have called Minnesota home. Finally, this book is for those who are interested in public history, American Indian history, suburbanization, and Minnesota history. As such, I use an innovative methodology to weave together autoethnography, personal and family narratives, archival analysis, comparative federal policy analysis, and quantitative methods. As an interdisciplinary scholar, I bring together these methods to tell a more complete and nuanced narrative about the entanglement of federal Indian and federal housing policy that has not yet been explored or told. These methods allow me to keep a narrow focus on federal policy and how broadly federal Indian and federal housing policy has affected the lives of Native people, both historically and today.

My reliance on autoethnography as a framework and mode of analysis helps to make sense of the diverse experiences and complex histories of contemporary suburban Indians in the Twin Cities. I draw on Malinda Maynor Lowery's definition of *autoethnography*: "a method of exploring one's own relationship to research that begins with questioning how culture and society have affected one's experiences. . . . Often I am telling someone else's story and not my own. . . . I have examined my own place in my family and culture."[37] However, I diverge from Lowery's use of autoethnography because instead of using my or my family's experience as a guide, I use it as a foundation or starting point. I begin and end this project with my own self-awareness and my family's story. I am writing about both history and a social process— something that is very personal for me and thousands of others like me. My experiences brought me to this project and inform how I think about it and the people contained within it; therefore, it is very much shaped by autoethnography as a suburban Indian. As a suburban Indian who grew up and continues to reside in suburban geographies, I am not able to objectively separate my own personal experiences, and those of my family, from my research. I also firmly believe my personal history and experience as a suburban Indian add a level of complexity and enhance my research and writing. My use of autoethnography in this way is significant because my research and writing stem from an Indigenous perspective and are largely meant for the Native community.

This project incorporates archival materials, including local histories of place, oral histories, personal and family narratives, government documents, letters, photographs, and public history. A close analysis of these sources reveals the ways American Indian people have participated in the many processes of suburbanization. Simultaneously, these archival materials document the tensions at play in federal policy and the many ways that land changed through settler colonialism. I consider the legislation of federal Indian policies and federal housing policies as primary source documents and thus as crucial aspects of the historical archives that have often been underexamined. The wide variety of sources I use helps me to analyze and to make sense of numerical data from the census, to fill in gaps, and to complete a more thorough and accurate narrative of suburban Indians.

I examine U.S. Census data from the nineteenth century to the present as a quantitative base to illustrate the continuous presence of American Indians in suburbs over time. I use the Minnesota Population Center's Integrated Public Use Microdata Series (IPUMS) to access population and socioeconomic data from decennial censuses, as well as publicly available U.S. Census data.[38] The earliest census records I examine are those from 1860 and the latest are from the 2010 decennial census. U.S. Indian Census Rolls (1845–1940) also inform a substantial part of my quantitative research, while military records and Relocation records inform a smaller, though equally significant, aspect of this research. Records that predate the mid-1940s are publicly available in their entirety and in their original format.[39] I use individual and family names from this period without pseudonyms, as records are considered public data; however, I note when pseudonyms are used in the manuscript. The decennial census microdata from 1950 onward in this book was accessed through IPUMS.[40]

Though I rely heavily on the census as a quantitative framework, I also recognize its limitations. In 1879 U.S. Congress passed an act to hire and train enumerators to travel to households to collect census data; prior to hiring enumerators as federal employees, the U.S. Census was conducted by U.S. Marshals.[41] Ultimately, it was an enumerator's responsibility to interpret the census instructions and then make a final decision to record a racial identity for each individual and family. The year 1960 marked the U.S. Census Bureau's debut of mail-out census forms to residences, finally allowing respondents to self-identify. By 1970, the Census Bureau worked to streamline the census questionnaire, and the U.S. Post Office delivered census forms that were to be mailed back to the Census Bureau. Race on the census has been a contentious topic and has received recent scholarly attention, particularly for American Indians.[42] Census-based racial identification can be problematic and difficult to analyze because many individuals change how they identify over time, from one census to the next. In 2000, for the first time ever, the U.S. Census invited individuals to identify as more than one race. Though this move is correctly celebrated and allows individuals to describe their race and ethnicity more accurately, it also allows for many combinations of multiple-race peoples with often differing ancestry. Despite its drawbacks and criticisms, the U.S. Census offers one of the most consistent and extensive data sources on population demographics across time and place. A final limitation of census data, particularly for American Indian population counts, is mobility. Over time, American Indians have been marked by a high degree of mobility compared to other racial and ethnic groups; much of this can be attributed to removal and the reservation system, which unduly and excessively sought to manipulate and curtail the movement of American Indian people.[43] In reality, we know American Indians resisted such impositions and regularly sought ways to return to their homelands while others left reservations, even if temporarily, for many of the reasons outlined in this book.

Overview

American Indians and the American Dream analyzes the ways in which American Indians, as individuals but more commonly as families, have worked to access homeownership, particularly in suburbs, while working with and against federal Indian and federal housing policies. In the chapters that follow, I pay attention to the longer history of land tenure and property rights as American Indians were dispossessed of their land— land that was first sold to settlers and would eventually find its way into the hands of developers a century later for mass home construction. Each chapter centers on a family story or stories of place and placemaking. These stories not only reveal where people come from and when, where they arrived to and how, but they also expose historical links to the violence of Indigenous dispossession and ask us to question our own place—how do we get to where we are? Perhaps more importantly, this book is not only about history and historical processes but also about the thousands of people, just like me, who have worked to carve out lives for themselves and their families in suburban communities that, in many ways, were designed to exclude them. Through ethnography, each chapter is a case study of encounter, and this book is very much about Indigenous encounters with settler colonialism, past and present.

In chapter 1, "Land of Loss and Survival: The Homestead Act of 1862 and the U.S.–Dakota War," I examine the historical Dakota and Ojibwe claims to space. This chapter begins in 1862 with the passage of the Homestead Act and examines the rapid arrival of non-Native settlers, the policies that allowed for and supported the rapid dispossession of Native land, and the resulting U.S.–Dakota War. In this chapter, I juxtapose the rapid shift away from Indian places and the erasure of Indian people from the landscape.

The second chapter, "Pivotal Policies: The Creation of the Federal Housing Administration and the Indian Reorganization Act," begins with American Indian participation in World War I and the creation of the Snyder Act in 1921. I consider the ways the Snyder Act, which authorized federal spending on Indian affairs, must also be read as a precursor to Indian housing programs and policies. In this chapter, I offer a critique of the Federal Housing Administration, the first official intervention into the housing sector, created within one week of the passage of the Indian Reorganization Act. This is significant, as both resulted from the New Deal legislation that dramatically altered the course of housing policy (primarily for white Americans) and Indian policy.

Chapter 3, "'We Must Do This Ourselves': American Indians and the American Dream in the Twin Cities," focuses on postwar suburbanization and the dual Indian policies of Termination and Relocation alongside the GI Bill. This chapter opens with an overview of the suburbanization boom that began after World War II and lasted well into the 1960s. I pay particular attention to the seeming whiteness of new suburbs and the roles of family, domesticity, and race. Here I analyze the ways that Indian people were excluded from processes of suburbanization, but I also acknowledge the ways that Indian families were able to participate in suburbanization. The second half of this chapter is devoted to the Termination and Relocation Policies. I examine the role of Termination on Indian communities across the state of Minnesota and interrogate the Relocation Program that moved thousands of Indian people to exclusively urban areas. I argue that both Termination and Relocation contributed to Indian suburbanization, though indirectly, and that those Indian people who did participate in the processes of suburbanization did so on their own.

Chapter 4, "Intersections of Responsibility: Federal Housing Policy, Indian Policy, and Minneapolis's Little Earth Housing Complex," centers on Little Earth, a housing complex in Minneapolis. Little Earth is the first and only American Indian preference housing program in the United States. In this chapter, I argue that Little Earth was a direct response by urban Indians in the cities to the Indian Relocation Program. I see Little Earth as a Native-led effort to house Indian people in the urban core of Minneapolis. I examine the creation of Little Earth alongside the creation of the Department of Housing and Urban Development as a cabinet-level agency in 1965. This moment is crucial as it marked a shift toward Great Society programs and the civil rights era more broadly, as well as the birth of the American Indian Movement in Minneapolis and the larger Red Power Movement.

Finally, in chapter 5, "Indian Homes and Indian Loans: Suburban Indians and the Section 184 Indian Home Loan Guarantee Program," I use autoethnography, both as a self-identified suburban Indian and based on my professional experience, to examine what it means to be a suburban Indian family in Minnesota today. I focus on one contemporary Indian family in a suburb north of Minneapolis as a case study to guide my analysis. This chapter takes a close look at the only federally administered off-reservation home loan program for Indian people today: the Section 184 Indian Home Loan Guarantee Program created in 1992.[44] In this chapter, I offer an analysis and critique of suburban American Indian homeownership by comparing the Section 184 program to Clinton-era policies to promote access to home loans and homeownership, as well as the advent of subprime mortgages. Here, access to capital and mortgages was clearly marked by race and income, as were the geographic places (on and off reservation and more specific counties) Indian people had access to through government and tribal home-ownership programs.

In the Conclusion, "Racializing Public Space: American Indian Homelessness as Houselessness and Exclusion," I bring together contemporary efforts of tribal communities and intertribal organizations based in the city to provide housing for unhoused American Indian community members. I focus on the growth and visibility of the Wall of Forgotten Natives. This American Indian community encampment took shape along Highway 55 in South Minneapolis, just adjacent to Hiawatha Avenue and what has become known as the American Indian cultural corridor. The visibility of American Indian homelessness again drew statewide and national attention after the police murder of George Floyd in May 2020. During the months that followed, Minneapolis, Saint Paul, and the surrounding suburbs were rife with racial tensions further complicated due to the Covid-19 pandemic and high unemployment rates combined with increasing numbers of evictions. Both the Wall of Forgotten Natives and the homeless encampment at Powderhorn Park, which received national attention, developed and expanded as a place of refuge for American Indians (and others) experiencing homelessness in the Twin Cities. This Conclusion offers a brief reflection on contemporary struggles to house American Indian community members, efforts that have been led by tribal nations and American Indian community members. This space is a way to reframe and rethink access to housing and land for American Indian people who have always called the Twin Cities home.

1

LAND OF LOSS AND SURVIVAL
THE HOMESTEAD ACT OF 1862
AND THE U.S.-DAKOTA WAR

> The Sioux Indians of Minnesota must be exterminated or driven forever beyond the borders of the State. . . . They must be regarded and treated as outlaws. If any shall escape extinction, the wretched remnant must be driven beyond our borders and our frontier garrisoned with force sufficient to ever prevent their return.
>
> —GOVERNOR ALEXANDER RAMSEY, September 9, 1862

> [The Homestead Act] is one of the most successful endeavors in American history, causing the great land rush to the Wild West. . . . Abraham Lincoln's Homestead Act empowered people, it freed people from the burden of poverty. It freed them to control their own destinies, to create their own opportunities, and live the vision of the American dream.
>
> —PRESIDENT GEORGE H. W. BUSH, November 28, 1990

IN 1788, Háza Íŋyaŋke Wiŋ, a Bdewákhaŋthuŋ Dakota woman, was born near the confluence of the Mnísota Wakpá (Minnesota River) and Wakpá Tháŋka (Mississippi River). Háza Íŋyaŋke Wiŋ—or Runs for Huckleberries Woman, as her name translates—married Mázasagye (Iron Cane) and had several children together, including their son Thaópi (His Many Wounds). Only a handful of Euro-American explorers had passed through the area when Háza Íŋyaŋke Wiŋ was a young girl, growing up at Kap'óža, today known as Little Crow's or Kaposia village, along

Wakpá Tháŋka, just south of present-day downtown Saint Paul. During the early nineteenth century, over four hundred Dakota people lived at Kap'óža, a well-developed village with frame buildings, large bark homes, established methods of food preservation, and well-tuned labor and social systems based on gender roles. The Bdewákhaŋthuŋ community who lived here remained at this village site and nearby areas along the Mnísota Wakpá and Wakpá Tháŋka until 1851. Through the 1851 Treaties of Mendota and Traverse des Sioux, signed just days prior, near present-day Saint Peter, Minnesota, the Bdewákhaŋthuŋ, Waȟpékhute, Sisíthuŋ, and Waȟpéthuŋ bands of Dakota were forced to leave their homelands. As a result of these treaties, Háza Íŋyaŋke Wiŋ and her family, along with other Dakota, were removed to a reservation near the Lower Sioux Indian Agency, located near present-day Morton, Minnesota, in 1853.

One decade later, in the summer of 1862, Thaópi, who was born at Kap'óža, spoke out in opposition to the simmering U.S.–Dakota War. During the war, Háza Íŋyaŋke Wiŋ cared for many of the non-Native settler women and children who were captured by the Dakota, and Thaópi worked to protect captives. Both Háza Íŋyaŋke Wiŋ and Thaópi were perceived to be assimilated by the non-Native settler community, a classification that likely spared their family from death during the war and the brutalities inflicted on Dakota during the forced removal by settlers, military, and government officials. In fact, Thaópi received a certificate of commendation from Henry Sibley, a clear indication that he was considered by many non-Natives to be a civilized man. After the war, Thaópi's family was allowed to remain in the state on land owned by Alexander Faribault, south of the Twin Cities. Eventually Háza Íŋyaŋke Wiŋ and her husband would make their way back to the area of her birth and early life, near Saint Paul. It is here that Háza Íŋyaŋke Wiŋ, today more commonly recognized in historical writing and local lore as Old Bets or Old Betsy, and her family would face the rapid influx of non-Native settlers to the region head-on.[1] As Háza Íŋyaŋke Wiŋ, Thaópi, and their family remind us, despite the history of removal and exile of Dakota, Ojibwe, and Ho-Chunk people throughout the nineteenth century, Native people remained in what was to soon become the Twin Cities. The story of Háza Íŋyaŋke Wiŋ and Thaópi underscores the resiliency of Indigenous people in Minnesota Territory and, later, the state of Minnesota throughout the nineteenth century—a story that is often lost, forgotten, untold, and hidden under the violence of removal, war, and exile across a place long known as Mnísota Makhóče.

This family narrative represents the hundreds, and eventually thousands, of Native people who would not be left behind or excluded from the swift development and growth of towns, cities, and suburbs along the Mnísota Wakpá, Wakpá Tháŋka, Ókhižu Wakpá (Saint Croix River), and Wakpá Wakháŋ (Rum River) valleys during the final decades of the nineteenth century and into the early twentieth century. In fact, despite the well-worn narratives of colonization, war, and dispossession, handfuls and pockets of Dakota and Ojibwe were able to remain in their traditional homelands, and they continued to claim and reclaim the ever-changing landscape as their own. This chapter focuses on the crucial years of the late nineteenth and early twentieth centuries, as the aftermath of the U.S.–Dakota War unraveled and gave way to sweeping transfers of land through the Homestead Act, the Pacific Railway Act, and the Morrill Act, all of 1862. Taken together, the war and federally subsidized land transfers worked in tandem to remake Indian places into white settler communities. It is this time period, between 1862 and the first decade of the twentieth century, that witnessed the supposed founding of a plethora of new, non-Native villages as more and more Indian land was stripped from tribal hands and opened up for settlement and development. Therefore, during this relatively early temporal window, the nascent suburbanization of the Twin Cities began. It is also in this region, the Twin Cities, where non-Native settlers reimagined and remade Indian places as their own, as they literally and figuratively inscribed their names across place, through the process of "firsting and lasting."[2] Yet the remaking of place by non-Native settlers would not diminish the centrality of place and belonging for Native people.

The suburbs of Minneapolis and Saint Paul have lengthy and well-documented Indigenous histories that have long been ignored, overlooked, and written over by dominant society—white settler community members and scholars alike. Ojibwe historian Jean O'Brien affirms this when she reminds us that the written narrative, through place-based histories, has significantly contributed to the erasure of American Indian people from place.[3] In fact, the written record has maintained a near exclusive focus on non-Native settlers, to the exclusion of Native people and other people of color. Indigenous histories and claims to space, as

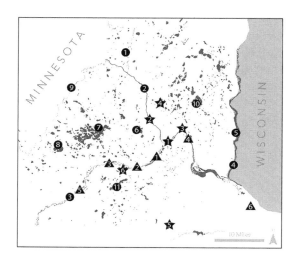

▲ Wičhóthi - Villages

1 Thitháŋka Thaŋnína
"Penichon Village"
2 Oháŋska
"Black Dog Village"
3 Thíŋta Othúŋwe
"Shakopee Village"
4 Kap'óža
"Little Crow Village"
5 Wiyáka Othídaŋ
"Sandbar Village"
6 Ȟemníčhaŋ
"Red Wing Village"

★ Ohé Wakháŋ - Sacred Places

1 Bdóte
Creation Origin Site
2 Owámniyomni
"St. Anthony Falls"
3 Wakháŋ Thípi
"Carver Cave"
4 Bdé Wakháŋthuŋ
"Long Lake" - 1700s Village
5 Íŋyaŋ Bosdáta
"Castle Rock"
6 Makhá Yušóša
"Boiling Springs"

● Bdé k'a Wakpá - Lakes and Rivers

1 Wakpá Wakháŋ   7 Mní lá Tháŋka
"Rum River"   "Lake Minnetonka"
2 Wakpá Tháŋka   8 Bdé Wakhóniya
"Mississippi River"   "Lake Waconia"
3 Mnísota Wakpá   9 Khaŋǧí Wakpá
"Minnesota River"   "Crow River"
4 Ókhižu Wakpá   10 Mathó Bdé
"St. Croix River"   "White Bear Lake"
5 Hoǧáŋ Waŋké Kiŋ   11 Bdé Mayá Thó
"St. Croix Lake"   "Prior Lake"
6 Bdé Makhá Ská
"Bde Maka Ska"

Map 2. Dakota places located throughout the Twin Cities, with place-names and English translations. Map by Katherine Koehler with Dakota places and place-names by Dawí Huhá Máza.

simple or complex as they may be, have been disrupted, erased, and, in many cases, denied by those who write history.

The assaults on Indian people, particularly those in Minnesota, throughout the late nineteenth century and into the early twentieth century have been well documented. However, the profound ability of American Indian people to remain present in and return to Indian places throughout southern Minnesota has remained largely ignored in popular and scholarly writings. Often, these Indian people worked as farmers and laborers while others relied on more traditional sources of livelihood, including fishing, hunting, trapping, and mitten and moccasin making, all the while adapting to a changing environment and living alongside increasing numbers of white settler families. While considerable forces worked to break apart American Indian communities, including military campaigns like the U.S.–Dakota War and the exile that resulted, a forced program of assimilation, and the denial of treaty rights, many Indian individuals and families remained together, working and often living in intergenerational homes. The movement of Indian people, as observed in census data, from and across Indian places like Kap'óža and into spaces that were becoming increasingly white, like Saint Paul, suggests a level of mobility among Indian people that has been ignored during this period. The presence of Indian people in southern Minnesota from such areas as Canada and Maine, in tandem with Dakota and Ojibwe peoples' continuous presence in the face of dispossession, removal, war, and exile, forces us to reconsider what an Indian place truly is.

Indeed, Native people have always lived across the entirety of Mníšota Makhóčhe. Of the Dakota who were able to remain in the state after the U.S.–Dakota War, many were protected and sheltered by white Christian families. Other Dakotas, including those who had served as scouts for the United States Army during and after the war, were allowed to stay on land owned by Henry Sibley in Mendota and on land owned by Bishop Henry Whipple and Alexander Faribault in what would become Faribault, Minnesota.[4] Yet many more Dakota were able to remain in the state, some by hiding or passing as white, and still others remained who put distance between themselves and the Mníšota Wakpá valley, often more supposedly assimilated Dakota. The survival of Dakota people in their homelands after removal, war, and exile in addition to the simultaneous and dramatic influx of non-Native settlers and their continued expansion, through policies like the Homestead Act, underscores the reality that these spaces within and around the Mníšota Wakpá and Wakpá Tháŋka valleys were, and remained, inherently Indian places despite the numerous forces that have worked to remake the region.

This chapter begins with a brief and basic overview of the lead-up to the U.S.–Dakota War. Then, I shift focus to the aftermath of the war, which very much continues to reverberate across the landscape today.

I consider the ways the U.S.–Dakota War was representative of the more expansive federal Indian policies of this era, policies that centered on military violence, conquest, and Indigenous dispossession. Next, I examine the ways federal policies, specifically the Homestead Act of 1862, worked as a tool to promote and advance Native dispossession across not only Minnesota but the whole western portion of the United States, across portions of the U.S. South, the Midwest, and Alaska. It is my contention that the Homestead Act must be viewed as a precursor to more familiar housing policies that took shape during the twentieth century. In many ways, the Homestead Act has grounded subsequent housing policies that have largely centered on access to homes and homeownership for some, but not all, based on race. Indeed, the Homestead Act was a significant land-based policy that opened vast swaths of Native land across the U.S. West to non-Native, overwhelmingly white settlers who hoped to claim land and build homes on the seemingly open prairie. Together, the Homestead Act and the U.S.–Dakota War must be considered federal policies that, though managed from Washington, were carried out on the ground in Minnesota. The efforts and results of each were to sever Native ties to land while simultaneously allowing for, encouraging, and supporting white settlement across Minnesota. This chapter ends with resistance. I center the many ways and many Native people who remained in the Twin Cities despite the efforts of policy makers, settlers, and military campaigns to remove them. To do so, I offer a close reading of local, place-based histories and a detailed analysis of U.S. Census data to reveal the complex interplay of Indigenous dispossession, first through the U.S.–Dakota War and then through the Homestead Act, and the multilayered stories of Native presence across Indian places that we now know as the Twin Cities.

Treaties, Land Loss, and the U.S.–Dakota War

By the mid-nineteenth century, the landscape and demography of Minnesota were undergoing dramatic change. The unparalleled settlement of non-Native persons on land made available by treaty with Native nations coincided with the removal of thousands of Ojibwe and Dakota people from the southern and central regions of Minnesota Territory. Eventually, as was the case for thousands of Dakota people, removal would tragically turn to exile. Though the U.S.–Dakota War of 1862 has received much local attention, and rightly so, we must not overlook what was unfolding during the first half of the same century. To make sense of the magnitude of the U.S.–Dakota War and the ensuing exile, we must have a solid understanding of the events that led up to the spring and summer of 1862 along Mnísota Wakpá, and we must be able to place it within a larger, national narrative. To not consider the significance of this larger and longer history is to deny the dispossession and ongoing colonial violence that is settler colonialism.

Though European explorers, missionaries, fur trappers, and traders had long traversed Mnísota Makhóčhe during the eighteenth century, tracing the shores of Mnísota Wakpá and Wakpá Tháŋka, few would establish long-term settlement in the region. This changed in 1805 when Zebulon Pike, an agent of the U.S. Army, arrived at the confluence of Mnísota Wakpá and Wakpá Tháŋka. Pike's supposed major accomplishment here was his treaty negotiation that secured approximately one hundred thousand acres of land, above the river bluffs, for construction of a military fort. Though this marked the first treaty in what is now known as Minnesota, this transaction remains contested as the treaty was not authorized prior to the arrangement, nor did it receive official presidential proclamation by President Thomas Jefferson.[5] Construction on Fort Saint Anthony, as it remained until 1825 when its name was changed to Fort Snelling, began in 1820 and was completed under the direction of Colonel Josiah Snelling in 1825.[6] Occupying the bluff that overlooks the confluence of the two rivers, Fort Snelling was the westernmost fort on the settler frontier at the time of its construction. This military fort was geographically significant as it was a way for the federal government to regulate not only the fur trade, a booming multi-million-dollar business at the time, but also American Indian bodies. In addition to the military fort, an Indian agency was also constructed—Saint Peters Indian Agency, located just outside the fort's stone walls. The first Indian agent at Fort Snelling, Lawrence Taliaferro, was stationed there between 1820 and 1839. Taliaferro served as the diplomatic face of the federal government in interactions with local Dakota and Ojibwe.

It is no coincidence that the same year construction on the fort was complete, the Treaty of Prairie du Chien was negotiated and signed

Figure 2. View of Fort Snelling, looking north, from the confluence of the
Minnesota and Mississippi Rivers (near the present-day Sibley Historic Site).
Painting by John Caspar Wild, circa 1844. Courtesy of Minnesota Historical Society.

just downriver from Fort Snelling. This 1825 treaty set boundaries on
tribal land long held by Dakota, Ojibwe, Menominee, Ho-Chunk, Sac
and Fox, Iowa, Potawatomi, and Odawa as homelands in a federal effort
to further regulate Native space and the movement of Native bodies.
Then, twelve years later, in July 1837, Ojibwe from across the region
convened at Fort Snelling for the purpose of yet another treaty negotiation. Here, they would cede over twelve million acres of their land between
Wakpá Tháŋka and Ókhižu Wakpá. Only two months later, in September 1837, a delegation of Bdewákhaŋthuŋ Dakota traveled to Washington, D.C., where they too were coerced into a treaty that relinquished
their triangle of land between Wakpá Tháŋka and Ókhižu Wakpá. These
treaties of 1837 were soon followed by the Treaties of Mendota and
Traverse des Sioux, both of 1851, when the Dakota ceded virtually all of
their land that covered the entire southern portion of Mnísota Makhóčhe
to the federal government. It was also during this time frame that the
Ojibwe in this region were removed to designated reservation lands in
the northern tier of the state. The federal government's efforts to remove
Native people from the southern half of Minnesota were made nearly

complete when the Dakota were removed to a small tract of reservation land in the western portion of the state.[7]

It is to this backdrop of dramatic and rapid land loss, largely coercive in nature and based on one-sided, heavy-handed treaties that many tribes felt pressured into, that the U.S.–Dakota War unfolded. The history of the U.S.–Dakota War has been well examined, especially over the last decade and a half, by Dakota scholars and community members who have sought to write and right the historical narrative from an inclusive and Dakota perspective.[8] Rather, my focus here is the years and decades that followed the war and the violent separation of so many Indian people, Dakota, Ojibwe, and Ho-Chunk, from their homes and tribal lands. In the immediate aftershock of the U.S.–Dakota War, Indian policy in Minnesota changed dramatically and rapidly. Noncombatant Dakota women, children, and elders were force-marched along Mnísota Wakpá from the western and southern portions of the state to the river bottoms just below Fort Snelling, at Pike Island, during the fall of 1862. Approximately 1,600 Dakota were held in rudimentary stockades between November 1862 and May 1863 under the watchful eye of the military stationed above at Fort Snelling. Approximately one-quarter of those who arrived at Fort Snelling that fall did not survive the military concentration camp they were held in. Meanwhile, Dakota men who remained in the region were immediately rounded up by military and settlers alike. Over 390 civilian Dakota men were placed on military trial for war crimes. When their rapid-succession sham trials were complete, some lasting only minutes, 303 Dakota men, who were convicted for participation in the war based on shoddy evidence and unreliable witness testimony, were sentenced to death by hanging. Then, in the midst of the Civil War and half a continent away, President Abraham Lincoln was called on to review the trial transcripts. In doing so, he single-handedly reduced the number to be sentenced to death, while simultaneously giving his full knowledge, permission, and the go-ahead for thirty-nine Dakota men to be hanged. On December 26, 1862, thirty-eight Dakota men were hanged at Mankato. One of the convicted men was granted a last-minute reprieve just moments prior, sparing his life. This remains the largest mass execution in U.S. history. The brutality and death would not end here.

Swift action against the Dakota and other Indian people in Minnesota would continue. On February 16, 1863, Congress passed legislation

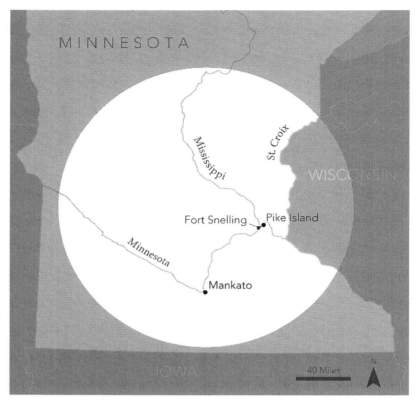

Map 3. Locations of Mankato, Fort Snelling, and Pike Island, where Dakota survivors of the U.S.–Dakota War were force-marched following the war. Map by Katherine Koehler.

to "abrogate and annul" all treaties that had been made with Dakota in Minnesota. The act stated the following as justification for termination of all Dakota treaties within Minnesota: "Aforesaid bands of Indians made an unprovoked, aggressive, and most savage war upon the United States, and massacred a large number of men, women, and children within the State of Minnesota, and destroyed and damaged a large amount of property, and thereby have forfeited all just claims to the said moneys and annuities to the United States."[9] This treaty abrogation included the elimination of Dakota reservation lands within the state. Soon after, on February 21, 1863, the Ho-Chunk were also dealt the war's

Figure 3. One of the few remaining photographs of the concentration camp just below Fort Snelling that held Dakota survivors of the U.S.–Dakota War. Photograph by Benjamin Franklin Upton; image created by Edward A. Bromley. Courtesy of Minnesota Historical Society.

aftershocks as Congress passed the Act for the Removal of the Winnebago Indians and for the Sale of Their Reservation in Minnesota for Their Benefit.[10] This even though the Winnebago, today more accurately known as the Ho-Chunk, did not participate in the U.S.–Dakota War. Yet their neutrality did not spare them their land in Minnesota, and in April 1863, the Ho-Chunk were notified that they were being moved to Crow Creek in South Dakota. One month later, in May 1863, under military escort, the Ho-Chunk were removed from their reservation in southern Minnesota along the Mnísota Wakpá to a new parcel of land in South Dakota. Over five hundred Ho-Chunk died during this forced removal and relocation.

The removal of Ho-Chunk from the state of Minnesota coincided with the Act for the Removal of the Sisseton, Wahpaton, Medawakanton, and Wahpakoota Bands of Sioux or Dakota Indians and for the Disposition of Their Lands in Minnesota and Dakota on March 3, 1863.[11] Then, in May 1863, the Dakota women, children, and elders who had been held at Fort Snelling over the winter were forced to leave their

PUBLISHED BY WHITNEY'S GALLERY, ST. PAUL, MINN.

TEPEES OF THE SIOUX INDIANS,

MINNESOTA.

Figure 4. Photograph of Dakota tipis within the concentration camp that held Dakota survivors of the U.S.–Dakota War during the winter of 1862–63. Photograph by Whitney's Gallery. Courtesy of Minnesota Historical Society.

homelands for Crow Creek. Large boats transported the Dakota women, children, and elders down Wakpá Tháŋka and then up the Missouri River to what became their new reservation. The Dakota men who had been held as prisoners over the winter also left the state of Minnesota in the spring of 1863. These 265 Dakota men were similarly loaded onto steamers and transported to Camp McClellan in Davenport, Iowa. Dakota men and women were not reunited as families and communities for four years. Together, these actions and policies of elimination and exile allowed for continued and unbridled non-Native settlement across what has long been Dakota homelands. The U.S.–Dakota War has since come to mark the violent stripping of Native bodies from their homelands. Though we must trace and examine a longer history of Indigenous dispossession in this region through treaties, the war and exile remind us of the violence of settler colonialism, past and present. Indeed, it was settlers and politicians alike who claimed land that was not theirs for the taking.

1862: The Homestead Act, the Morrill Act, and the Pacific Railway Act

The U.S.–Dakota War and exile did not exist in a vacuum. Rather, at the national level and in addition to the Civil War, there was much policy change and development that was largely intended to fund war efforts and to extend the reach of the Union. This includes the Homestead Act, signed into law by President Abraham Lincoln on May 20, 1862, only weeks before the outset of violence on the Minnesota prairie. The Homestead Act is widely accepted and recognized as pivotal legislation that opened millions of acres of land across the western half of the United States, virtually for free, for white settlement. In addition to the Homestead Act, additional major land redistribution programs—the Pacific Railway Act and the Morrill Act—were passed within weeks of one another, each with a similar objective. Significantly and revealingly, each of these three major land programs were funded with so-called public land with the objective to redistribute this land as a means of generating financial resources for a financially struggling nation at war, a nation that continued to push westward expansion and freedom for some but not all.[12]

Not long after the Homestead Act became official policy, President Abraham Lincoln signed into law the Pacific Railway Act on July 1, 1862, "to promote settlement and to boost construction of railways and telegraph lines."[13] A means of U.S. expansionism, the Pacific Railway Act authorized land grants to the Union Pacific Railroad, running west from the Missouri River, and the Central Pacific Railroad, running east from Sacramento, in their efforts to complete a transcontinental railroad. The act, which relied virtually entirely on public land, "granted the railroads public lands in alternate sections along their routes upon completion of a specified number of miles," as well as a two-hundred-foot right-of-way from the side of the track.[14] Additionally, the act allowed the railroads to take lumber and stone, as natural resources, from lands within the public land domain along the tracks. In the ensuing years, subsequent railroad acts were passed, and, in total, over 174 million acres of public domain lands were transferred to large railroad companies for their right-of-way access. By May 1869, the transcontinental railroad was complete, bringing the East and West Coasts together. The railroad was now a vehicle to move bodies and ideologies of civilization, assimilation, and development.

Only one day after the Pacific Railway Act became law, the Morrill Act was passed on July 2, 1862. The Morrill Act, sponsored by Senator Justin Morrill of Vermont, transferred millions of acres of public domain lands to colleges and universities that have become known as land-grant institutions. The act granted each state thirty thousand acres of public land per senator and representative in Congress. Each of the fifty states, as well as Washington, D.C., soon became recipients of the Morrill Act land grants to establish new colleges and universities. Additionally, the Morrill Act has subsequently been used across U.S. territorial possessions such as Guam, American Samoa, Puerto Rico, the U.S. Virgin Islands, and the Northern Mariana Islands to establish land-grant institutions. The College of Micronesia was also established with Morrill Act funding. The land that was used to fund the land-grant system was the very same land that tribal nations and Indigenous peoples had all too recently been dispossessed of, from coast to coast. It was this land, stolen land, that would go on to fund institutions of higher education and establish university and college endowments, to the tune of billions of dollars over the next century and a half. In part, the Morrill Act stated:

That all moneys derived from the sale of lands aforesaid by the States to which the land are appropriated, and from the sales of land scrip hereinbefore provided for, shall be invested in stocks of the United States . . . not yielding less than five per centum upon the par value of said stocks; and that money so invested shall constitute a perpetual fund, the capital of which shall remain forever undiminished . . . to the endowment, support and maintenance of at least one college where the leading object shall be . . . to teach such branches of learning as are related to agriculture and the mechanic arts . . . in order to promote the liberal and practical education of the industrial classes in the several pursuits and professions of life.[15]

In sum, the Morrill Act acquired so-called public land via land seizure and treaty from 245 tribal nations across the United States.[16] In Minnesota, over 1.2 million acres of Dakota land was distributed under the Morrill Act. An additional 53,738 acres of Ojibwe land in Minnesota was used for Morrill Act land parcels.[17] The University of Minnesota benefited from 94,631 acres of Native land and earned over $579,000 by land sales, a return on investment 251 times greater than the $2,309 paid for said land.[18]

The aims of the Morrill Act, to fund colleges and universities, must not be overlooked. From the passage above, drawn directly from the Morrill Act legislation, we know that beyond the sale of public land to fund institutions of higher education, the specific intent of those colleges and universities was to "teach such branches of learning as related to agriculture and the mechanic arts."[19] Of course, agriculture and agricultural education had long been cornerstones of the assimilationists, objectives of federal Indian policy. Therefore, the Morrill Act, established and sustained on Indian dispossession, is ironic in the most unfortunate of ways. Euro-American systems of land use and management, including agriculture, had been forced upon tribal communities and individual Indian people as markers of assimilation, as prerequisites for participation in new, supposedly American civic life. Yet, when desire for land grew and non-Native settlement expanded, these same Native people would be dispossessed of their land through legal and manipulative means and removed to smaller and smaller reservations, where the same pressures of agricultural production remained under the watchful gaze of

Bureau of Indian Affairs agents. It was this same land, once transferred out of Indian hands, that was now considered public land—land that Native bodies had only recently been stripped from—that helped fund the creation and maintenance of colleges and universities to teach agriculture as a valuable trade for the benefit of predominantly white students. Native students would not be given this opportunity; rather, this opportunity was closed off from them as they were removed to reservations. Educational opportunities for non-Natives were built off the backs of American Indians.[20] Taken together, the Homestead Act, the Pacific Railway Act, and the Morrill Act—each passed within weeks of one another during the Civil War as outstretched arms of Indigenous dispossession—mark the first time anywhere in the world a nation so thoroughly and broadly committed to such scale the resources (land and money) for the purpose of settlement and higher education.[21]

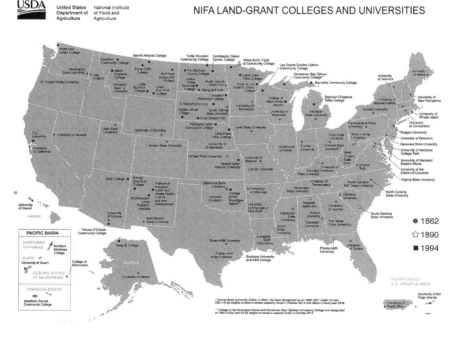

Figure 5. Locations of land-grant universities, funded through the 1862 Morrill Act, throughout the United States. Courtesy of U.S. Department of Agriculture.

Together the Homestead Act, the Pacific Railway Act, and the Morrill Act were in many ways the federal government's response to the American public's calls to open so-called public domain lands for purposes of settlement, development, and U.S. expansion. More precisely, the Homestead Act declared:

> That any person who is the head of a family, or who has arrived at the age of twenty-one years, and is a citizen of the United States, or who shall have filed his declaration of intention to become such . . . who has never borne arms against the United States Government or given aid and comfort to its enemies, shall . . . be entitled to enter one quarter section or a less quantity of unappropriated public lands . . . at one dollar and twenty-five cents, or less, per acre; or eighty acres or less of such unappropriated lands, at two dollars and fifty cents per acre.[22]

Indeed, since the United States had achieved independence less than one hundred years prior, its land area had grown vastly from 512 million acres to over 2 billion acres.[23] Land had long been a commodity, and its monetary value and necessity for settlement and expansion purposes only increased during the 1860s when the young nation was at war. The Homestead Act served a relatively simple purpose—to allow would-be settlers a chance to claim land as their own. The act allowed citizens and immigrants who sought U.S. citizenship, ages twenty-one and over, the opportunity to settle up to 160 acres of land, provided they live on it as a "homestead" for a set number of years (generally five), build a home on and farm the land ("proving up" the land), and pay minimal processing fees. Interestingly, despite a heavy reliance on citizenship, the Homestead Act did not lay out stipulations around race.[24]

Yet, in reality, the Homestead Act contributed to the dispossession of millions of acres of land that tribal nations, from coast to coast, had already lost to dubious treaty negotiations and encroaching settlers. In Minnesota, as the aftermath of the U.S.–Dakota War made clear, Native bodies would not stand in the way of white settlement, and the Homestead Act simply could not exist without the dispossession of Native peoples. The Homestead Act, which existed as a land-based federal policy until 1974 (1986 in Alaska), ushered in white settlement; those settlers, or homesteaders, went on to claim approximately 270 million acres of land across thirty states. During the Homestead Act's 123 years of existence, four million land claims were made, with over 50 percent of homesteaders proving successful. In Minnesota, there were over eighty-five thousand homesteads, representing a total of nearly 10.4 million acres of land. In total, homestead settlers in Minnesota claimed and took as their own 20 percent of the state's entire land base. This is significantly more than Minnesota's neighbors to the south and east (in Wisconsin 3.1 million acres and in Iowa 900,000 acres were settled under the Homestead Act). However, to the west of Minnesota, even more public land was usurped by eager settlers, with 17.4 million acres claimed under the Homestead Act in North Dakota and 15.6 million acres settled in South Dakota.[25]

The Homestead Act has become a defining piece of land-based legislation, outlining what settlement, landownership, and housing should and would look like, and who it was available to, for decades and centuries to come. In fact, the Homestead Act must be considered an early housing policy, a federal policy that set the tone for federal housing programs and policies that were to come. As such, these policies dictated who had access to land and property, who had access to financial resources, including mortgages, who had access to single-family dwellings, and who had access to homeownership. It is here, then, that we must look to understand the complexity and entanglement of property or landownership and whiteness or race, a theme that runs through the entirety of this book, as it is represented and revealed in the Homestead Act.

If we consider the Homestead Act as an early federal housing policy, we are able to peel back the layers to look at the relationship between so-called civilization, property or landownership (commonly understood as settlement), housing, and citizenship as they existed in the 1860s. Civilization and assimilation had long been objectives of federal Indian policy. When Thomas Jefferson exalted the supposed virtues of private property and farming nearly a century prior, efforts had long been made to push Euro-American agriculture on American Indian people. Those who acquiesced to these efforts were deemed civilized, some even acquiring U.S. citizenship along the way. For those who resisted or were removed before such efforts could be made, their land—tribal homelands—was almost always in jeopardy. A prime example of this is the Removal Act in the Southeast and the designation of the Five Civilized Tribes. Citizenship hinged on assimilation and agriculture, with those deemed more assimilated or civilized able to hold onto their land longer. The Homestead Act made clear the linkage between landownership and citizenship. The act was initially only available to U.S. citizens and immigrants, primarily from Europe, who sought U.S. citizenship and desired to establish a home. At the same time, very few Native people had access to U.S. citizenship, as citizenship was closely tied to American Indians' degree of assimilation. Throughout the late nineteenth century and into the twentieth century, citizenship was granted to American Indian individuals primarily on a piecemeal and individual basis, largely revolving around their degree of perceived assimilation. It was not until 1924 that the Indian Citizenship Act was passed and U.S. citizenship theoretically became available to all American Indian people.[26] Therefore, the Homestead Act was largely closed off to Native peoples as noncitizens.[27] It was the precise disenfranchisement of American Indian people that allowed for the settlement of public lands—once Indian lands—through the Homestead Act. In essence, and as a double standard, American Indians had to prove they were "American enough" through assimilation to keep or own land while immigrants were given land and the ability to claim "Americanness" by working the (Indian) land and building a home on the government's dime.

Not only was access to the Homestead Act limited by citizenship status, but it also reaffirmed and cemented the relationship between citizenship and property (land) ownership. If we consider the basics of the Homestead Act as who has control or access to land, the federal government deliberately excluded some while including others. American Indians, who were not yet U.S. citizens, were closed off from individual property or landownership through the Homestead Act. American Indians, as noncitizens, were also read as nonwhite and as not capable of owning or managing land, as revealed in the decades-long efforts of assimilation policies and land-based policies designed to strip them of their land—including such policies as the Homestead Act and Allotment. Indeed, the General Allotment Act, only twenty-five years after the Homestead Act, in many ways mirrored the Homestead Act. For American Indian people, Allotment policy was promoted as a way to offer individual parcels of land to Native people with the promise of eventual U.S. citizenship so long as the Indian allottee could maintain or prove up their allotment. Just like the Homestead Act, Allotment offered 160-acre parcels of land to American Indian adult male heads of household for establishing a home and for agricultural purposes. And unfortunately, just like the Homestead Act, Allotment had the same devastating effects of breaking up tribal land bases while directly contributing to the loss of tribal trust land on reservations.[28] It was the Homestead Act then, where we witness the ways that whiteness hinges on property and the ways property is thus a tool to regulate identity. As Indigenous studies scholar Aileen Moreton-Robinson affirms, "white propriety rights were cemented in law through the appropriation of Native American lands and the subsequent enslavement of Africans. . . . As a form of property, whiteness accumulates capital and social appreciation as white people are recognized within the law primarily as property-owning subjects. As such, they are heavily invested in the nation being a white possession."[29] Indeed, the Homestead Act was a mechanism to regulate who had access to land or private property and U.S. identity or belonging.

The citizenship and racial dynamics of the Homestead Act run deep. When the act was passed in the summer of 1862 and signed into law by President Lincoln, it was not the first time the bill had been introduced and explored by Congress. Just three years prior, President James Buchanan vetoed the same bill during his presidency. At the time, Buchanan, who represented the view of many white southerners, feared the Homestead Act would be used to settle lands by those who opposed slavery, already a contentious and long-simmering issue.[30] Indeed, as the Civil War unraveled, the Homestead Act became a means to expand (white) settlement across the nation, thereby securing an antislavery, pro-Union base. Once the Civil War ended, the 1866 Civil Rights Act and the Fourteenth Amendment of 1868 theoretically granted freedmen and freedwomen access to the Homestead Act as well. Though Black people went on to successfully homestead in every state, they did so at significantly lower rates than their white counterparts. Approximately 3,500 Black people successfully claimed land under the Homestead Act, for a total of 650,000 acres.[31] Then, in 1898, the Homestead Act was opened to Asian Americans who were born in the United States, a direct result of the Supreme Court birthright case *United States v. Wong Kim*

Ark. However, despite these cases, the Homestead Act remained largely exclusionary.

Less explored than the property and racial dynamics of the Homestead Act are the ways the act worked as an early housing policy. Yet, when closely examined, it becomes clear that the Homestead Act established precedent linking homeownership and citizenship. As discussed above, citizenship has, in many ways, served as a stand-in for race, specifically in thinking about who had access to citizenship and who had access to the Homestead Act. With this in mind, the actual legislation of the Homestead Act made clear that those who claimed a homestead were required to build a residence on their parcel of land. Section 2 of the 1862 Homestead Act states, "for his or her exclusive benefit, and that said entry is made for the purpose of actual settlement and cultivation."[32] Here, we need to consider what "actual settlement" was to mean at the time. By looking to a later section of the act, we are provided more guidance. The act required the homesteader to file an affidavit to change "his or her residence" and to not leave the homestead plot for more than six months at one time.[33] With this information, we know that homesteaders were expected to build a residence or, as we commonly understand today, a home, a place to provide long-term shelter, a place that one returns to.

The act expected would-be homesteaders to prove up the land not only by agricultural or farming means but by building a home on the land and making it their primary and permanent residence. Thus, the Homestead Act provided what many have described as "free land" to build a house and attain homeownership. This is in sharp contrast to the available options for American Indians at the time, who were largely confined to reservations, where the land is held in trust, and with virtually no financial support or incentive for home construction. Though we do know that many American Indians would build family homes on reservation land, those homes did not come with the guarantee of property ownership the way the Homestead Act did. It is precisely the trust status of reservation land that has historically and significantly limited property ownership and homeownership that operates in opposition to the Homestead Act's guarantee of land and house as property.[34] In this way, American Indians were further excluded from the possibility of becoming homeowners on homesteaded land—land that we know today is tied to the accumulation of generational wealth. The Homestead Act was not simply about settling land and claiming it as your own; it was about making that land your home.

Remaining and Returning: Indian Presence in Indian Places

Despite expansive federal Indian policies of the mid- to late nineteenth century, much of which centered on military violence, conquest, and Indigenous dispossession, we know American Indian people sought out creative ways and fought to remain in their homelands, despite what the historical narrative tells us. Though significant land-based federal policies, like the Homestead Act, worked as tools to promote and advance Native dispossession across places like Minnesota to overwhelmingly white settlers, we must remember the Indian people who remained across this landscape. Here, I transition to examine primary-source local histories and federal census data to reveal the Indian people who remained across this landscape, participating in the processes of change, despite policies that specifically worked to remove them.

If focus is given to modes of transportation linking places, self-sufficient economies, and an intentionally arranged residential living pattern as markers of a metropolitan and even suburban environment, then certainly the Dakota and Ojibwe were the first suburbanites in this region, and their stories must not be overlooked and ignored for the larger and more dominant narratives of white settlement. The stories of these Indian people—those who remained in an ever-changing environment, rendered invisible and incomplete by the forces of colonialism, including war, exile, and rapid non-Native settlement—highlight the complexity of a continuous Indian presence, over time, in Indian places that were rapidly reimagined as a white, suburban Twin Cities. Though Indigenous place-names became Americanized and non-Native settlement increased, Dakota, Ojibwe, and other Native people, as well as their families and descendants, who were forced from the southern half of Minnesota, returned, remembered, and reclaimed the land that they have always called home, Mnísota Makhóčhe. The end of this chapter is about those Indian people who remained and returned to an ever-changing landscape, pushing back against and challenging state and federal policies.

Though popular and dominant historical narratives continuously tell us of the "vanishing Indian," Native people were active participants and residents in the development of the Twin Cities as we know them today. Yet, perhaps more significant and revealing than the mere presence of American Indian people on early census documents is that the places where they were located were seemingly, or outwardly perceived to be, white towns and cities. However, when I peel back the layers to reveal Indian peoples' residential, familial, and work patterns, we see that Indian people continued to live as neighbors to one another and that many Indian families also lived in the same place or town for decades. The Indian people who lived in these constantly changing places were employed; some worked as farmers and laborers, while others adjusted to capitalism and found work in industrial jobs. Perhaps even more remarkable are the Indian people whose occupations reflected more traditional sources of income during this era of dramatic assimilation efforts. Those who worked as hunters, fishermen, trappers, and even mitten and moccasin makers did so in an increasingly capitalistic environment, when their land and resources for traditional rounds and sustenance-base activities were also rapidly depleted and shifted hands to new owners. Yet it was this variety of reliable income sources that, according to census record, afforded American Indian individuals and their families to live in "fixed" and "civilized" dwellings, just as their new white neighbors.[35]

In addition to census data, local place-based histories offer a glimpse into the lives of American Indian people in the Twin Cities at the turn of the twentieth century. Edward D. Neill is only one example of a regional place-based history writer of Minnesota. Born in 1823, Neill served as a chancellor at the University of Minnesota and as president of Macalester College in Saint Paul; he was also a Presbyterian minister, serving as a chaplain to Minnesota soldiers during the Civil War. As a scholar, Neill regarded himself as a historian, particularly of colonial America, and gathered an extensive archival collection, including various so-called artifacts and resources on American Indians as well as correspondence with numerous political figures.[36]

Neill wrote a flurry of county-based histories during the 1880s, many of which are considered the first such histories of place; his histories include Washington, Hennepin, Ramsey, and Dakota Counties.[37] Perhaps unsurprisingly, these primary-source, place-based histories obscure

Native histories and claims to space by superseding them with a Euro-American history and claims to space through the process of firsting.[38] Yet the writing of Neill and other white males is representative of scholarly and popular writings of place during the late nineteenth and early twentieth centuries, particularly in their descriptions of Indian people. In the creation of such narratives, these texts claim to tell an official history and thereby further contribute to the firsting discourse as they work to assert their own nativity to the land itself. It is here that I push back against these erasure narratives that have long been told and retold. Instead, I juxtapose these written narratives alongside census data to document Native people who remained in the region despite federal and state policies that sought to remove them.

Today the suburban bluffs of Mendota overlook both Mnísota Wakpá and Wakpá Tháŋka, just across from Fort Snelling, an area long known by the Dakota as Bdóte. It is much smaller both geographically and in terms of population than neighboring Mendota Heights. Mendota is home to the Sibley Historic Site, what was once the American Fur Company post during the fur trade era of the nineteenth century, right along Mnísota Wakpá.[39] The city of Mendota prides itself on its history as beginning "in 1805 when President Thomas Jefferson sent Lt. Zebulon Pike to the upper Mississippi to acquire a site for a fort."[40] Though the American history of Mendota may have begun in 1805 with the signing of a treaty, the Indian history and presence certainly did not end. According to local historical records and common place-based historical narratives, Dakota people have lived in and around Mendota since at least the eighteenth century. However, Dakota oral histories and archaeological evidence suggest an Indigenous presence much earlier. Archaeological evidence, gathered from the Sibley Historic Site at Mendota, documents human habitation of the area during the "Paleoindian, Archaic, Woodland, Late Precontact, Contact and Historic" periods, with over 61,000 items collected, confirming Dakota oral histories.[41] It was in this same area that Euro-American explorers arrived during the seventeenth and eighteenth centuries and began to transcribe *Bdóte,* the Dakota name for the area that surrounds the mouth of Mnísota Wakpá, to English as *Mendota.* The entirety of Bdóte includes numerous Dakota sacred sites, such as Oȟéyawahe (Pilot Knob), Wakháŋ Thípi (Carver's Cave), and Mní Owe Sni (Coldwater Spring).[42] These Dakota places increasingly came under American colonial control during the early to mid-nineteenth century as forces of colonialism spread west.

In 1881, Neill wrote of Mendota in his *History of Dakota County* as the site of the first settlement in what is now the state of Minnesota with the "first inhabitation" by "a half-breed Sioux, by the name of Duncan Campbell" in 1826.[43] He recalls that though the area was once inhabited by "Sioux," it "only assumed importance after the building of Fort Snelling" and that its name was "formed from the Sioux word 'mdo-te,' which signifies the junction of two rivers."[44] In Neill's own description of Mendota, he at once confirms an Indian past and presence,

Map 4. Locations of the suburbs discussed in this chapter, each located along riverways. Map by Katherine Koehler.

particularly through Háza Íŋyaŋke Wiŋ, the Dakota woman born there in 1788, the same woman who opens this chapter. Though Neill portrays her as the "last Indian," census data certainly contradicts this claim.[45] The 1880 U.S. Census documented at least twenty Indian people who lived in Mendota, the same geographic area Neill claims is virtually absent of Indian people in 1881.

Not only have Indian people always been present at Mendota, they also actively engaged with the changing economies and worked to maintain cultural ties. According to census records, the Indian people who lived in Mendota at the turn of the twentieth century were involved in various forms of labor, work that varied from keeping house and working as laborers to those who earned money making mittens, hunting, and tanning hides. Importantly, Indian people in Mendota lived as neighbors in homes located next to each other; this is significant because it shows that the American Indian people here were able to maintain community bonds as neighbors. In 1900 and 1910, the Indian people who lived in Mendota included Dakota and Ojibwe people who lived in "fixed," "civilized" dwellings just as their white neighbors.

Shakopee, located along the southern shore of Mnísota Wakpá just before it curves north toward Saint Paul, is home to seven burial mounds, including those in Memorial Park, some dating back two thousand years. Originally home to twenty-nine burial mounds, the burial sites of the Dakota people at this Indian place were gradually destroyed over time as roads and parking lots were constructed and housing and commercial development ensued. The name *Shakopee* is an Anglicization of the name of the Dakota leader Šákpe. Šákpe's village was located along Mnísota Wakpá, near present-day Shakopee, and was known as Thíŋta Othúŋwe or Shakopee Village. It has long been an area where Dakota gathered to play lacrosse against one another and often against neighboring tribes. Šákpe's village on Mnísota Wakpá had "the largest population in the mid-nineteenth century" of Bdewákhaŋthuŋ Dakota people.[46] It was here that in 1842 the "first steamboat came down the river" and Oliver and Harriet Faribault, a mixed-blood fur-trading family, built a log cabin. During the 1840s, Samuel Pond, a missionary, established himself in the area. It was not long before the 1851 Treaties of Mendota and Traverse des Sioux opened this land for non-Native settlement and the Dakota who lived here and called this place home were removed. Only a few years later, in 1854, the white village of Shakopee was platted and grew rapidly; it was incorporated for the first time in 1857.[47]

In local histories, Shakopee has been written about as a notorious battle site between the Dakota and Ojibwe, as "the largest village of Med-day-wah-kawn-twawn-Sioux," as a site where early traders and missionaries were located, as "the county seat, [and] the site of a Sioux village which was ruled by a hereditary line of chiefs, bearing the name of Shakpay or Shakopee (six)," and as a village passed through on a mail route following Indian trails.[48] Although these written narratives describe a significant Indian presence in Shakopee, many of these accounts end in the mid-nineteenth century. Yet census data from the late nineteenth century picks up where the written record ends to reflect a sizable Indian population in Shakopee, even after the U.S.–Dakota War. Though only eight Indian people were documented in census records as residing within the town of Shakopee in 1875, by 1880 that number had grown to exceed thirty people across seven familial households. Almost all the married Indian women were neighbors and worked keeping house in 1880.[49]

Interestingly, the Dakota who were recorded in the 1900 census were absent from Shakopee when the enumerator came through. The census record, recorded by enumerator Henry C. Schroder states, "Owing to the fact that the above indians left town a few days before the above date the information is not complete which was gotten from the neighbors."[50] We are left to speculate as to why the "above indians" were absent. The census enumeration form is dated June 26, 1900; perhaps the family recently left town to participate in tribal ceremonies, which often occur in the summer months, or to contribute to the summer's seasonal round activities of fishing and gathering, or even to partake in a community event or visit relatives. That the information, documented on official census forms was gathered from neighbors, who are also Indian, is also revealing. The information provided by the neighbors suggests they knew their Indian neighbors well—they were able to tell the enumerator whether they could read or write, that they were all "ration Indians," their places of birth, and each family member's blood quantum, a very personal matter; perhaps they were even kin or extended family.[51] Further, the information provided describes a single household that was a multigenerational family of seven. Interestingly, this family was not present in census records for Shakopee in 1875, 1880, or 1885, though this does not mean they were not there—simply that they were not recorded as Indian.

Though certain Indian places, like Mendota and Shakopee, were able to maintain a distinct Native population, not all Indian places are as easy to identify and define in historical narratives and census records between 1875 and 1910. Landscapes have been altered, place-names have changed time and again, and settlers eventually became suburbanites. Before Bloomington was founded, it was home to at least two Dakota villages, Thithánka Thannína (Penichon Village) and Ohánska (Black Dog Village).[52] Dakota burial mounds continue to dot this landscape four miles upriver from Fort Snelling, overlooking Mnísota Wakpá, known as the Bloomington Ferry Mound Group. However, in Edward D. Neill's Hennepin County history he describes "Peter Quinn [as] the first white man to settle and cultivate the soil of the town [of Bloomington]. He was an Indian farmer, in accordance with the treaty with the Indians."[53] In this brief statement Neill emphasizes the whiteness and masculinity of the first settler: "Peter Quinn was the first white man." This of course fails to consider the prior occupation of Dakota people. As an "Indian farmer," Peter Quinn was hired by the U.S. government in 1843 to teach the Dakota in the area Euro-American farming techniques. Similarly, Neill later points out "[the] first school in the township [of Bloomington] was at the Dakota Mission. . . . Though organized for the Indians, some white children of early settlers attended."[54] Again, though Neill draws the reader's attention to the whiteness of the first and early settlers of Bloomington, he simultaneously confirms a prior Indigenous presence.

While Neill alludes to and sidesteps a Dakota presence in Bloomington throughout the mid- and late nineteenth century, U.S. Census data affirms an Indigenous presence. A territorial census from 1875 documents at least eighteen Indian people living in Bloomington across three neighboring households; by 1880 there were four separate Indian households. Like Mendota, the Indian residents of Bloomington worked as laborers, farmers, and home keepers. In 1880 Alice Lawrence (age six) and Henry Lawrence (age seven), likely cousins, were both described as "scholars." Another Indian girl, named Hannah (age fourteen), was also described as a scholar. The Indian residents of Bloomington in the late nineteenth century were families who lived as neighbors, next door to one another, and often resided in the city for several decades. Interestingly, several of the Indian people who lived in Bloomington during the late nineteenth century maintained their Dakota names, which were recorded in census data. On June 16, 1880, the enumerator recorded four Indian families; members of two of these families used their Dakota names. A widowed Apulakewin (spelled Aputakewrie on the 1875 census) was seventy-five years old and headed a household of her children, including daughter Sakemazawin. One of Apulakewin's neighbors was Wadata Lawrence (simply listed as Wadata on the 1875 census), also a widowed head of household.

West of Bloomington is Eden Prairie, a Dakota place whose southern border is formed by Mnísota Wakpá. The description Neill offers of Eden Prairie echoes that of Bloomington, particularly as he continues the practice of firsting. Even as he does this, Neill again reaffirms an Indian presence in the area as he states, "the first claim on the north part of the prairie, immediately after the treaty [of 1851] was made with the [Dakotas]."[55] In essence, this acknowledges the Dakota ties to place and their residence in (and around) Eden Prairie prior to white settlement and presumably after the removal treaty of 1851. Neill follows up with an interesting narrative of an incident that occurred on May 27, 1858, shortly after the town was formed: "A fearful Indian battle was fought, which was witnessed by several of the settlers. It took place between the old enemies, the Sioux and the Chippewas."[56] This passage simultaneously confirms an Indian presence in Eden Prairie after removal while also casting American Indians as savage through the rhetoric of "battle" and "enemies" at war. Despite the narrative portrayal of Dakota and Ojibwe in this instance, what is significant is that both were present at Eden Prairie after the Treaties of Mendota and Traverse des Sioux, signed in 1851, sought to remove Indian people from this landscape to the western fringe of Minnesota Territory. Here, Neill's use of language reveals common stereotypes of the period, often drawing on stereotypes of American Indians as hyperviolent and aggressive rather than expressing empathy or recognizing the history of intertribal violence; for example, Neill states that "the Chippewas formed an ambush" and "though inferior in numbers, [the Sioux] fought with characteristic vigor and desperation."[57] Yet, his writing also offers valuable evidence of Dakota people present in Eden Prairie and nearby localities, including Shakopee, in the mid-nineteenth century.

Where Neill's written history ends, census data makes clear there was a lengthy presence of Indian people in Eden Prairie at least through the turn of the twentieth century. In 1880 there were at least twenty-seven Indian people who lived across seven home groups clustered together in Eden Prairie, including the Bluestones and Otherdays. Several of the Native male heads of household worked as farmers. Each of the Indian homes in Eden Prairie was owned by their Indian occupants in 1900 and 1910. Of the families recorded in census materials, the most common occupation of male heads of household was farming. The youngest Indian resident of Eden Prairie was a newborn baby boy, only one month old. All the Indian residents of Eden Prairie documented in the census were born in Minnesota; this is crucial when thinking about the exile of Dakota people from the state. The fact that individuals in their mid- to late teens were born in Minnesota signifies that some of these families likely never left the state after the U.S.–Dakota War and resulting exile.

The Indian presence in southern Minnesota, though continuous, has often been overshadowed and concealed by dominant Euro-American histories, making it difficult for the untrained eye to locate American Indian people. Larger non-Native communities often masked the less numerous presence of Indian people in Minnesota during these difficult years. Though the Indian presence at Minnetonka and Anoka at the turn of the century differs dramatically from those previously described, their Indian presence is perhaps a sad reminder of colonialism and land loss. Located west of Minneapolis, Minnetonka, which originates in the Dakota name for the body of water Mní Iá Tháŋka, became a resort and tourist destination for wealthy white settlers. Scores of white visitors flocked to the shores of Mní Iá Tháŋka throughout the late nineteenth century and well into the twentieth. In fact, white settlers began arriving as early as 1852, just one year after the Treaties of Mendota and Traverse des Sioux opened the region for settlement. These early settlers likely encountered Dakota regularly since "[the] Indian chief, Little Six, and his band of braves, camped at Wayzata Bay, near the present site of Wayzata village during the winter of 1853, returning every winter following the outbreak of the Sioux of 1862. . . . Little Six was considered an exemplary Indian, who was cleanly, manly, and brave."[58] This descriptive passage in Neill's text emphasizes the presence of Dakota people at Mní Iá Tháŋka, including areas today that are considered parts of suburban Minnetonka and Wayzata, both before the U.S.–Dakota War and after. During the late nineteenth century and into the twentieth, Mní Iá Tháŋka continued to gain popularity as a tourist and resort destination for the wealthy. Perhaps it is ironic, then, that during the late nineteenth century, Minnetonka, an Indian place of increasing white affluence, also became the home of the Hennepin County Poor House. Census records show that in 1880 an Indian woman named Lizzie Radcliffe resided at the Hennepin County Poor House, unfortunately described, and remembered, only as an Indian and as a "pauper."

Wakpá Wakháŋ (Rum River), which flows out of the southern corner of Mille Lacs Lake in central Minnesota, twists and turns its way south until it empties into Wakpá Tháŋka at Anoka. The name *Anoka* stems from the Dakota word *Anúŋkha* and loosely translates to "on both of something." Both the Dakota and Ojibwe resided in this area prior to any white settlement. It was this benefit of being on two major rivers that also drew early white settlers to Anoka for exploration, commerce, and homesteading. Published in 1905, Albert M. Goodrich describes "the last battle in Minnesota between the Sioux and Chippeway tribes" as approximately 150 Ojibwe made their way down Wakpá Wakháŋ to Anúŋkha.[59] "Here they held a war dance on the east side of Rum river. . . . The white boys turned out in large numbers to view the spectacle as if it had been a circus performance, little thinking in what deadly earnest the Indians were."[60] This battle, which Goodrich richly describes, is more than one decade after the 1837 treaties with the Dakota and Ojibwe that were to effectively remove them from this area.

As in numerous other Indian places, Indian people continued to reside in Anoka throughout the late nineteenth and early twentieth centuries. Although Anoka was a place the Dakota and Ojibwe traveled to and through, and occasionally camped in for lengthier periods, in 1880 Anoka was home to an Indian woman named Hattie Worchester. She was recorded in the census as being the wife of a white male head of the household. More interesting, however, Hattie Worchester is recorded as an Indian who was born in Minnesota, yet her parents were both born in Maine. In 1880 the census did not record tribal affiliation, but considering that both of Hattie Worchester's parents were born in Maine, she most likely was not Dakota or Ojibwe. This case represents an interesting and important example of the direction Indian affairs was headed in Minnesota as Indian people from across the country began to call Minnesota and, more specifically, the Twin Cities home.

When the Dakota, Ojibwe, and Ho-Chunk were forcibly removed from their tribal homelands and reservations in the central and southern portion of Mnísota Makhóčhe during the mid-nineteenth century, they often also vanished from the historical narrative of the state and local histories. These historical erasures have been clouded and overshadowed by the significance of the U.S.–Dakota War and the dramatic influx of non-Native settlers to the same areas. In fact, Minnesota saw exponential population growth ahead of and leading up to the years of the U.S.–Dakota War and the Homestead Act. In 1860, two years after Minnesota statehood, the population of Minnesota grew exponentially by over 2,700 percent from the first federal census conducted in the territory in 1850. This dramatic growth in a white settler population also coincides with a declining American Indian population.

Year	Population
1850	6,077
1860	172,073
1870	439,706
1880	780,773
1890	1,310,283
1900	1,751,394
1910	2,075,708

Figure 6. Minnesota's population growth during the second half of the nineteenth century was dramatic. Between 1850 and 1910, the non-Native population grew by more than 34,000 percent.

Yet, as this chapter shows, despite the increasing numbers of non-Native settlers across the Twin Cities region, American Indian people have always been present, even as their traditional homes and the landscape around them rapidly changed and settlers quickly outnumbered Indian people. The Dakota origin story places their point of entry into this world at the mouth of Mnísota Wakpá, and ample evidence exists that demonstrates the significance of both Mnísota Wakpá and Wakpá Tháŋka for trade and economic purposes between Indian people and later between Indian people and Europeans. Likewise, archaeological and written accounts of early European explorers from the seventeenth century onward document Dakota and Ojibwe villages throughout what is considered today to be suburban Minneapolis and Saint Paul. The survival and endurance of Indian people, particularly the Dakota, to continuously live in Indian places during times of vast and rapid dispossession, removal, war, exile, and increasing settlement throughout the late nineteenth century is nothing short of remarkable. And, as I contend, both local county histories and census records offer an opportunity to rethink suburban places and first residents. More, the seemingly inevitable erasure of Indian people from suburban places becomes preventable and fixable. As Coll Thrush contends, Indian people adapted, as they always had: they chose to "stay near traditional territories and make a go of it. . . . They and their homes would remain important landmarks for indigenous people."[61]

This story of American Indian land loss and survival across Mnísota Makhóče must also be situated among a context that engages with federal policies to better understand that what happened to American Indians here was similarly happening to Native people across much of the country. In this way, Minnesota is a microcosm to better understand such federal-level land-based policies as the Homestead Act, the Pacific Railway Act, and the Morrill Act. These three policies in tandem with the U.S.–Dakota War, all of which occurred midway through 1862, are a marker of sorts of dispossession and yet simultaneous and remarkable American Indian survival and revival. By looking at the evidence shared here, we see a more complete and accurate history; we see the ways so-called public land has been framed, used, and remembered. We are also then forced to think about the irreconcilability of place and place-making for American Indian people and settlers. While the U.S.–Dakota War led to Dakota exile, the opening of land for settlement, and the expansion of the Homestead Act across the state, the places non-Native settlers created would not and did not diminish the value and meaning of home for the Dakota and Ojibwe. Instead, we see a dialectic, an ongoing push and pull of sorts, between the world the policies created, the ones settlers made, and the one American Indian people have always known and continue to know.

2

PIVOTAL POLICIES
THE CREATION OF THE FEDERAL HOUSING ADMINISTRATION AND THE INDIAN REORGANIZATION ACT

> An overwhelming majority of the Indians are poor, even extremely poor. . . . The homes are characterized by poor structure, poor repair, overcrowding, lack of sanitation, and bad housekeeping. . . . The primary duty of the government in dealing with its Indian wards is to aid them in adjusting themselves to white civilization.
>
> —LEWIS MERIAM, *Meriam Report: The Problem of Indian Administration*

> But there has been also the *American dream,* that dream of a land in which life should be better and richer and fuller for every man, with opportunity for each according to his ability or achievement. . . . A dream of social order in which each man and each woman shall be able to attain the fullest stature of which they are innately capable, and be recognized by others for what they are, regardless of the fortuitous circumstances of birth or position.
>
> —JAMES TRUSLOW ADAMS, *The Epic of America*

ACCORDING TO HIS 1917 World War I draft registration card, Louis Gruette, an Ojibwe man from the White Earth Reservation in northern Minnesota, lived at Ogema, a small reservation town in northern Minnesota, where he was a carpenter. Three years later, at the time of the 1920 census, Louis Gruette, a citizen of the Pembina Band, still lived at

White Earth but was now employed as a laborer for the railroad.[1] By 1930, Louis Gruette was married, and he and his wife, Mary, who was also Ojibwe from White Earth, had moved to Mound, Minnesota. Today, Mound is widely recognized by most locals as a suburb west of Minneapolis, hugging the western shores of Lake Minnetonka. The name Mound comes from the numerous Dakota Indian mounds that dot the landscape of the city. Prior to the arrival and settlement of Euro-Americans during the mid- to late nineteenth century, Mound was home to Dakota people, specifically those of the Bdewakanton band.

When the 1930 census was conducted in Mound on April 14, the Gruette family was the 178th family visited in the township, not quite a city or a suburb by today's standards. It is here that Louis Gruette worked as a building mason while his wife, Mary, though described as not employed on census documents, certainly contributed to if not oversaw the day-to-day operations of their household and cared for the couple's five children, ranging in age from two to eleven years old. Though Mound was still a place in flux, gradually shifting away from farming homesteads, in 1930 the Gruettes owned their home, valued at $1,500, and it was not considered a farm like several of their neighbors. These neighbors, who likewise owned their homes, had home values that ranged between $1,000 and $5,000; two of the Gruettes' neighbors rented, and two lived on homesteads that continued to operate as farms. Though Louis was employed, several of his neighbors were not. Of those who were, almost all had occupations requiring manual labor—a mechanic, a caretaker, a gardener, two carpenters, and one male head of household who worked as a stenographer at a local loan company. But each of the neighbors' wives, like Mary, was listed as having no occupation. Every one of these neighbors was white, coming from Swedish, Norwegian, and German backgrounds.

The Gruette family was not alone in their migration to the Twin Cities during the early decades of the twentieth century. Rather, their family story of migration across Indian spaces to places that were becoming predominately white suburbs is representative of numerous American Indian families. Many of these families and individuals left their home reservations for the first time, as a method of survival on the cusp of the Great Depression, and moved to the growing cities and predominately white suburbs of the United States during the early to mid-twentieth century, a time of rapid change. When the Gruettes left an Ojibwe place, the White Earth Reservation, to establish a home in Mound during the early decades of the twentieth century, they were migrating to another Indian place—this time a Dakota place.[2] Similarly, hundreds of other Indian individuals and families migrated to Minnesota's Twin Cities as a way to access education, secure employment or job training, for housing opportunities and economic advancement, and, perhaps, to make and shape new Indian communities.

Spaces and places were changing dramatically at the turn of and into the twentieth century. After Minnesota achieved statehood in 1858, Euro-Americans rapidly settled the south-central portions of the state, aided and abetted by the Homestead Act of 1862.[3] In Minnesota, over eighty-five thousand homesteads accounted for over ten million homestead acres across the state. After the U.S.–Dakota War, non-Native settlers and second-wave settlers, many benefiting from the Homestead Act, continued to flood the region. By the late nineteenth century, railroads crisscrossed the state, virtually all of which had stops in the increasingly urban Minneapolis and Saint Paul. The growth of urban enclaves was largely spurred by the rise of the flour mill and hydroelectric industries, which benefited from the power generated by the Mississippi River that runs through the heart of each city. As industry boomed across Minnesota, with mining to the north in the Iron Range, the population of Minneapolis and Saint Paul and their surrounding metro area continued to swell. It was during this period, the first decades of the twentieth century, that the suburbs of the Twin Cities, as we most commonly understand them to be, took shape. Building on Kenneth T. Jackson's characteristics of suburbs that he uses throughout *Crabgrass Frontier,* my use of *suburbs* includes places that have lower population densities than their urban counterparts (in this case, Minneapolis and Saint Paul), areas marked by higher rates of homeownership and the desire for such, places that are generally socioeconomically better off than the urban core, and commuter places that rely on accessible, reliable, and relatively speedy transportation.[4] However, the many American Indians who reside in suburbs push back against and force us to consider Jackson's definition in new and important ways. Indeed, as I argue throughout this book, suburbs across the entirety of the United States are inherently Indigenous places that were rapidly (re)made and (re)populated through the historic and ongoing settler colonialism of the nineteenth, twentieth, and now twenty-first centuries. This is significant as scholars and Native community members alike work to denaturalize the seeming inevitability of settler colonialism.

With this background in mind, in this chapter I examine significant and enduring pieces of federal housing policy and federal Indian policy of the 1920s and 1930s. I begin with a careful review of the Snyder Act of 1921 and the Indian Citizenship Act of 1924. Here, I intervene in housing studies and American Indian studies scholarship to examine the ways the Snyder Act offers a legal lens or framework from which to critically examine Indian housing programs and policies as they have unfolded over the last one hundred years. At the same time, I consider the ways Indian citizenship, and lack thereof, fit into this post–World War I period when homeownership was widely promoted by the federal government as the key to a strong citizenry. Next, I juxtapose the 1934 creation of the Federal Housing Administration alongside the passage of the Indian Reorganization Act, which unfolded within days of one another. By examining a longer history of the Indian Reorganization Act and the Federal Housing Administration, beginning with the Snyder Act of 1921, moving on to the Indian Citizenship Act of 1924, and then the Meriam Report of 1928, I do the important work of unpacking and highlighting the complexity and entanglement of Indian policy and housing policy at the same political moment, a time of "relief, reform, and recovery." More, this chapter draws on census data from 1920, 1930, and 1940 to better understand the ways American Indian people actively worked to assert their dual citizenship status as members of tribal nations and as newly declared citizens of the United States in the wake of World War I, the economic crisis of the Great Depression, and in an increasingly metropolitan and automobile-oriented society.

It was in the midst of this changing environment that American Indian people left their reservations, many for the first time, to seek out a life in the Twin Cities. Hundreds, if not thousands, of Indian individuals and families, much like the Gruettes, migrated to Minnesota's Twin Cities, joining Indian people already there, as a way to secure an education or job training, to gain employment, to reconnect with family, and for improved housing opportunities—futures that were certainly ripe with opportunity. Much like Native American and Indigenous studies

(NAIS) scholars Douglas K. Miller and Nicolas G. Rosenthal demonstrate in their examinations of American Indian mobility and arrival to urban areas, it is important to look to the ways Indian people participated in this early wave of suburbanization of the Twin Cities precisely because of the numerous factors that pushed back, challenged, and often worked against them.[5] The personal and family stories offered in this chapter provide a glimpse into the often highly invisible and overlooked histories of Indian people in places that were becoming increasingly suburban, places outside the urban core yet connected via transportation, and places read as white, between 1920 and 1940. Many of these family stories have never been told, examined, or documented before. Taken together, these prove to be common family stories of labor and homeownership, movement, and migration. Census data and archival records allow us to piece stories and histories together to consider why, when, and where Indian people moved into the metropolitan area in the early decades of the twentieth century to the backdrop of shifting federal policies that established subsidized homeownership and, for Indian people, granted a seemingly new level of autonomy to tribal nations and Indian people on reservations across the country.

However, the Indian stories of migration and movement to a developing and growing metropolitan environment shared here must be considered alongside earlier movements and migrations of Indian people. Here, I am specifically referring to those movements and migrations of Indian people that occurred throughout the nineteenth century as a process of seasonal rounds, rather than thinking of twentieth-century migrations to cities as somehow distinct and different, as if occurring in isolation.[6] The wave of American Indian mobility that the Gruettes participated in, to a built, developing, and rapidly changing metropolitan environment, marks the first major wave of post-removal, post-reservation American Indian movement away from reservations and toward increasingly urban and white areas. In the process, Indian people shifted the focus of their seasonal rounds from natural resource procurement and sustenance to access to a seasonal round market marked by steady employment and improved housing opportunities, thereby altering earlier practices to suit an economy based on capitalism and wage labor. This mobility and movement of American Indians away from reservations and to metropolitan areas, and often back, during the 1920s and

1930s is the often-overlooked precursor to the more well-documented Indian urbanization that occurred during the 1950s and 1960s. Indeed, this early wave of Indian mobility and migration is often passed over, concealing American Indian participation in the development and growth of the suburban Twin Cities that rapidly occurred during this time frame.

The Gruettes, who moved away from their reservation and toward the increasingly metropolitan environment of the Twin Cities, are not always remembered as Indian, drawing our attention to the complexity of place and identity. Louis Gruette passed away in 1938, fifteen years after his family arrived in Mound. His death certificate, dated April 23, 1938, recorded his race as white, even though his place of birth was listed as the White Earth Reservation and he (and all his family) had been listed as Indian on the 1920 and 1930 censuses. Two years later, at the time of the 1940 census, the last year for which census data is publicly available, his widow, Mary, and each of the couple's six children, who still lived at home, were captured in time and remembered as white. Mary, who was also from White Earth, seems to have remained in the suburb of Mound until her death in 1976. Similar to her husband, her death certificate listed her race as white, even though she was born at White Earth and Mary's mother, who was listed on the 1895 White Earth Indian census rolls, was a member of the Gull Lake Mississippi River Band of Chippewa Indians.[7] These inconsistencies, revealed and documented in federal census and state death certificate records, highlight the shifting nature and ambiguity of race and race-making during the time of the policies examined in this chapter. The Gruette family, then, is representative of other American Indians who moved away from their reservations and into the Twin Cities, as well as other metropolitan areas nationwide, and who were forced to reconcile with, and adapt to, a predominately white environment. Indeed, this was a time and place where race was increasingly fluid and contested, particularly for people of color. This is especially true for American Indians, who had long been pressured to assimilate. The Gruette family story demonstrates the difficulty of piecing together family narratives, particularly for Indian people who moved to the Twin Cities in the early decades of the twentieth century—the very people who have been rendered invisible through exclusionary federal policies, an ever-growing non-Native settler population, and the erasure of Indigeneity in census records that had long been controlled by federal enumerators.

Setting the Policy Stage

Ahead of the Great Depression, as technological advances and available forms of transportation increased in the form of gas-powered vehicles and new roads, so too did the accessibility and affordability of travel by vehicle. American Indian people were not to be left behind in the new age of automobility. They did not just move across national, state, county, or municipality lines—they moved across, up, and through social class lines as well. In fact, as Philip J. Deloria reminds us of this time period, "[Indian] mobility called into question the very idea of colonial containment, cultural transformation, and eventual subservience to the United States."[8] The Indian people who were able to take advantage of new forms of accessible mobility and make their way to the Twin Cities, and other metropolitan areas across the United States, encountered new opportunities for employment and homeownership, thereby transcending social class by their work and where they lived, both of which had become and continued to grow as predominately white environments.

The Twin Cities became increasingly accessible for all people during the first decades of the twentieth century. As recounted by local historians, "Automobile traffic significantly altered the suburban areas of both Anoka and Hennepin counties. . . . With the addition of affordable mass-produced automobiles, road and suburban expansion was a natural outlet for increased economic activity."[9] Similarly, in *Indians in Unexpected Places,* Deloria emphasizes "the *auto* and the *mobility* that made up the word *automobile* pointed exactly to the ways in which mobility helped Indian people preserve and reimagine their own autonomy in the face of the reservation system."[10] The reservation system, an unfortunate mainstay of American Indian life since the mid-nineteenth century, had left many Native people desirous of more by the early twentieth century. With one world war underway and increasing technological advancements, specifically automobiles, in many ways the world felt smaller, or at least more connected and accessible. Now, American Indians were no longer resigned or limited to the reservations or to the scraps of Indian land that remained after treaties and Allotment. This was the atmosphere American Indian people chose to engage with and participate in when they left the reservation for the Twin Cities during the 1920s and 1930s, a world of new and exciting change. Yet, the economic prosperity, autonomy, and suburban growth American Indian people encountered in the Twin Cities soon grew to a halt with the arrival of the Great Depression by late summer 1929.

As the 1920s drew to a close and the nation continued to reel from the effects of a severe economic downturn brought on by the shifting postwar economy, so too would American Indian communities. In an attempt to stymie economic decline, the federal government strove to enact policies that would stabilize the economy and promote fiscal spending. It was during this time that a handful of the most recognizable and relied-upon federal policies took shape. Guided by President Franklin D. Roosevelt, the New Deal sought to alleviate the economic tensions so many Americans were experiencing, with a focus on the "relief, recovery, and reform" of financial and lending institutions across the United States. In fact, many of the programs born out of the Great Depression and subsequent New Deal era remain active today, including the Securities

Figure 7. An American Indian man in a headdress rides on an automobile during the Minnesota winter. Photograph by William Bull. Courtesy of Minnesota Historical Society.

and Exchange Commission, the Social Security system, the Federal Housing Administration (FHA), the Federal Deposit Insurance Corporation, and the Federal Crop Insurance Corporation.

The move to increasingly urban and suburban areas by Indian people in Minnesota in the early decades of the twentieth century must be placed within the political, social, and economic atmosphere of the time. By the end of World War I, hundreds of Minnesota Indians had enlisted to serve in the armed forces, even though many Indian people were not yet U.S. citizens. Importantly, during these same decades rapid urban population growth and development overlapped with ongoing efforts of American Indian assimilation. Indian children continued to be sent to boarding schools, and in Minnesota the ongoing process of Allotment had already and severely depleted the tribal landholdings. Perhaps the most devastating effects of the Allotment era can be seen at White Earth, where the Gruette family was from, once the largest reservation in the state. During Allotment, much of the Indian land at White Earth was taken illegally and through dubious means, reducing tribal trust land held by the federal government for the Indians to only approximately 6 percent of the entire reservation, with the remainder of the land within the borders of the reservation usurped by white land purchasers and other interests.[11]

When World War I ended in 1918 and U.S. servicemembers returned home, the seeds of the Great Depression had been sown as the booming war-related economy came to a staggering halt. It is estimated that over ten thousand American Indians served in the military, in various capacities, during World War I. For many American Indian servicemembers, World War I became a path toward U.S. citizenship. On November 6, 1919, Congress passed legislation that provided a pathway for honorably discharged American Indian veterans of World War I to acquire U.S. citizenship. Prior to World War I, American Indians had only limited access to U.S. citizenship, access that centered around the degree of perceived assimilation. Long guided by landownership and then the Allotment process, assimilation was gauged on an American Indian person's ability to maintain and farm their land, ability to speak English, willingness to adopt Christianity, and successful engagement with capitalism. Access to U.S. citizenship for all American Indian people would not occur until 1924.

In the years following World War I, Congress passed the less well-known and less-remembered Snyder Act. The Snyder Act, generally viewed as the legislation that allows for the appropriation of federal funds for Indian health care and Indian education, was signed into law on November 2, 1921, sponsored by New York Representative Homer P. Snyder. The Snyder Act arose from the state of New York's challenge of congressional authority to spend funds on American Indian people's health and education needs. Since then, the Snyder Act has come to be viewed as a sort of consolidation of earlier treaties between tribal nations and the federal government. Originating from the federal–tribal political-legal relationship, the Snyder Act allows for the administration and disbursement of federal moneys for the provision of services to Indian peoples. This is in line with the federal government's trust responsibility, as a sort of compensation or payment for Indian people's land cessions during the treaty-making era. As federal Indian policy scholars David E. Wilkins and K. Tsianina Lomawaima and federal Indian law scholar Felix S. Cohen each articulate, the federal government's provision of services to Indian people rests on treaties.[12] Legally binding treaties between tribal nations and the federal government have subsequently formed the backbone of the Snyder Act.

Though the 1921 Snyder Act has been widely studied through the lens of Indian health care and education, I center it in Indian housing.[13] Here, I position the 1921 Snyder Act as a tool to examine and analyze the federal government's responsibility to provide more accessible and improved housing programs and policies to American Indian people— on and off reservations. A close reading of the 1921 Snyder Act reveals how and why American Indian housing should similarly fall under the purview of federal "obligations and services," much like Indian health care and education.

> The Bureau of Indian Affairs, under the supervision of the Secretary of the Interior, shall direct, supervise, and expend such moneys as Congress may from time to time appropriate, *for the benefit, care, and assistance of the Indians throughout the United States for the following purposes: General support and civilization,* including education. For the relief of distress and conservation of health. For industrial assistance and advancement and *general administration of Indian property*. . . . For the enlargement, extension, improvement,

and repair of the buildings and grounds of existing plants and projects. . . . And for the general and incidental expenses in connection with the administration of Indian affairs.[14]

Though the above passage does contain ambiguous language, the Snyder Act deserves more attention in the context of Indian housing and federal trust responsibility. If one examines the language of specific treaties, we are provided a clearer roadmap of sorts. For example, the February 27, 1855, Treaty with the Winnebago (today, more accurately termed the Ho-Chunk) articulates how treaty and annuity payments were to be spent: "In subsisting [the Ho-Chunk] a reasonable time after their removal; in making improvements, such as breaking and fencing land, and building houses."[15] In the same treaty, it was explicitly stated that not only would homes be built for the Ho-Chunk but any federal moneys from the 1855 treaty and prior treaties with the Ho-Chunk may be used for the "furnishing of houses." A similar story unfolds in the 1859 Treaty with the Winnebago: "For the purpose of procuring the means of comfortably establishing the Winnebagoes upon the lands to be assigned to them in severalty, by building them houses, and furnishing them" in exchange for land.[16] In no uncertain terms, the federal government, through treaty negotiation and obligation, made promises to the Ho-Chunk to not only build them houses but also to furnish those homes. Significantly, the Ho-Chunk were not the only tribal nation the federal government made such promises to. Indeed, a review of treaties from the mid-nineteenth century reveals this was a relatively common practice and assumption of responsibility on behalf of the federal government. In this way, the federal government paved the way to cement in treaty their responsibility to house Indian people, making it, much like health care and education, a trust responsibility.

Here, Wilkins and Lomawaima draw a clear connection between the trust doctrine and the federal government's responsibilities to Indian people as emanating from the Snyder Act. In reference to the trust doctrine, they state: "in general congressional policies and specific acts applicable to all Indian tribes (such as the 1819 Civilization Act and the 1921 Snyder Act)."[17] They go on to elaborate that "the trust doctrine, in this view emanates from the unique relationship between the United States and Indians in which the Federal Government undertook the obligation to insure the survival of Indians. . . . [The trust doctrine's] broader purpose . . . is to protect and enhance the people, the property, and the self-government of Indian tribes."[18] It is through this lens, then, that the Snyder Act not only serves as the legislation that provides for the mechanisms of the federal government to provide the necessary federal funding for Indian health care and Indian education but also, as I contend here and emphasize in subsequent chapters, must be read as supporting and authorizing federal funding for Indian housing across the United States, both on reservation and off, which rests on a long and legally binding history of treaty-making that affirms the federal government's trust responsibility. Indeed, while "three components define the trust relationship: land, self-governance, and social services," my attention here is on what *social services* entails.[19]

Such spending, though viewed as an unnecessary expense and unearned entitlement by some, has been carefully explained by federal Indian policy and legal scholar Felix S. Cohen. In his 1942 *Handbook of Federal Indian Law,* he contends:

> Federal services which the United States provides for the Indians are frequently viewed as a matter of charity. The erroneous notion is widely prevalent that in their relationship with the Federal Government the Indians have been the regular recipient of unearned bounties. In reality, federal services were, in earlier years, largely a matter of self-protection for the white man or *partial compensation to the Indian for land cessions or other benefits received by the United States.* In recent years such services have been continued, partly *as a result of the failure of the states to render certain essential public services to the Indians,* because of the special relation to the Federal Government.[20]

This "special relationship," upheld by the Constitution, cemented through treaties and in court cases, morphed over time to the guardian–ward relationship at the time of Cohen's writing. Based on the failures of state governments to "render certain essential public services to the Indians," and as a direct result of the federal–tribal relationships established in treaties, the Snyder Act should be read as a tool or intervention to direct federal moneys to tribal nations, money that should be made accessible to tribal citizens, for housing and homeownership programs, on and off reservation, much like Indian education and Indian health-care programs. Thus, federal Indian housing programs should not be considered needs-based housing; rather, moneys allocated for Indian housing should more accurately be viewed as based in treaty-making and an obligation of the federal trust responsibility—to fulfill promises made in treaties in exchange for land.

Moving on from the Snyder Act, the year 1921 also marked an entry point for the federal government's explicit interest in homeownership as a matter of federal policy. In 1921, then secretary of commerce Herbert Hoover cosponsored the short-lived, and little known, homeownership campaign with the National Association of Real Estate Boards, aptly titled the Own Your Own Home (OYOH) campaign. Though the homeownership campaign originally began as a public-relations initiative led by the National Association of Real Estate Boards, the Department of Labor joined forces with the campaign in 1918.[21] The efforts of the OYOH campaign centered on encouraging middle-class American families toward homeownership as a desirable, preferable, and secure financial investment, much like the Homestead Act advocated for landownership fifty-five years prior. In an architectural journal article from 1919, the program is advertised as a means to "provide better living conditions, increase efficiency, encourage thrift, give greater comfort and happiness and create individual reserves for misfortune and old age. Every house owner with his family, whether rich, poor or well-to-do, becomes thereby a better citizen, with increased self-respect, independence and responsibility to the city and nation and are more vitally interested in the welfare and prosperity of both."[22] Perhaps not surprisingly, this push for homeownership was widely supported by individual cities, lumber companies, and mortgage lenders.[23] Eventually, the federal government set aside funds to publish an informative OYOH booklet that was distributed across the country to interested parties and communities while OYOH advertising simultaneously flourished in local newspapers. Many of the newspaper advertisements for the OYOH campaign espoused the virtues of single-family homeownership, linking homeownership to a responsible citizenry, affirming gender roles, and as a supposed responsibility to the nation. Similarly, the accompanying booklet published by the federal government guided readers on how to establish their own localized campaigns and once again affirmed the many values and virtues of homeownership. By the time Hoover, who had long championed the OYOH campaign, became president at the end of the decade, he was known as a staunch and vocal advocate for homeownership.

Despite the promises of homeownership through the OYOH campaign, as noncitizens who lived on reservations and were thus geographically removed from metropolitan areas where housing development was underway, American Indians were largely excluded from the prospect of homeownership through the new initiative. In fact, American Indians as a whole did not have access to U.S. citizenship until the 1924 Indian Citizenship Act (ICA), which in many ways proved a limiting factor in the quest for homeownership.[24] Once U.S. citizenship was available and granted to American Indians, for many a new level of complexity was added to their own identity. Since tribal nations are sovereignty entities, tribal citizens had to negotiate what it meant to be a U.S. citizen, particularly within the settler colonial United States built on the dispossession of Native people. Though American Indian people were benevolently granted U.S. citizenship on paper, voting was still off-limits as it was regulated by state law until the late 1950s. Thus, citizenship did not equate to full democratic participation in the political system at the state or national level. At the same time, homeownership, promoted through such programs as the OYOH campaign and eventually through Federal Housing Administration policies, gradually became a stand-in for citizenship, something that remained off-limits for American Indians. Indeed, as political theorist and American Indian studies scholar Kevin Bruyneel reminds us, the Indian Citizenship Act was not about social concerns but was regulatory in nature. Moreover, "the ICA created and confirmed a form of US citizenship for indigenous people that neither denied their citizenship in tribes nor fully incorporated them into the American polity. It affirmed dual citizenship status as well as a citizen-ward status. Taken alone or together, the dual citizenship and citizen-ward interpretations of the ICA show that, from the US perspective, indigenous people were ambivalent Americans, neither fully inside nor fully outside the American polity."[25] In this way, the ICA was more symbolic in nature than of actual substance. The act and citizenship did little to advance the needs and treatment of Indian people. For example, though they were full citizens under federal law, many

American Indians were not granted the freedom to vote under state law until the 1965 Voting Rights Act. Even today, in some states, like South Dakota and Arizona, American Indians continue to face barriers to voting in local, state, and federal elections.[26]

The ICA revealed, or brought to the surface, the tensions that existed between states and American Indians as citizens. Here, states had individual objectives as they worked to incorporate Indian people into the state citizenry (or exclude them from it). For decades to come, American Indians only had access to a certain kind of citizenship, one that was heavily surveilled and looked a certain way, often revolving around specific forms of property and highly dependent on where they lived—whether on reservation or off, and whether they lived in a rural, urban, or suburban geography. This is in line with the many ways land use, property, and landownership were linked to the Homestead Act's requirement of citizenship and the ways Allotment could lead to citizenship for some American Indian people. However, and importantly, each of these policies (the Homestead Act, Allotment, and the ICA) came with their own caveats, which were revealed as they unfolded. For Indian people, policies like the Homestead Act were a sort of catch-22. American Indians were seemingly left out of access to property (and thus access to homeownership) because they were not full U.S. citizens, yet they could not gain or access full citizenship status because they did not own land or property. In the coming decades, we would see the complexity of this sort of dual citizenship, and the role of property and place, come to a head when federal Indian policy shifted toward Termination and Relocation.

Shifts in Indian policy of the 1920s, from the Snyder Act of 1921 to the ICA of 1924, were not over, and by the final days of the decade, the federal government was at work, aiming to dramatically alter its Indian policy once again, this time in response to the horrific findings of the Meriam Report. Published in 1928, the scathing 850-page report reveals the high rates of disease and death among Indian people who lived on reservations and children who attended boarding schools, the poor sanitary conditions of boarding schools, and the rampant poverty that plagued reservations post-Allotment:

> An overwhelming majority of the Indians are poor, even extremely poor, and they are not adjusted to the economic and social systems

of the dominant white civilization. . . . The prevailing living conditions among the great majority of the Indians are conducive to
the development and spread of disease. . . . The housing conditions are likewise conducive to bad health. Both in the primitive
dwellings and in the majority of more or less permanent homes
which in some cases have replaced them, there is great overcrowd-
ing, so that all members of the family are exposed to any disease
that develops.[27]

It is important to point out that the Meriam Report was published seven
years after the passage of the Snyder Act, which theoretically authorized
the federal government's appropriation of funds to provide social services to Indian people, and four years after American Indian people supposedly became full American citizens through the ICA. While the 1921
Snyder Act authorized federal appropriations, it did not stipulate the
amount of funds to be paid out, a time frame to ensure action, or mea-
surable benchmarks for evaluation. Similarly, though the ICA granted
citizenship to American Indian people, it did nothing to remedy the
economic hardships Indian people faced as a direct result of removal
policy and the reservation system. That the Meriam Report considers
and mentions the status of Indian housing is also significant. However,
from the passage above, attention given to Indian housing is largely
through the lens of Indian and public health, specifically as poor housing is linked to increased "disease." Later, the Meriam Report makes
clear the linkages between housing and health in reference to the "inadequate provision of ventilation" throughout government-subsidized
homes on reservations, the lack of "education in housekeeping" offered
to Indian individuals, the close proximity of sanitation to Indian homes,
the lack of furnishings, and the "primitive arrangements for cooking and
heating."[28] Throughout, the report emphasizes the great need to invest in
and dramatically improve the housing stock across reservation communities while ensuring any new Indian homes are conducive to community
and cultural needs. In many ways, the Meriam Report put Indian housing on the federal government's radar, thus making it hard to ignore.

The direct critique of Indian housing throughout the Meriam
Report similarly emphasizes the growing urban American Indian population and their need for housing. In this way, the publishing and widespread circulation of the Meriam Report must be taken as a push factor

that spurred the movement of Indian people away from reservations and toward growing metropolitan areas, including the Twin Cities. Indeed, the Meriam Report notes, "Indians with much white blood, or to state it in another way, whites whose dash of Indian blood permits their enrollment as Indians," are most commonly found in the cities, and a "considerable proportion of these Indians visited are automobile owners."[29] In fact, Indian families who were working to navigate their own identities, much like the Gruettes, were captured in the Meriam Report. American Indian organizing was already occurring in the cities in the mid-1930s to "deal definitely with enrollment rights and property rights" of tribal members who had already arrived to the metropolitan environment and "[the] Indians in other Minnesota cities [who] are interested in the Twin Cities councils."[30] Similarly, Pauline Brunette Danforth points out how "the Meriam Report noted the presence of Indians in Minneapolis and said Minneapolis-St. Paul attracted Indians because of the number of Industries that call for large numbers of unskilled laborers," and the report itself "pushed" additional Native people to leave their reservation communities for cities by emphasizing the deplorable on-reservation living conditions.[31] So while it is certainly true that most Indian people in the Twin Cities lived in predominately white areas and neighborhoods, they also sought out opportunities to form their own communities, however small. The policy changes that occurred during the 1920s, including those brought about because of the Meriam Report, set the stage for changes that were to come in the 1930s.

1934: Two Months, Three Policies

On June 8, 1934, President Franklin D. Roosevelt delivered his presidential message to Congress, setting the tone for the policies and programs that were to rapidly unfold:

> People want decent homes to live in; they want to locate them where they can engage in productive work; they want some safeguard against misfortunes which cannot be wholly eliminated in this man-made world of ours. In a simple and primitive civilization homes were to be had for the building. The *bounties of nature in a new land* provided crude but adequate food and shelter. When land failed, *our ancestors moved on to better land.* It was always possible

to *push back the frontier,* but *the frontier has now disappeared.* Our task involves the making of better living out of the lands we have.[32]

He continued: "Millions of dollars have been appropriated for housing projects by federal and local authorities, often with the generous assistance of private owners. . . . There is ample private money for sound housing projects. . . . We are working toward the ultimate objective of making it possible for American families to live as Americans should." FDR similarly emphasized the need for legislation "to improve conditions for those who live in houses, those who repair and construct houses, and those who invest in houses." Moreover, he declared that "many of our homes are in decadent condition and not fit for human habitation. They need repairing and modernizing to bring them up to the standard of the times. Many new homes now are needed to replace those not worth repairing."[33] In one single speech, FDR shared with the nation his hopes and dreams to house the masses.

Eager to secure a stable economy following the Great Depression, the first term of Franklin Roosevelt's presidency has been noted by scholars and citizens alike for his efforts at relief, recovery, and reform. As the prior passages demonstrate, FDR and his administration were concerned with efforts to modernize the housing stock available to Americans, thereby making the most effective use of lands acquired by their ancestors centuries prior—land that tribal nations and Indian people had long called home. To do this, he called upon an idyllic view of American civilization—ideals that paralleled Thomas Jefferson's views of property and land rights over one hundred years prior. These ideals, as observed in the Homestead Act and the OYOH campaign, rang true once again in FDR's words. By the same token, FDR's declarations of housing and home needs, and the rhetoric surrounding his administration's support for the New Deal, ironically affirmed those same ideals that had long dictated Indian policy: assimilation via modernization, appropriate use of land, the preference for and preeminence of nuclear families, and civilization as an easily reached tangible reality. This ideology would also undergird the Indian New Deal that was taking shape and unfolding at the same political moment.

Signed into law during summer 1934, the Indian Reorganization Act largely eclipses the passage of the Johnson-O'Malley Act (JOM). The

Johnson-O'Malley Act of April 16, 1934, authorized federal contracts with states to be made whereby the federal government would be financially responsible for the educational, medical, and other "welfare" services provided to Indians by individual states. In this way, JOM "eased the jurisdictional restriction against states dealing with their Indian peoples," arguably very much in line with the objectives of the Snyder Act of 1921 over a decade prior.[34] In fact, the wording of the Johnson-O'Malley Act explicitly states that "the Secretary of the Interior is authorized, in his discretion, to enter into a contract or contracts with any State or Territory having legal authority so to do, for the education, medical attention, agricultural assistance, and social welfare, including relief of distress."[35] Today, the Johnson-O'Malley Act is primarily referenced in terms of Indian education, where individual public school districts receive federal funding for Indian education programming based on the number of tribally enrolled students who attend that district's schools. Summarily, the Johnson-O'Malley Act was a way to subsidize state governments for the provision of services, specifically education, for American Indian people who lived off reservation, calling for federal–state cooperation in the administration of Indian services.

Only weeks after the passage of the Johnson-O'Malley Act, the Indian Reorganization Act (IRA) was passed into law on June 18, 1934. More formally known for the two sponsoring senators, the Wheeler-Howard Act was signed by FDR as an act "to conserve and develop Indian lands and resources; to extend to Indians the right to form business and other organizations; to establish a credit system for Indians; to grant a certain right of home rule to Indians; to provide for vocational education for Indians; and for other purposes."[36] Recognized widely as the "Indian New Deal," the centerpiece of the IRA, as an Indian policy, was that it put an end to the Allotment process that began in 1887. Brought together by Harold Ickes as the "architect," John Collier as the "spokesman," and Felix Cohen as the "legal skill, [with] a quick mind, and a strong desire to work for social justice," the IRA gave tribes the ability to "reorganize" their tribal governments.[37]

Though the IRA was widely promoted as a tool to put tribal governments in control of tribal affairs, and to allow American Indian people more freedoms to exercise their inherent right to sovereignty, the IRA has also been critiqued as a tool to further assimilation and advance federal paternalism. For example, the federal government provided templates for the (re)organization of tribal governments that were largely designed by the federal government, rather than allowing for tribal input and consultation. These new IRA governments also furthered a Western model of governance and left virtually no space for traditional tribal governing structures. In this way, the IRA has been viewed as disrupting historic forms of tribal decision-making, in some cases wreaking havoc across tribal communities as factions developed and new struggles for power began. Moreover, the IRA set in place parameters for tribal nations to serve as corporations for economic purposes while allowing for Indian preference hiring in the Bureau of Indian Affairs. Although some tribes did benefit from the increasing level of autonomy that IRA tribal governments brought about, much of this was short-lived as federal Indian policy shifted toward Termination less than two decades later.

Now nearly a century old, the IRA has been examined by many scholars of NAIS and is often noted as a turning point in federal Indian policy. In the context of federal Indian policy and federal housing policy, attention must be given to the ways the IRA sought to supposedly retribalize Indian land, through a return to trust status, and to the nearly simultaneous passage of more sweeping New Deal–era policies—namely, the passage and creation of the Federal Housing Administration. Indeed, a major component of the IRA allowed the secretary of the interior to place tribally held land, which had previously been subject to Allotment, back under federal trust for tribal nations. This retribalization of Indian land was intended to protect said land from further sale and loss through the Allotment process, via the federal government's trust responsibility, which extended to land. This retribalization is important in terms of time. The Allotment process, which officially began in 1887, though in some instances much later, came with a twenty-five-year term whereby American Indian allottees had to prove their ability to manage their land allotment before outright fee simple ownership would be granted to them. Ahead of that twenty-five-year term, American Indian allottees only had the right to occupy and use the land; they could not sell or lease their allotments as they were not seen as fully capable or competent of doing either (hence the guardian–ward relationship). However, Commissioner of Indian Affairs John Collier and his collaborators in Washington recognized the potential for additional land loss once the twenty-five-year terms reached their maturity, many of which were coming due in the 1930s, and many already attained. The IRA, then, was described and promoted as a tool of the federal government to keep Indian land in trust and under a sort of protected status.

The retribalization of Indian land, as it arose out of the IRA, is significant in terms of place and legacy. Historically, and problematically so, only certain kinds of Indian land have been eligible for the federally protected trust status. Though in many ways trust status seems to make sense, as a protective mechanism to ensure that tribally held land cannot be bought or sold, and to prevent the taxation of tribal land by states and localities, there are limits to trust land designation. Traditionally, Indian land has been described as "held in common" and has been without individual private property ownership as exists under capitalism, though this can vary greatly by tribe and region. Instead, land has been cared for and managed through a more broad and inclusive community investment in and responsibility for the land.[38] This responsibility to the land has not been taken up in the management of trust land under the auspices of the federal government. Rather, under the trust land arrangement, Indian people have the "right to occupancy," while the federal government holds title to, or owns, the land.[39] Under this arrangement, the federal government can unilaterally remove Indian land from trust status. We also know that the federal government, despite its trust obligation to Indian people and their land, does not always act in the best interest of Indian people. Today, tribal nations must apply for any newly acquired land to be placed under trust status, a process that can become quite lengthy, and depending on where the land is located and what is at stake, applications are often denied.[40] So, while the IRA made efforts to return tribal land to trust status, as it was prior to Allotment, we know the whims of the federal government dictate what happens next. Though trust status in many ways protects tribal land, it does not give tribal nations full autonomy over that land. The retribalization of Indian land under the IRA, as a means to end the Allotment process and land loss, only narrowly applied to reservation lands. In more recent years, we have seen the limits to the retribalization of Indian land under the IRA and in case law—for example, the 2009 Supreme Court case *Carcieri v. Salazar*.[41]

Rather than clarify or even simplify land status, in many ways the IRA further complicated Indian land status on reservations. That the

IRA came out of the New Deal era, and only days before the creation of the Federal Housing Administration, is significant, as federal policy rapidly changed as the federal government worked to stymie the financial downturn of the Great Depression. While clear linkages can be observed between the U.S. economy and the goals and objectives of the National Housing Act of 1934, less clear is the relationship between the IRA and the economic downturn Indian people on reservations experienced. Though Collier worked closely with Ickes and Cohen to create the IRA, what passed and became law was an extremely pared-down version of the bill that the three men originally proposed. Congress had strong opposition to the initial version of the bill—specifically to the proposed efforts to create a stronger tribal court system, the efforts to increase the amount of tribal land being placed into trust, and the relinquishment of increased federal oversight. Indeed, while the IRA is viewed as a sort of emancipatory era of federal Indian policy, the bulk of the bill's efforts to further liberate Indian people was eliminated prior to passage. Rather, the IRA that was passed had much more to say about maintaining federal authority over Indian people. Indeed, when it was time to appropriate funds to the Office of Indian Affairs, Congress made clear their "dislike of the IRA by cutting the Office of Indian Affairs appropriations from nearly $53 million for 1934, before the act was passed, to less than $38 million in 1937."[42] This drastic reduction in funding for Indian policy coincided with the passage of the sweeping National Housing Act of 1934 and the U.S. Housing Act of 1937.

Despite the federal government's attempts to stimulate the economy and the well-documented history of urban slums and tenement housing in the country's early industrial cities, the government did not make a formal or significant intervention into the housing sector until the Federal Home Loan Bank Act of 1932. This legislation worked to make homeownership more accessible and affordable by establishing a network of federally supported lenders to provide mortgages and established the Federal Home Loan Bank Board. The same year, the federal government created the Reconstruction Finance Corporation to provide financial assistance to state and local governments, financial institutions, corporations, and the railroads. However, the Federal Home Loan Bank Act and the Reconstruction Finance Corporation were not enough to provide the necessary support to homeowners who faced high mortgage interest rates, high home loan down payments, and rapid three- to five-year repayment terms.[43] Then, two years later, to enact more sweeping change, the federal government passed the National Housing Act of 1934, which thereby created the Federal Housing Administration. The FHA is the primary federal agency handling mortgage insurance, essentially acting as a government guarantor of mortgages and protecting individual citizen lenders from default. Significantly, the FHA regulates interest rates on home loans and established a national mortgage association that continues to provide a market for home mortgages to be bought and sold by banks and investors, thus increasing the availability of money and potential for lender profit.[44]

With FDR's clear calls to stimulate the housing market and Americans' increased thirst for homeownership, the FHA worked to bolster the housing market and therefore the larger U.S. economy. Yet, prior to the passage of the National Housing Act of 1934 and the creation of the FHA, there was a near complete lack of regulation or standardized building codes across the United States. In many cases, homes were regularly in disrepair and of shoddy construction. This was similarly affirmed on reservations in the Meriam Report, which described Indian housing across the United States just six years prior. While the creation of the FHA captured the federal government's attention for the need for sound housing, an overwhelming majority of home loan moneys went to white families.[45] Though the federal government was aware of the need for housing across Indian Country, it instead focused its efforts on white families through home loans and accessible finance terms to support and expand homeownership. In this way, the FHA was not intended for the use and benefit of American Indians or other people of color. For many at the policy-making level, just as it had been with the creation and enactment of the Homestead Act, property ownership was white.

Intended to make home loans more accessible and affordable for most Americans, the policies of the FHA did little to assist lower-income people, including many people of color, in attaining home loans. In fact, despite its promises, the FHA contributed to a major aspect of racial discrimination in the housing market. The FHA's *Underwriting Manual* created and established the long-entrenched process known as redlining.[46] In order to determine the individual properties to approve for mortgages, the FHA used a standardized set of "quality standards," including physical characteristics, geographic location, and the racial and ethnic makeup of specific neighborhoods. The quality standards corresponded to a series of color-coded maps where neighborhoods ranged in color from green (considered "most desirable") to red (considered "least desirable"), with Black and lower-income neighborhoods deemed most risky for lending—hence the term *redlining*.[47] Edina, an inner-ring suburb on the southwest fringe of Minneapolis, is an oft-cited example of redlining. As James W. Loewen points out in *Sundown Towns,* the Country Club district of Edina is a well-known case where racially restrictive covenants were built into the deeds of many homes to ban "any person other than the one of the white or Caucasian race" from owning a home in the area.[48]

Though the process and practice of redlining have been more well-documented in terms of Black exclusion, American Indian people were simultaneously and deliberately excluded from specific neighborhoods and homeownership opportunities through the same process. In fact, the programming supported by the National Housing Act of 1934 "cannot be understood apart from the changing racial composition of US cities during the second and third decades of the twentieth century."[49] Though much focus and attention has been given to the Great Migration of Black people to the urban north, and rightly so, the temporal overlap with federal Indian policy must not be overlooked. The ways the FHA prevented and curtailed American Indian people's access to homeownership opportunities were carried through the remainder of the twentieth century as historically entrenched lending procedures and racial discrimination added another layer of complexity to the movement of racialized groups to urban and suburban areas.

In addition to the practice of redlining, FHA lending policies and programs born of the 1930s also allowed for home deeds to include racially discriminatory covenants that explicitly prevented people of color from purchasing homes in increasingly white suburban developments. The Supreme Court case *Shelley v. Kraemer* (1948) held that racial covenants, which prevented "people of the Negro or Mongolian race" from owning property, were legally unenforceable.[50] However, the Supreme Court ruling simultaneously asserted the validity of race-based covenants

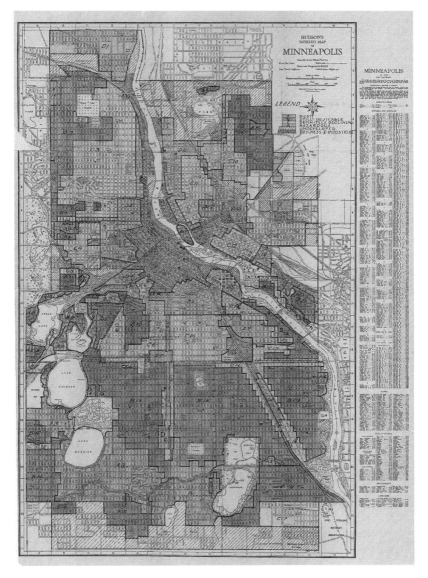

Figure 8. Minneapolis redlining map. Areas of the city designated as "hazardous" for home loans were the least desirable for lending. Other areas ranged from "definitely declining," "still desirable," and finally to "best" as candidates for home loans. *Hudson's Indexed Map of Minneapolis,* retrieved from Mapping Inequality: Redlining in New Deal America [database, accessed October 2022], https://dsl.richmond.edu/panorama/redlining/#loc=5/39.1/-94.58.

as a "freedom" of private parties, which is guaranteed under the Fourteenth Amendment of the Constitution. In 1948, a second case concerning the legality of race-based covenants reached the Supreme Court, *Hurd v. Hodge,* a companion case to the more well-known *Shelley v. Kraemer.* At issue in this case from a Washington, D.C., neighborhood was a 1906 racially restrictive covenant that stated, "Said lot shall never be rented, leased, sold, transferred or conveyed unto any Negro or colored person, under a penalty of Two Thousand Dollars."[51] The defendant in this case, James M. Hurd, purchased his property from a white owner. However, his white neighbors refused to allow Hurd to peacefully reside in this predominately white neighborhood, relying on each home's racially restrictive covenant. The neighbors filed suit in court to dismiss Hurd's deed to the property, based on the racial covenant. Importantly, throughout the court case and in legal commentary, Hurd is consistently described as a "Negro"; however, as revealed in the buried footnotes of the case, Hurd identifies as a Mohawk Indian.[52] This case reveals the racial tensions that enveloped housing and homeownership policies of the FHA for all people of color, including American Indians. Even with the court cases settled, segregation and discrimination remained active throughout much of the country, and in many cases, including across the Twin Cities, segregation remained legal throughout the housing, employment, and education sectors.[53]

Certainly, there were other race-based covenants that specifically precluded Indian occupancy, those that expressly excluded "any of the nonwhite race," as well as the many others that considered American Indians as "Negro" precisely for the purposes of exclusion. These racially restrictive covenants added to the burden of finding adequate housing for many American Indians, including Native people living in the Twin Cities, by further reducing their housing options.[54] Nearly all major metropolitan areas of the 1930s and 1940s, inclusive of new suburban developments and existing urban rental properties, imposed a version of racially restrictive housing ordinances. Both 1948 court cases make explicit the blurring of the color line and the efforts homeowners and neighborhood organizations would go through to maintain their whiteness. Although the Supreme Court struck down the legal enforceability of race-based restrictive covenants, it did not prevent them from being enforced on a local, neighborhood level.

Racially restrictive property covenants, white flight, and redlining have carved out a legacy across many of America's communities by preventing people of color, including American Indians, from purchasing property. This legacy is obvious today in the racial makeup of suburbs from coast to coast. Adding another level of complexity, in 2014 subprime lending continued to be directed toward communities of color; in Minneapolis, this includes the historically and largely American Indian Phillips neighborhood where 38 percent of all home loans between 2004 and 2006 were subprime. In the same neighborhood that grew out of postwar Indian urbanization and Relocation, 63 percent of home loan applicants of color were denied mortgage financing, compared to 54 percent of whites of the same income levels.[55]

In an early attempt to address the inherent and recognizable racism and segregation that emerged in the housing market, Congress passed the U.S. Housing Act of 1937, which established the Public Housing Program. Intended to provide assistance to lower-income families, the Public Housing Authority authorized loans to local public housing agencies for low-rent housing projects.[56] This is in stark contrast to the homeownership opportunities that were readily available to middle-class white Americans under the aims and provisions of the 1934 National Housing Act, further confirming the ways access to housing is marked by both race and class. There has never been an equal playing field in terms of housing and federal policy. As numerous scholars from the field of critical race studies argue, including George Lipsitz, "by channeling money away from older inner-city neighborhoods and toward white home buyers moving into segregated suburbs, the FHA and private lenders after World War II aided and abetted the growth and development of increased segregation in US residential neighborhoods."[57] So, though the FHA did not build the houses or design the suburbs, they did determine who was able to receive a government-backed loan with lower down payments and longer repayment terms, thus making homeownership more accessible for some while excluding others. In this way, the American Dream was almost always out of reach for many, and certainly for American Indians who had only recently gained access to U.S. citizenship. This revealed the tensions at play around assimilation through land and property ownership, citizenship, and homeownership. American Indians have long been excluded from land and property ownership, citizenship, and homeownership while always subject to assimilation.

Though the National Housing Act of 1934 articulated a rhetoric of housing American citizens as a mission that was progressive, positive, and prudent, using descriptions of advancing civilization and modernization, American Indian people were seemingly, and perhaps intentionally, left out of its purview. Then only recently enveloped into the U.S. citizenry, the rhetoric and goals of the 1934 National Housing Act, as carried out by the FHA, in many ways echoed the calls of the Meriam Report. Yet it seems that instead of applying, or expanding, the National Housing Act to American Indians and Indian reservations, the federal government instead created the Indian Reorganization Act as a way to deal with the so-called Indian problem. While white American citizens seemed to be entitled to federal financial support, guidance, and a whole host of rules and regulations for their benefit, American Indian people— whose land was rapidly swindled away through the treaty-making process with the federal government, later to be allotted and opened to white settlement, where homes and cabins were built for white families—were ultimately excluded from the benefits of the National Housing Act of 1934 and policies and programs of the FHA. This exclusion occurred on at least two levels. First, FHA policies and programs were never intended for Indian land or reservation land, particularly Indian land held in trust by the federal government. Second, off-reservation Indians were directly excluded from FHA homeownership programs and policies due to racism, redlining, and lack of access to full citizenship. Instead, American Indians were thrust into the driver's seat of newly formed and often very foreign tribal governments.

Indeed, the racialized and classed housing legislation and policies of the 1930s were widely supported and promoted by real estate and lending interests—individuals who studied and relied on property taxes, property values, and home prices for their own livelihood. Perhaps it is no surprise, then, that this is also the very same era that the idea of the American Dream became popularized in the writing of James Truslow Adams's 1931 book *The Epic of America*. Fundamental to the notion of the American Dream are land and property ownership. The irony for

American Indian people, of course, is that the American Dream, much like Manifest Destiny, has been built on land Native people have been dispossessed of. As the century marched on, the American Dream became, as it remains today, much more conflated with capitalism and consumption in that it "is continually (re)produced and reconstituted to maintain consumer demand and support the profitable investment of capital in the built environment."[58] The American Dream, then, has been aided and abetted by federal housing policy, specifically as it emerged in the 1930s in the wake of the Great Depression. In fact, the American Dream in many ways cannot be separated from federal policy, especially as it relates to exclusionary land practices when one reads the "landscape as a text" (for example, not only who has access to homes but the increasing size, stature, and cost of homes; not only who has access to land, broadly speaking, but limiting access to land via cul-de-sacs and privacy fences; not only creating new subdivisions but limiting access to subdivisions with gates and homeowners' associations, etc.).[59] Despite these obstacles and barriers, American Indians were not left out of the American Dream; instead, they navigated homeownership and early suburbanization on their own terms.

When the Gruette family arrived in Mound from the White Earth Reservation in 1930, they came as active participants in the early suburbanization that swept the Twin Cities. Like many other American Indian individuals and families, the Gruettes had arrived at a predominately white metropolitan area. The Twin Cities were rapidly developing, growing, and changing and necessitated a steady flow of willing workers. From agricultural work to industrial work to domestic work, American Indian people filled a need in the labor market. However, the work American Indian people did in the Twin Cities' suburbs between 1920 and the end of World War II cannot be separated from their migrations to and movements within the metropolitan area that allowed them the opportunity for employment. Surely reservation conditions, including high unemployment and poverty, served as a push factor that influenced many Indian people to migrate away from the confinement and isolation of reservation communities.

Though Indian people were also able to transcend social class by working and living in predominately white suburbs, it is difficult to determine how many American Indian individuals or Indian families were able to trade in a working-class lifestyle for something solidly middle class. However, through census data, we can observe the American Indian people in the Twin Cities who were able to access homeownership between 1920 and 1940. Indian people like Arthur Hamilton, who lived in a home valued at $3,000, double that of his neighbors, had made the suburban Twin Cities home. Similarly, Charles Brunelle, a Native man who was employed as a laborer for General Electric and eventually by the City of Minneapolis in 1930, owned a home in Minneapolis valued at $4,000. These mobile Indians who became homeowners had homes near equivalent in value to those of their neighbors. This is not to say that suburban living for Indian people in the early to mid-twentieth century was without its problems. During the early decades of the twentieth century, when homeownership was highly valued, race was a crucial marker of inclusivity, and a nonwhite identity could immediately deny an Indian person the chance of homeownership and suburban belonging. Though we cannot be certain if early racial shifting, not to be conflated with assimilation but to be read as occurring alongside it, was occurring because of or in response to suburban residence, it certainly reveals the complexity and interconnectivity of race, citizenship, and identity during this period—something all people of color faced, particularly those in newly shaped and developing cities and suburbs. Early twentieth-century American Indian migrants to the increasingly urban environments of Minneapolis and Saint Paul were by no means the first, but they certainly came as active participants in a shifting housing market largely meant to exclude them. They participated in a growing labor market and participated in new and developing urban Indian organizations. Most importantly, for many Dakota and Ojibwe, their reimagining of Indian Country was a remembering, remaking, and reclaiming of an Indian place.

3

"WE MUST DO THIS OURSELVES"
AMERICAN INDIANS AND
THE AMERICAN DREAM
IN THE TWIN CITIES

As with any group . . . the housing of the Indian population varies
greatly. Some live in well-equipped, modern homes; others reside in
poorly furnished, poorly constructed homes; and others exist under
the most deplorable conditions. Since the number living under good
housing conditions is extremely limited, no attempt will be made to
consider them. These homes are generally found in the Twin City area
or in towns or cities where an Indian office is located. Here, the occupants are well established economically and enjoy security.

—GOVERNOR'S INTERRACIAL COMMISSION,
*The Indian in Minnesota: A Report to Governor
Luther W. Youngdahl of Minnesota*

This land is your land, this land is my land. . . .
This land was made for you and me.

—WOODY GUTHRIE, *This Land Is Your Land*

ON THE EVENING OF JUNE 30, 1953, area placement officer Kent
FitzGerald visited the family of Gerald Owens, an American Indian man
from the White Earth Reservation in northern Minnesota who had come
to Minneapolis as a participant in the Bureau of Indian Affair's Relocation
Program. Owens was employed at a manufacturing job and was earning
steady pay of $90 per week.[1] Despite his work and take-home pay, it was
difficult for Owens to secure adequate housing, and his family "[was]

living in a rather crowded quarters—a two room furnished apartment" in South Minneapolis.[2] The Owens family was not satisfied with the promised opportunities of the Relocation Program, nor was the family interested in returning to their reservation in northern Minnesota. Instead, during the same June 30 family visit, Owens informed the area placement officer that he had plans to move elsewhere. Kent FitzGerald relayed this message to J. W. Kauffman, superintendent of the Consolidated Chippewa Agency. In a letter dated July 2, 1953, FitzGerald shared:

> Mr. Owens informed me that he is arranging to purchase a home under contract at Hamm Lake, a suburb north of Minneapolis. This is a five room house, and the present owner is going to permit the Owens family to move in with the understanding that they will do some necessary repair work on the building. The monthly payment will be the same as rental payments but they will be applied on the purchase of the house.[3]

Just days later, on July 6, 1953, placement and Relocation officer Carl J. Cornelius penned a letter to Owens congratulating him on his new home:

> We are likewise happy to learn that you are planning to purchase a home at Hamm Lake. This will no doubt provide you with larger living quarters, but in addition to the comforts you will derive from such housing, you have taken an important step in the improvements of your social and economic standing. . . . We wish to commend you for your excellent efforts and we will be most happy to hear from you from time to time telling us of your work, housing and any other items of interest that we may pass on to other families who are interested in moving to the cities.[4]

The Relocation agents, who were to provide guidance and support to Owens and his family during the Relocation process, had assumed a benevolent yet paternalistic position. Moreover, these Relocation agents took personal pride in the presumed success of the Owens family, as indicated by the family's recent move to a large suburban home and "improvements" to their "social and economic standing," as they worked to make this family a symbol of the Relocation Program.

When Gerald Owens applied for Relocation and moved his family away from the White Earth Reservation south to Minneapolis, they were participating in the ongoing process of American Indian sub/urbanization that rapidly occurred in the wake of World War II. As a veteran, Gerald Owens had the off-reservation experience that the Relocation Program desired of its applicants, and he sought to take advantage of his skill set by moving to the city for improved employment and housing opportunities. However, like most relocatees to Minneapolis, the Owens family was quickly disappointed by the opportunities and improvements the Relocation Program advertised; this was true of both employment and housing. Rather than return to their home reservation, like many who took advantage of the Relocation Program eventually did, or remain uncomfortable and unsatisfied in cramped living quarters in urban Minneapolis, the Owens family chose to move north and out of the city to Ham Lake, "19 miles north of the Minneapolis loop." When Gerald Owens moved his family to a "larger house" with "ample space for a garden plot" in Ham Lake, he did so independently of the Relocation Program.[5] The Owens family story and move to the suburban Twin Cities, outside of Minneapolis, reveals a more critical and unexamined history of American Indian suburbanization and the Indian Relocation Program during the mid-twentieth century.

In this chapter, I intervene in Relocation and early Indian urbanization scholarship to make several key arguments. First, despite the proclaimed aims and idealized notions of the American Dream that were embedded in the Relocation Program, specifically as it pertained to housing, Relocation failed to integrate American Indian people into mainstream suburban communities. Rather, the Relocation Program moved American Indian participants into almost exclusively urban areas and almost always into rental housing, and very often this housing was substandard. The Relocation Program, a component of the sweeping Termination era, must be understood as a racialized housing policy. Here, it is important to examine the stated goals of the Relocation Program as policy and the way the program operated on the ground. Relocation worked to racialize American Indian people by dictating and restricting which Indian people were eligible for the program and through the close surveillance of relocatees once they arrived in the city. This is evidenced in the way individuals and families who wanted to participate in the Relocation Program were required to complete an in-depth application process, including invasive and intimate health questions and medical histories. Moreover, those who participated in Relocation were expected to adhere to regular postmove home visits by a Relocation officer who inspected their home or apartment, the yard and landscaping, their physical appearance and that of their children, their school and church attendance, and their economic knowledge (i.e., participation in capitalism; have they purchased a television or a car) to determine whether they were making a supposedly successful adjustment. This policing of American Indians on Relocation reveals the ways the program worked to racialize Native people, by viewing them as inherently different and in need of paternalistic oversight, rather than allowing them the autonomy to live in the city as they chose to do.

Instead, and despite the supposed integration the Relocation Program advertised, the Indian people who participated in the rapid suburbanization of the United States that followed World War II, whether through employment or homeownership, did so on their own. Further, American Indian suburbanization in the postwar years reveals the inconsistencies between the Relocation Program and the more dominant and far-reaching federal housing policies of the postwar period, including those administered by the Federal Housing Administration (FHA) and Veterans Affairs (VA). In this chapter, I center the Relocation Program alongside FHA and VA housing and home loan programs, specifically the GI Bill, to expose the dramatically unequal access to homeownership American Indians faced and the failure of the federal government to truly integrate Indian people, a main pillar of Relocation. The introductory family story of the Owens serves as a starting point to examine and consider the suburbanization process for other American Indian people who lived and worked in the Twin Cities from WWII into the 1960s. The many American Indians who moved into the suburbs in the years and decades following WWII chose where and how they wanted to live, often making a conscious choice to improve their housing and employment opportunities, even if it meant moving away from family or tribal communities.

Postwar Policies and Suburbanization

While the Relocation Program was working to move Indian people away from reservations and into rental housing units, the VA closely followed the FHA's efforts to design a new program to support homeownership for military veterans. The Servicemen's Readjustment Act became law on June 22, 1944, just before the end of WWII and nearly one decade to the day after the FHA was first created. The American Legion, seeking to streamline veterans' benefits and to avoid the confusion that followed WWI, pushed Roosevelt for a designated and accessible program to administer veterans' benefits earned during wartime. Among the many benefits and entitlement programs available to veterans of WWII through the Servicemen's Readjustment Act was a low-interest, government-insured home loan program. Eventually, the home loan benefit of the GI Bill would be compared to the Homestead Act of 1862 in its ability to dramatically alter the landscape through the expansion and growth of new settlements and housing.[6] While it is impossible to know when and with what speed postwar suburbs would have developed and grown without the GI Bill, it certainly sped up and supported the process.

In contrast to the Relocation Program, the GI Bill was an extensive and expensive strategy to reintegrate WWII veterans. The $14 billion spent on the GI Bill of 1944 was to provide medical, education, temporary cash assistance, and home loan programs to military veterans—the most expansive returning veteran benefits package to date. By 1955, 4.3 million homes—20 percent of all new home construction—were built using the GI Bill's home loan guarantee for new construction or purchase, worth a combined market value of $33 million.[7] Within the terms of the GI Bill home loan guarantee, the federal government assumed responsibility for the first year of interest, stipulated that the loan's interest rate was not to exceed 4 percent, allowed for a twenty-year repayment period, and required only 10 percent down. Almost one-third of WWII veterans took advantage of the GI Bill's home loan guarantee. Though the GI Bill promoted and supported homeownership for all veterans, it also bolstered already-occurring white flight to the suburban fringes while further limiting housing options for veterans of color.

In the wake of WWII and on the heels of the GI Bill, the Housing Act of 1949 was authorized with the stated goal of providing "a decent home and suitable living environment for every American family."[8] The main pillars of the act included federal funding for "slum clearance" (Title I), increased authorization for FHA mortgage insurance (Title II),

Figure 9. A Veterans Administration promotional flier advertises home loans available to eligible veterans. The GI Bill had a significant home loan component that many veterans of World War II took advantage of to purchase single-family homes in newly developing suburbs. National Archives and Records Administration.

and extended federal funding to build over eight hundred thousand public housing units (Title III). As scholars of U.S. housing policies acknowledge, the legislation of the 1949 act was inherently contradictory.[9] Though described as a way to alleviate housing shortages, particularly for lower-income people, the Housing Act of 1949 placed the burden of finding adequate and affordable housing most acutely on people of color, specifically Black people. Indeed, the United States Commission on Civil Rights "made it clear that the government and its minions were more contributing architects than passive bystanders in the residential isolation of African Americans."[10] Urban Black people, caught up in the "historical inertia" of residential race-based segregation, were forced to decide between the push of urban renewal efforts to get out of the city and the pull to move to public housing projects in the city rather than to truly integrate into growing (white) suburbs.[11]

While the VA worked diligently to determine the exact housing benefits veterans of WWII would receive through the GI Bill, Congress, the Hoover Commission, and Republican leaders in Washington considered eliminating the Bureau of Indian Affairs (BIA), optimistically described as a pathway to save the federal government millions of dollars.[12] In the effort to reduce federal spending, the dual Indian policies of Termination and Relocation were born, though certainly the sentiment undergirding them had long been simmering. Touted as a means to "reintegrate" Indian people into mainstream society, particularly Indian veterans who were deemed more "prepared" for "full-integration," policymakers crafted Termination and Relocation as benevolent, using the rhetoric of American Indian emancipation from federal wardship. Indeed, policymakers intentionally used liberatory language to frame Termination and Relocation as congruent with the democratic ideals of freedom and independence, a "freeing" from Indian policy. Kenneth R. Philp points to the ways that, in Termination-era policies, the federal government strove to maintain American idealism "reflected [in] Cold War beliefs about the superiority of Euro-American civilization and political ideology."[13] Ending the federal government's guardian–ward relationship with Indian people, as was intended of Termination and Relocation, was seen by conservative politicians as the final necessary step for Indians to fully assimilate and "enjoy" the benefits of American citizenry.[14]

When Termination was passed in 1953, the bill made clear "it is the policy of Congress, as rapidly as possible, to make Indians within the territorial limits of the United States subject to the same laws and entitled to the same privileges . . . to end their status as wards of the United States, and to grant them all of the rights and prerogatives pertaining to American citizenship."[15] In this way Termination was intended to sever all ties between the federal government and sovereign tribal nations. This included all treaty-negotiated responsibilities of the federal government, such as promised federal aid, services (such as health care and education), and "protections" (i.e., federal recognition and the resulting political/legal relationship). Perhaps most significantly, Termination eliminated the trust status reservation land had long been under as a sort of "protective" mechanism of the federal government. To determine whether a tribe was ready for Termination, Congress looked to the degree of intermarriage, assimilation to white customs, and literacy rates, as well as the military participation of tribal members—in many ways, a parallel to the Allotment era. Thus, as Termination unfolded, the federal government revealed the ease with which it was prepared to refuse acknowledgment of tribal sovereignty.

Termination was devastating to tribal nations and American Indian people. Between 1953 and 1964, 109 tribes lost their status as federally recognized tribal nations, and over thirteen thousand individuals lost their status as members of federally recognized tribes, a severe blow to sovereignty. Today, most tribal nations have since been restored to a federally recognized political/legal status, but the effects of Termination linger, particularly through land loss.[16] Through Termination, over 1.36 million acres of Indian land, once held in trust by the federal government, lost its protected status and quickly slipped out of tribal hands, with much of the land being sold for massive profit.[17] Though the tribal nations located in Minnesota escaped Termination, the Menominee, our neighbors to the east in Wisconsin, were not as fortunate.[18] Government officials and supporters, including many in the BIA, had long pushed assimilation as the ultimate goal of Indian policy, a goal well-entrenched since at least the mid-eighteenth century. Essentially, by way of Termination, Indian people were pushed to give up their tribal identity, which would legally no longer exist, and "[conform] to the values and attitudes of mainstream, Anglo-American society."[19] Undergirding

Termination Policy was the hope that Indian people would move away from their reservation communities, which would legally no longer exist, and to a more metropolitan area to further assimilate and integrate. For those individuals who, upon Termination, did not relocate, they would no longer be reservation Indians but "Indians" with no land, no formal recognition, and no rights as such.

Relocation, a main tenet of Termination, and supposedly voluntary Indian-initiated migrations to metropolitan areas were underway long before Termination and Relocation became official Indian policy. Federal and local support for Indian relocation to urban areas began to take shape in the 1930s as a response to the dramatic loss of Indian land, a direct effect of Allotment. As a result, by the 1940s a new and dramatically different Indian policy took shape. In 1948, the Hopi and Navajo participated in an early job placement and relocation program, which became a model for what was to come. Then, in the early 1950s, the program expanded to tribal nations across the United States and was available to all members of federally recognized tribes. Finally, in 1956 the Indian Relocation Act was enacted as law, though it had been in operation for several years prior. American Indians who participated in the Relocation Program, later to coincide with the Adult Vocational Training Program, were provided a one-way bus ticket to a federally designated urban relocation area. These predetermined destinations initially included Chicago, Dallas, New York, Los Angeles, and Oklahoma City, though other large cities were later added.[20] The relocated Indians, and sometimes entire families, were provided short-term financial support and temporary housing in rental units in the city. In Chicago, this included $10.10 per week for "temporary shelter," possibly at the YMCA.[21] Although voluntary, the BIA marketed the Relocation Program to Indian people using images of single-family homes, "with shutters in suburban America," that would work to entice women and families into relocating to cities.[22] This is in stark contrast to what they actually received.

Government housing reports from Minneapolis describe the semi-permanent rental units relocated families occupied as often overcrowded, accommodating extended family, in disrepair both inside and out, lacking adequate plumbing and electrical features, and, more often than not, overpriced.[23] According to a 1947 report from Minnesota, "recent

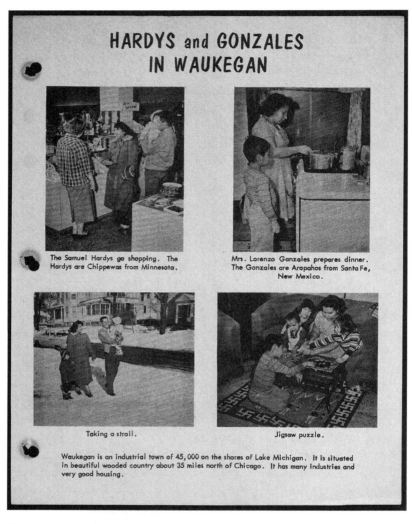

Figure 10. A Bureau of Indian Affairs promotional flier advertises the American Indian Relocation Program. Images of single-family homes, shopping, automobiles, family life, and cooking were often used to entice American Indians to participate in the program and to leave reservations for city living. Edward E. Ayer Digital Collection, Newberry Library, Chicago.

THE BURNS FAMILY IN WAUKEGAN

Edward Burns, Chippewa from Redby, Minn., reports to work at plant.

The Hardys, Chippewas from Ponemah, Minn., pay the Burns a visit.

Son, Peter, chats with new classmates at High School.

Burns Children at play.

Waukegan is an industrial town of 45,000 on the shores of Lake Michigan. It is situated in beautiful wooded country about 35 miles north of Chicago. It has many industries and very good housing.

Figure 11. A Bureau of Indian Affairs promotional flier advertises the American Indian Relocation Program. Images of single-family homes, shopping, automobiles, family life, and cooking were often used to entice American Indians to participate in the program and to leave reservations for city living. Edward E. Ayer Digital Collection, Newberry Library, Chicago.

migrants to the cities were crowded into homes in blighted areas" and "in at least one instance the multiple structure into which families have moved have been condemned."[24] American Indians who participated in Relocation were largely unsupported upon arrival to the city. Rather, Relocation became about movement—movement away from and off reservation land. Relocation would not last, and today the program has largely been deemed unsuccessful in its objective to permanently relocate Indian people to urban areas. Of the American Indians across the country who participated in Relocation, conservative estimates claim that 30 percent would return to the reservation, while others suggest the return rate was likely closer to 60 percent.[25]

After moving nearly twenty miles north of the Twin Cities to a home under contract in Ham Lake, Gerald Owens specifically expressed to the placement and Relocation officer that he was "interested in securing a VA loan to improve the place." Rather than offer support or guidance to Owens, the placement and Relocation officer simply told him to contact the Loan Division of the VA at Fort Snelling.[26] It is here that Owens's Relocation records end and, likely, so too his appeals for financial guidance and federal support for homeownership as an American Indian veteran. Though based in California, David Dowd, who was from Bemidji, Minnesota, contacted the Minnesota Chippewa Agency Relocation Department about down payment assistance after his relocation to Oakland, only a few years after Gerald Owens's similar effort. In his August 1956 letter, Dowd writes:

> I am writing in regards to information on the bill that was passed for down payment assistance on houses for relocated Indians. The Indian office in San Francisco will not give us any information. They told us to write your office to see if we are entitled for a down payment. It is very hard to find places to live, and rent is very high. Will you please let us know as soon as possible. We've been out here a year and a half, and would like to know if we are entitled to this. Have worked steady since we've been out here.[27]

In response, the agency Relocation officer wrote, "As I understand it, there has been no full procedure set up for this program" and that regardless, it would be Dowd's responsibility to contact and work with the local San Francisco office to pursue such matters.

Despite their best efforts, American Indian people under Relocation never had the same opportunity for suburban homeownership that many white Americans—including WWII veterans, who had access to FHA and VA loans, like the expansive GI Bill—had. Rather, American Indians continually faced bureaucratic red tape and discrimination as they pursued suburban homeownership. Whereas postwar ideologies, including the American Dream, maintained specific imaginaries of home as domestic space with clearly defined gender roles, the Relocation Program, despite its portrayal as a tool of assimilation, stood in direct opposition, preventing American Indians from accessing suburbia and homeownership, a key marker of upward mobility. Unfortunately, Gerald Owens and David Dowd were not alone. Thousands of American Indians faced similar circumstances in the post–World War II environment as they struggled to further integrate into the dominant society and achieve the American Dream and homeownership. The Relocation records of Gerald Owens and David Dowd document the more common, yet complex, issues that arose as American Indian individuals and families tried to use the Relocation Program to improve their housing and employment opportunities. The Relocation records of these men and their families draw attention to the inconsistent and unequal access to long-term suburban housing for Indian people, even when that help was specifically requested.

Relocation as a Racialized Housing Policy

The rapidity with which suburbs were built, grew, and eventually populated after World War II, largely to the exclusion of people of color, including American Indians, underscores their careful orchestration by the federal government. The U.S. government's visible role in the housing market, specifically through the creation of the FHA, continued throughout the second half of the twentieth century. Cleared of American Indians during the nineteenth century through Removal and the reservation system, then supported by FHA policies of the 1930s and 1940s, suburbs became preferable and desirable sites for new homes by an increasing number of white Americans in the postwar atmosphere. At the same time, the FHA preferred the construction of new suburban homes rather than the improvement of older structures in urban areas.

These were the very places Black people and American Indians, through the Relocation Program, were moving into. Indeed, Michael J. Bennett notes that 85 percent of the nation's growth after World War II occurred in suburbs:

> Starting in 1950, almost all of the nation's cities lost population while the suburbs gained 60 million new residents. The [GI] bill, like all laws, had unintended consequences; in this instance, it helped accelerate the concentration of blacks and minorities in the cities. If people were leaving the cities to find a better life, they were also fleeing them to avoid shadows cast by urban blight— and people of darker skin.[28]

Though the programs and policies of the FHA were promoted and advertised to support homeownership for all, they bolstered already-occurring white flight to the suburban fringe. Racially biased deed restrictions and racial covenants—commonplace in housing programs throughout the twentieth century, including suburban communities in Minnesota—went largely unchallenged, even after the 1948 *Shelley v. Kraemer* Supreme Court ruling prohibited their legal enforcement.[29] In 1954, Minnesota became one of the first states in the nation to pass a law that specifically banned racially restrictive covenants, though, similar to the earlier Supreme Court ruling, informal segregation and discriminatory attitudes remained largely unchanged. Though Black people were the most common targets of this racism, American Indians also felt the burden of the color line. In 1940, Helen Lightfoot, a twenty-nine-year-old Indian woman from South Dakota, worked as a live-in maid for a white family in Edina, Minnesota.[30] Though the neighborhood's racially restrictive covenant prevented anyone other than "one of the white or Caucasian race" from purchasing or renting a home in the community, the covenant did allow people of color to "[serve] as domestics for the owner or tenant of said lot."[31] This caveat was in line with neighborhood deeds that sought to "maintain a high class, restricted, residential district, free from objectionable or value-destroying features" by prohibiting livestock and "objectionable trees or shrubbery" and keeping all garbage and waste hidden from view.[32] The racialization and dehumanization are clear, and the only place for nonwhites in this Twin Cities suburban community was exclusively as hired help.

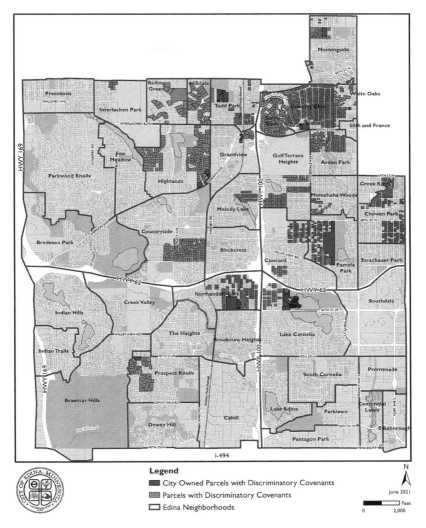

Figure 12. Racial covenants throughout the suburb of Edina (shaded in medium to dark gray). The Country Club district, where Helen Lightfoot (Dakota) worked as a live-in maid, is in the upper right corner. Nearly all homes in this neighborhood contained racial covenants. Other neighborhoods with high concentrations of race-based covenants include Hilldale, Rolling Green, Normandale Park, Highlands, Golf Terrace Heights, and Pamela Park. Just Deeds Project, Edina, Minnesota.

Similarly, lenders and builders in the postwar years were heirs to millions of dollars, funneled their way by the FHA and the GI Bill. Relocated Indians, however, were almost always relegated to cramped quarters in the urban core. A 1956 report on the Relocation Program describes the typical housing available to Indian people as "passable to working-class standards, inadequate according to middle-class standards," where "the rooms [are] shabbily but not wretchedly furnished" with the hope for "improvement" coming "as more relocated families find their way into the racially mixed public housing developments."[33] In considering Relocation housing, Philp points out:

> Relocation officials could not always keep their promise of finding adequate housing for the Indians. After 1945 most of the new housing stock was located in middle-class suburbs. Desirable rental property often cost too much for low-paid, unskilled Indian workers who faced frequent layoffs. Consequently, Indians usually had to move into public housing projects or shabby unfurnished ghetto apartments in lower-class neighborhoods where slum landlords charged excessive rent.[34]

Access to housing during the mid-twentieth century, for differing racial groups, makes clear the intentions of the federal government through their well-organized and well-funded efforts to move white and nonwhite people. The same 1956 report by the Association on American Indian Affairs made clear: "Much good housing at reasonable cost will never be easily found. It is not here. This is a community problem and the Relocation Office cannot solve it."[35] As was true nationwide, this was also true of the available housing in the Twin Cities. Like most other metropolitan areas across the country, Minneapolis and Saint Paul saw a severe shortage in adequate housing in the wake of World War II. Despite the promises of earlier housing programs, including the U.S. Housing Act of 1937 and the Housing Act of 1949, by the mid-1950s there was not yet enough public housing units to house those who were unable to access home loans, and this included American Indians who arrived on Relocation—a problem the BIA well knew existed. Instead, most of the FHA's attention was focused on efforts to support those (white) lenders and (white) developers who spurred on the postwar economy through new home construction in the inner-ring suburbs around Minneapolis and Saint Paul for (white) residents.

The Relocation Program must be considered alongside the mass exodus of white residents from urban, inner-city environments and into growing suburbs. In a process that was known as "white flight" by the 1960s, more and more white individuals and families moved out of the urban core and into more suburban geographies while American Indians and other people of color moved into recently vacated properties and newly constructed public housing facilities. White flight contributed to the ongoing processes of redlining that worked to keep people of color (and poor whites) out of newly constructed suburban neighborhoods by making home loans in areas occupied by people of color more difficult to obtain and financially risky for mortgage insurers. We cannot fully understand the processes and extent of white flight without also considering the Relocation Program. Likewise, we cannot fully understand the detrimental effects of Relocation without also considering how it worked in tandem with white flight. This is particularly significant because white flight has almost exclusively been examined through a Black–white binary. However, the Relocation Program, as a racialized housing policy, similarly contributed to the racialized white/nonwhite, urban/suburban divide, if not deliberately then as a by-product of postwar housing policies that were increasingly marked by race. In Chicago, the 1956 report on the Relocation Program documented that "white residents of neighborhoods" that were "becoming mixed" with Indians "[reported] panic selling" in response to the Relocation Program. Rather than a tool to integrate Indian people, Relocation limited the housing available to American Indians who participated in the program by predetermining the urban areas Indian people could move into and by adhering to the accepted racism of the time. Relocation in many ways foreclosed homeownership for American Indians and instead limited their housing opportunities to rentals.

Despite the odds against them, American Indian people certainly used Relocation as a tool to access improved, suburban housing rather than stay in urban areas with little access to appropriate housing, just as the generation before them who often left the reservation for the first time to find new opportunities. It is also likely many more Indian people sidestepped the Relocation Program altogether, instead moving directly to suburban communities on their own without any federal support. Damon James, an Ojibwe man born in 1932 at the Mille Lacs Reservation in central Minnesota, applied for Relocation in 1953 with his wife and two young daughters. After temporarily moving into "rather crowded quarters in South Minneapolis" with James's cousins in July 1953, "they [were] quite anxious to find housing of their own" and were waiting on their promised Relocation checks to do so. By early July, Damon James had secured employment at the Brooks Fruit Express, where he was paid $1.56 an hour working as a "truck helper and stock-clerk." James, also an army veteran, had difficulty finding higher-paying work, and his family continued to need assistance "for at least three weeks to get them on their feet" while they worked to secure an apartment and pay off the bills the family had accumulated while in the city. Soon after, on August 7, 1953, a memo from the area placement officer points out that the James family had finally secured their own apartment in the city, next door to James's aunt and uncle.[36]

The James family was getting by in the city, perhaps even con-sidered a success of the Relocation Program. Damon James and his young family stayed in Minneapolis for several months while he and his wife worked low-paying jobs that provided just enough to pay their monthly rent and purchase necessities for the family. Then, on May 15, 1954, area Relocation officer Kent FitzGerald was informed that Mr. and Mrs. James had worked to move their family to Elk River, nearly a year after they had initially arrived in the city. The official correspondence announces "that the James family had moved to Elk River, Minnesota where Mr. James is now employed by a company which sells minnows and other kinds of bait to fisherman. Mrs. James stated that Mr. James had lost his job with the Fruit Produce Company in Minneapolis be-cause he was late to work so frequently on Monday mornings after having spent the weekend at his wife's home on the Mille Lacs Reser-vation."[37] Elk River, a developing suburb north of Minneapolis, was a much shorter commute from the Mille Lacs Reservation for the family, who chose to maintain their reservation connection and remain in the metro area.

It is precisely here that we can observe how the home loan guarantee of the GI Bill was primarily designed for white veterans and (suburban) homeownership that operated in contrast to the Relocation Program, specifically designed and intended for American Indian people, centered on short-term (urban) housing. Each of these policies served a specific purpose: to move certain racialized peoples to specific geographic and residential locations. Unlike Relocation, FHA programs and the GI Bill worked to provide federally insured housing funds for the construction and purchase of single-family homes, and increasingly these homes were in suburbs. On the contrary, Relocation, as an Indian-specific housing policy, was a way for the federal government to further reduce its obligations to Indian people by moving them away from reservations to urban environments. In this way, the federal government could gradually sever its relationship with Indian people while moving them to cheaper short-term rental units with virtually no opportunity for homeownership. Rather than address the unique set of challenges many American Indian people faced in the housing market and on reservations, Relocation was shortsighted and underfunded, with almost no financial or social supports once the move or relocation occurred.[38]

In retrospect, if the federal government had truly intended and desired the full integration of Indian people into mainstream society, the BIA's housing policy, in the form of Relocation, would have more closely followed the policies of the FHA, much like the VA did with the design of the GI Bill's home loan component. Instead of moving Indian people into short-term rental housing, the federal government, through the BIA, would have allowed for, promoted, and provided financial support for homeownership programs for Indian people. Instead of moving Indian people to the urban areas that many whites were moving out of, the federal government would have encouraged the move to the suburbs for American Indians who were leaving the reservation. Instead of denying Relocation opportunities to many Indian families due to higher associated costs, the federal government would have allowed for the maintenance and stability of Indian families. The Relocation Program never intended to fully integrate Indian people into the dominant, white, consumer-oriented postwar society. Instead, it was designed as a means to reduce government spending and to move Indian people away from reservations. As a by-product of Termination, Relocation worked to simultaneously open additional Indian land for sale and purchase while reducing the obligations of the federal government—much like the earlier Allotment era.

The historic legacies of the Relocation Program as a targeted housing policy are easily observed today in the concentrated urban Indian neighborhoods that dot the designated Relocation cities Indian people were once encouraged to move to, including Minneapolis. Most urban Indians in Minneapolis today continue to rent and have little chance of homeownership because of oppressive and discriminatory housing policies. In April 2014, the Institute on Metropolitan Opportunity released a housing report that detailed the ways "toxic subprime loans were deeply embedded in the mortgage market in the Twin Cities and were highly targeted towards communities of color."[39] The same report examines the low rates of homeownership in the Phillips neighborhood, a historic American Indian community in Minneapolis. It cannot be ignored that the individuals and families who were able to benefit from federal housing programs and the policies of the postwar era—namely, FHA programs and the GI Bill—have been able to continuously reap generational advantages. These benefits take the shape of upward mobility—including home equity, suburban schools that generally draw on a larger tax base with supposedly more desirable teachers and facilities, and the housing stability homeownership provides, something urban Indians who participated in the Relocation Program did not have access to.

Relocation and the Surveillance of Indian Bodies

When American Indian people participated in the Relocation Program, they also unwittingly agreed to a certain level of government surveillance. This surveillance came in the form of detailed questions on the application for Relocation assistance and, later, through individual home visits conducted by BIA Relocation officers. The questions asked on Relocation applications ranged from general questions about age, gender, and education to more detailed questions pertaining to military involvement, marital status, children, and arrest records. Yet the most problematic and invasive questions probed each individual's medical records, including records about pregnancies and sexually transmitted infections. Native men and women were required to detail their physical and mental health as well as provide in-depth health histories of any children who would accompany them during Relocation. Further, the application process scrutinized family histories, paying close attention to interfamily dynamics and reputation, which was generally based on hearsay. These BIA Relocation application records were a way to affirm a level of authority and superiority over Indian people. Furthermore, the actual process of applying for Relocation, by stating your perceived level of and desire for assimilation, and the associated home visits, intended to gauge the applicants' level of assimilation, were directly in line with the stated goals of Termination. This was one way to encourage postwar and Cold War–era ideals of family and domesticity for Indian people to finally (and fully) assimilate during the Relocation process.

The notion of surveillance of Indian bodies is not new; it is part and parcel of the longer history of assimilation and the efforts of the BIA. In her book, Cathleen D. Cahill describes how "policy makers sought to transform Native peoples' intimate, *familial* ties by creating a new set of relationships between the nation's Indian 'wards' and government employees—the 'federal fathers and mothers.'"[40] The surveillance of Indian people has perhaps been most obvious at church- and government-run boarding schools where school administrators worked to condition Indian children to lose their Indian ways and adopt Euro-American ideals of dress, mannerisms, education, and language. However, early missionaries who chronicled the lives of Indian people, providing some of our greatest archival collections today, carried out meticulous surveillance of student behavior. Scholars, including Brenda Child and K. Tsianina Lomawaima, demonstrate the pervasive ways boarding schools detailed the daily lives of Indian students, and often entire families, in the name of assimilation.[41] This form of detailed and invasive observation and record-keeping carried over into other aspects of Indian peoples' lives throughout the twentieth century, particularly during the Cold War. As the heightened fear of difference and so-called perversion became increasingly linked to Communism, government surveillance of Indian people increased. The very domesticity that was encouraged and widely demonstrated in promotional images, on television shows, and in women's magazines throughout the 1950s was also tied to the expectation of men, women, and families who participated in Relocation.[42]

The actual application for Relocation assistance provided perhaps the first glimpse into the degree of surveillance and ensuing expectations relocatees would go on to face, even if they were unaware. Among the first questions asked on the application include those about "religious affiliation" with regular or sporadic attendance immediately designated as options to select; of course, the most desirable religious affiliation would be Christian. Additionally, the applicant was asked to specify their "degree of Indian blood," today a well-recognized means of statistical extermination.[43] The application then went on to request an itemized accounting of all personal belongings, including those that would remain on the reservation and those that the individual/family would take with them upon relocation, along with the value of each item. Revealingly, the application requests that each Relocation officer indicate the "general appraisal of individual and/or family group with detailed information on items not otherwise covered."[44] This "detailed" information often included a brief synopsis of the individual's or family's history, their appearance, their skill set, any arrest record, and their potential ability to successfully adjust to the city.

When Fred Wilkins, Fond du Lac Ojibwe, and his family sought Relocation assistance to move to California in 1959, they were described in detail on application materials as "an excellent family unit. They are very neat in personal appearance and converse intelligently. Their past record would indicate that they should experience no problem in adjusting to their new community." Similarly, in his October 1959 Relocation application, Howard Lawson and his family were described as "neat appearing; they converse easily. They are both extremely fond and proud of their baby daughter." Further, it was stated that Mr. and Mrs. Lawson were expected to be a "successful relocation unit." In contrast, the 1956 Relocation application of Ray Whitethunder, Dakota from the Prairie Island Indian Community, described his drinking and "trouble with self-confidence."[45] Remarkably, the application also noted that he "has a long way to go in learning to compete with the general public, but this is not unusual considering the majority of the Prairie Island group," revealing the obvious and unrestrained racism of Relocation agents and officers.[46] Each of these statements taken from individual Relocation records demonstrates the attention paid to Indian peoples' behavior, dress, and use of language and, more significantly, provides critical commentary about societal expectations and markers of supposed success. Further, this sort of surveillance of Native mannerisms became a single judgment made by a single Relocation officer at a single moment in time. This regimented surveillance of Indian peoples makes obvious the aims of the Relocation Program: to identify those Native people who were most likely to assimilate into or become a certain type of American. As such, the Relocation applications became a tool to search for imagined docile Indian bodies while simultaneously cataloging and documenting anything that could be perceived as successful assimilation along the way.[47]

Once Indian people arrived at their Relocation destinations, the surveillance did not end; rather, it intensified. Relocatees were expected to regularly check in with their assigned Relocation officers in their destination city, to notify and update their Relocation officer of their employment status (appointments, layoffs, firings, hirings, etc.), and to keep the Relocation office abreast of their living situation. Eventually, for those who remained in contact with Relocation officials, this also entailed home visits. Before Edward Bowers was able to arrange for his family from White Earth to join him in Minneapolis, he was required to secure employment and "suitable housing." Upon the Lawsons' arrival in suburban Huntington Park, California, they were interviewed for a home counselor's report in May 1960. The report, conducted by George M. Felshaw, field Relocation officer, states:

> [Their] apartment is located in one of the nicer residential areas in Los Angeles and rents for $65.00 per month plus utilities. . . . Mrs. Lawson is a very fine housekeeper and she expresses her appreciations for the help given them through the relocation services. . . . They recently bought a used television set; however, it was not working as it needs a tube. Watching TV was all their recreation amounted to at the time of the visit; however, they indicated after they get to know the area better they will get out more often. . . . The family appears very conscientious and it is assumed they will have no problems in adapting themselves to city life.[48]

Later, at the time of their six-month final report in October 1960, the Lawson family had moved. The family seemed to exceed the expectations of the Relocation officer:

> On this final visit to the Lawson home, they were well, happy, and progressing very nicely. Mr. Lawson is very well pleased with his job and is earning $2.22 per hour now. Mrs. Lawson is taking a correspondence course in Dental Assistance which she is finding very interesting. The course is covered in twelve months and costs $140 total. The school also has a placement service when a student finishes. . . . The family like their neighbors very much and were

invited to accompany them to the Pomona Fair, Lincoln Park and beaches this summer, which they did. . . . They are continuing to pay $11.00 per month on a bill at home and also have been saving a little money for a down payment on a car. Mr. Lawson's boss is going to help him select the car to be sure he makes a 'good buy.' . . . There seem to be no problems. The family is very enthusiastic about this area so have been able to adjust to their community easily.[49]

For the Lawson family, who was viewed as a potentially "successful relocation unit" and seemed to be "adjusting" to their new Relocation environment, government surveillance may not be so obvious. However, numerous records circulated back and forth between the Relocation office in Los Angeles and the Minnesota Agency at Bemidji about them, most likely without their knowledge. Similarly, for thousands of other Indian relocatees, the same applications, memos, letters, and home visits served as a way for the federal government, and the BIA in particular, to monitor the assimilation of Indian people through their everyday personal lives. As many of the records demonstrate, much of this surveillance was done at a workplace, through BIA interviews with employers and coworkers, conducted among neighbors, and with members of church parishes. The detailed Relocation records of the Lawson family point to the expectations the BIA set for the Lawsons and other relocatees. They were evaluated on such private matters as the arrangement of their home, their consumption of goods, and the ways in which they were deemed to be successful, including their home, which they had made in a suburban area of Los Angeles, and the purchase of a television set and an automobile—each of which were measures of domesticity and key markers of the American Dream during this time frame.

The experience with Relocation and surveillance was similar for another Minnesota Ojibwe family from Cass Lake. In July 1961, Elliot Carver applied for a repeat Relocation request. Carver, who was married with two children, had served in both the navy and the army. Having previously relocated to Los Angeles, the Carvers were forced to return to their reservation in northern Minnesota after an illness in the family. While temporarily in Minnesota, the Relocation officer noted, "They are presently living in a tiny one room house which has no cooking facilities. . . . They are becoming very discouraged as Elliot has been able to obtain only short-term employment and it was also necessary for them to resort to welfare assistance during winter months. This is a very nice family and we feel a second relocation is justified and that they are deserving of this chance."[50] In this brief passage, the presumed postwar ideals of domesticity and housing are clearly at play. The family is living in a "tiny one room house" forced to take dinners with Mrs. Carver's parents.

By October 1961, the situation had turned for the Carvers, who were approved for Relocation and were living in a home they secured in suburban Hawthorne, California. The 30-day report/home counselor's report describes the Carvers' "very modest two-bedroom house" as "unfurnished" with a "very large yard." When the Relocation officer inquires about the family's finances, Mr. Carver reveals that "they have been unable to put aside any portion of his wages into a savings account; however, they have been able to save enough money required for their rent and incidental expenses, such as utilities." The Relocation officer goes on to state:

> [They were] counseled on the advisability of saving a reasonable proportion of their income for emergencies. The children attend York Grade School which is one block from their residence. [Both children] have made new friends and seem extremely happy in their new surroundings. . . . [Mrs. Carver] is a good homemaker and the home was neatly arranged and very clean. . . . The Carvers attend St. Joseph Catholic Church regularly which is only three blocks from their home. . . . For recreation, they have been visiting relatives and attending movies. They have no television, but fully intend to purchase a used T.V. when they are able to set aside money to pay cash. . . . The Carvers display an earnest desire to make a success of their second relocation attempt and with continued employment, there is no reason why they will not make a successful adjustment.[51]

Just as the Lawsons were deemed successful based on their accumulation of household goods and residence in a suburban neighborhood, so too were the Carvers. Each family was judged on how their home was kept up (in both cases the upkeep of the home is described as the responsibility of the wife), whether they had or intended to purchase a television set, their outward appearance, their community engagement, and their financial situation. For the Carvers, and many other families who participated in Relocation, their church attendance is also noted as a point of success and adaptation. In the final six-month report for the Carvers, the Relocation officer points out that they finally purchased a "1954 Mercury," they continue to attend church regularly, the children "receive favorable reports from their school," and the family appears to "understand the desirability of accruing funds to meet emergencies." Most significantly, the report, and case file, closes with, "They are alert and capable and appear to be able to get along without assistance from the office." Perhaps this is the degree of assimilation and adaptation the Relocation Program had long envisioned.

FHA loan programs and the VA's GI Bill were strategically designed to foster suburban development while mass-home-construction firms benefited from the federal support that guaranteed low-interest rates to individual buyers, taking much of the financial fears out of buying. Suburbs, envisioned as the new frontier, were defined by homeownership and were widely promoted by a growing body of real estate developers.[52] However, in the postwar age of prosperity and suburbanization, not all people were allowed to participate. While the policies and programs of the FHA and the VA's GI Bill promoted an idyllic (white) suburban America, the dual Indian policies of Termination and Relocation prompted a new generation of short-term urban residence in the least desirable rental units for American Indians.

In the government's efforts to avoid financial crisis after the Great Depression and to promote the growth of capitalism in the wake of World War II, Indian people continued to be viewed along racial lines. Expansive federal housing programs and policies directly contributed to white suburbanization, while preventing American Indians and other people of color from residing in these same areas. Relocation Policy did not consider suburbs as residential options for Indian people. The contrasting policies of the FHA, the GI Bill, and Relocation during the same political time are astounding. As Kenneth T. Jackson discusses, the impacts of FHA mortgage funding after WWII were to "[hasten] the decay of inner-city neighborhoods by stripping them of much of their middle-class constituency" and contribute to the "neglect of core cities"; these were the precise areas Indians were placed during Relocation.[53] Though the government viewed Relocation as a tool to allow Indian people to leave reservations and to assimilate into white society, many were never given the opportunity to move to the suburban areas whites flocked to in the postwar environment. Instead, Indian people were encouraged, yet limited, by the federal government to move into urban areas—precisely the areas that had been designated "urban slums" needing "revitalization." Donald Fixico notes that Indian Relocation was less about opportunity and more about control and containment, directly opposite the goals of the GI Bill.[54] The work of maintaining suburbs as predominately white places after WWII entailed the active disregard of people of color and lower-income people, including American Indians in federal housing and Indian policies. Using postwar suburbanization as an example of a relatively new form of long-term, white settlement, Indians have again been erased by the dramatic increase of non-Natives in the suburban housing boom.[55]

Federal Indian policy at midcentury, when viewed alongside federal housing policy of the same postwar era, allows us to understand the choreographed nature of suburbanization. Rather than view American Indian people as absent from or invisible in suburbs, it must be remembered that both federal Indian policies and federal housing policies throughout the mid-twentieth century prevented them from moving into or accessing new, increasingly white, suburban developments and instead funneled them into shorter-term rental housing in urban areas. The deliberate movement of white veterans and American Indians to specific residential locations, suburban and urban, becomes clear when the Indian policy of Relocation is examined alongside the GI Bill and earlier housing policies of the FHA.

The personal narratives of Gerald Owens, Damon James, David Dowd, and each of their families demonstrate the difficulty many Indian people faced in accessing quality housing in the city once they arrived on Relocation. However, more significantly, these Indian families, and numerous others, succeeded in locating suburban housing that was more affordable, spacious, and accessible without the assistance of government programs. These stories of American Indian peoples' active engagement with the processes of suburbanization during the mid-twentieth century are significant because their participation was largely unexpected and unsupported by policymakers. American Indians pushed past numerous barriers, including racism, to access suburbia. Though the goals of Relocation hinged on assimilation and integration, the logistics of the program predisposed it to failure. However, the American Indian Relocation Program opened the door for an unknown number of relocatees to take advantage of and adapt the program to fit their needs and goals. This often included access to a middle-class lifestyle in the suburbs. The Twin Cities, and Minnesota more broadly, are microcosms of other metropolitan areas and states around the country and serve as a testament to the survivance of the Indian people in suburbs. Often, Indian people faced policies that sought to prevent such moves. However, as Susan Power, a Dakota woman who was born on the Standing Rock Reservation in South Dakota and relocated to Chicago, remarked in her interview for the Chicago American Indian Oral History Project, "We all know there never was a government program designed to make us independent or successful. We must do this ourselves and here in the cities we have more of a chance."[56]

4

INTERSECTIONS OF RESPONSIBILITY
FEDERAL HOUSING POLICY, INDIAN POLICY, AND MINNEAPOLIS'S LITTLE EARTH HOUSING COMPLEX

[It] was the Indians who became ultimately responsible for managing these programs. . . . While at one time the tribe dealt mainly with the BIA, it could now expect also to see HUD, IHS, EPA and sometimes other federal entities. These were additional responsibilities for a tribal government without added budgetary resources. New and uncharted areas for regulation presented themselves quickly and demanded attention.

—HOUSING ASSISTANCE COUNCIL, *Indian Housing in the U.S.: A History*

I would like to discuss some of the problems we confront in the world today, and some of the problems that we confront in our own nation by using the subject of the American Dream. I choose this subject because America is essentially a dream. . . . While the American Dream reminds us that every man is an heir of a legacy of worthfullness. But ever since the Founding Fathers of our nation dreamed this dream, America has been something of a schizophrenic personality.

—MARTIN LUTHER KING JR., "The American Dream"

DURING THE SECOND HALF OF THE 1960s, on the heels of the civil rights movement and in the midst of a steadily growing urban Indian community, American Indian community members in Minneapolis and Saint Paul began to meet to discuss the many issues urban Indians across the Twin Cities were facing. These community gatherings eventually became the foundation for the politically minded American Indian Movement, widely recognized as AIM. It would not be long before "AIM and its leaders saw the need for a native-oriented housing development to help American Indians transition from the reservation to the city without losing touch with their traditional values. AIM worked with government agencies and social service organizations to make this native-run housing community a reality."[1] Thus, the origins of the first and only Native-preference public housing complex in the United States, located in South Minneapolis, took root.

The initial and primary objective of the Little Earth housing complex, at the time known as the South High housing complex due to its location on the site of the old high school in South Minneapolis, was to provide housing and a variety of community services to a growing American Indian population in the city. Only one decade prior, the federally funded American Indian Relocation Program encouraged and temporarily sponsored the movement of American Indian individuals and families away from reservation communities to urban areas, including Minneapolis. In fact, Minneapolis became a de facto Relocation destination. As the city drew Native people from northern Minnesota and Wisconsin, a Relocation office was temporarily opened in Minneapolis to aid relocatees, though the city was not designated an official Relocation destination by the Bureau of Indian Affairs (BIA). It was also during this period that Minneapolis, and to a lesser extent Saint Paul, saw dramatic growth in the urban Indian population, largely spurred by the Relocation Program.[2] The 1960 federal census recorded 15,496 American Indian people in Minnesota, 2,077 of whom were located in Minneapolis. Yet during the same census year, the "Minnesota Chippewa Tribe estimates there [were] 5,000 Indians in Hennepin" County, where Minneapolis is located, and another "3,000 in Ramsey" County, home to Saint Paul.[3] These population records mark a dramatic increase in American Indians in the metropolitan area—the very areas American Indian people were removed from during the treaty-making era and Dakota exile one hundred years prior.[4]

In this chapter, I examine the early history and founding of the Little Earth housing complex in the decades following Relocation as a point of disjuncture from the larger policy objectives of the Department of Housing and Urban Development (HUD) during its formative years of the late 1960s and early 1970s to reveal the ways the federal government continued to stifle, and even ignore, the housing needs of American Indian people in urban areas. I analyze the creation and organization of HUD, including its predecessor agency, the Public Housing Administration, to demonstrate the ways in which American Indian people have remained ambiguous and often invisible in terms of federal housing programs, funding, and administration. In doing so, I reveal the complexity of tribes' sovereign status, even as they remain "domestic dependent nations." Moreover, I examine the limits of tribal enrollment and thus tribal citizenship for individual Indians who remain "wards" of the federal government and the ambiguity of off-reservation Indians in terms of housing.[5] It is here that I interrogate the administration of Indian housing programs. Why is Indian housing tied to public housing within HUD? Would Indian housing be better served if it were separate from HUD altogether? What would Indian housing look like if it were part of the BIA? Would this be a beneficial relationship or location for Indian housing? Why are Indian housing programs almost exclusively limited to tribes and tribal entities on reservations when most tribal members live in metropolitan areas away from reservation communities? How may Little Earth, as a Native housing complex, position itself to receive increased and much-needed American Indian–specific housing funds? What would Indian housing and funding look like if individual Indian people were eligible for Native-specific housing funds from HUD (rather than funds distributed via tribal entities)?

During the 1960s and into the 1970s, despite the numerous studies and government reports that regularly highlighted the great need for improved Indian housing both on reservations and in urban centers, the federal administration for Indian policy rapidly shifted. This disorganization allowed for a major gap in funding—the housing needs of off-reservation American Indians. This aspect of Indian housing was and continues to be overlooked despite the Relocation Program that moved thousands of Indian people to metropolitan areas across the country beginning in the 1940s and lasting into the early 1960s. To redress this negligence, I examine the creation and operation of the Little Earth housing complex, whose residents are predominately American Indian and enrolled tribal members. This focus underscores the ways the federal government has failed and continues to fail urban Indians, particularly in terms of housing. By centering urban Indians and Little Earth, I demonstrate the tensions present in the administration of HUD programs, barriers to housing caused by bureaucratic red tape that ties up housing resources, and the gap in housing programs for off-reservation Indians. The lack of federal funding available for providing safe and adequate housing for urban Indians is particularly troublesome when attention is paid to the activism of the 1960s and 1970s. The activism of communities of color and American Indian communities led to changes in civil rights and advances in racial equality, specifically for Black people. The 1970s also saw the advent of the Indian Self-Determination and Education Assistance Act (1975), which worked to give tribes more autonomy and voice in how federal funds were administered. Therefore, a close look at Indian policy and housing policy during the 1960s and 1970s reveals the disconnect between need and policy.

In this chapter, I demonstrate the ways the Little Earth housing complex has been a Native-led response to house Native people, including the hundreds who arrived in Minneapolis as participants in the Relocation Program. Here, I contend that Little Earth should be viewed as an urban Indian housing program akin to reservation-based housing programs with preferential placements, occupancy, and access to Indian-specific funding. By limiting the federal funding that Little Earth is eligible for, the federal government, through HUD, denies historic treaty obligations to tribal nations and Indian people. Instead, much of Indian housing falls under Great Society–era programs based on income and need rather than acknowledging the distinct and unique legal/political relationship that exists between tribal nations and the federal government—in essence, the foundation of trust responsibility. In this way, Little Earth, as the only nontribal American Indian–preference low-income housing complex in the United States, though multitribal, should be able to access Indian housing funds based on the tribal membership of its residents rather than be designated solely as a public housing complex. Individual Indian residents should be eligible for Indian housing funds off reservation, flowing directly from the federal government. Rather, the limitations imposed by the federal government and

HUD prevent access to a wide variety of funds that would otherwise be available to Indian people through the Office of Native American Programs (ONAP), which currently administers Indian housing programs for HUD. My focus remains on Little Earth as an Indian-preference housing project funded, developed, and constructed amid a political moment bookended by the 1965 creation of HUD and the 1988 Indian Housing Act to highlight the ways in which federal housing policies and federal Indian policy are constitutive of one another.

History of Little Earth

When construction on the $4.5 million South High housing complex for low- and middle-income families began in October 1971, the ground-breaking was accompanied by traditional drumming and Native singers. The housing project, set to include 39 apartments, 167 townhomes, and designated recreation areas, was to be finished within a two-year time frame. Interestingly, the original owner and sponsor of the housing complex was the Saint Paul–Minneapolis Archdiocese and the Minnesota Council of Churches who had established an Indian Housing Committee of various American Indian leaders from across the Twin Cities to provide guidance and serve as a board to oversee implementation. Created in 1948, the Minnesota Council of Churches has worked to build, strengthen, and connect faith communities with a focus on social justice across religious denominations. The Minnesota Council of Churches also continues to have a long history of working with American Indian communities and refugee communities in the state. The stated goal of the Archdiocese and the Minnesota Council of Churches, at the time, was to "provide initial support to accomplish building and occupancy of the project," and they also pledged to "support the resident corporation where needed."[6] With a $4.4 million Federal Housing Administration (FHA) mortgage, supplemental federal funds provided by the Model Cities program, and local funds secured through the Greater Metropolitan Housing Corporation, construction on the first, and only, urban housing project proposed by and for American Indians began.[7]

Local newspapers were abuzz with news of guaranteed financing for the landmark housing complex. Unlike any other, it was described as a "housing project to aid Indians," "the first of its kind in the United States to be conceived of and initiated by urban Indians," and a "groundbreaking" event. Today, the housing complex is widely recognized throughout the Minneapolis–Saint Paul region simply as Little Earth or, more formally, Little Earth of United Tribes, Inc. It remains the only American Indian "preference project-based Section 8 rental assistance community in the US."[8] Many non-Natives in the area erroneously conceive of Little Earth as a reservation rather than the predominately Native public housing complex that it is precisely because of the large number of American Indians who call it home and the cultural services in the immediate vicinity. Today, Little Earth houses approximately one thousand residents, 98 percent of whom identify as American Indian. Over thirty tribal nations are represented at the housing complex, and 65 percent of those who call it home receive public assistance. This is a dramatic increase in Native occupancy from the early 1970s when only 40 percent of the residents identified as Native American.[9] Today, limited by its size and ability to access funding, Little Earth maintains a waitlist of nearly five hundred family units, largely reflective of the demand for affordable housing in the Twin Cities, particularly for American Indian families.[10]

Though widely celebrated with community and financial support, the fervor over the construction of the first-of-its-kind Indian-preference housing project would not last. Due in large part to high vacancy rates, rent collection problems, shoddy construction, and poor management, by early 1975 the "financially troubled" housing development was "taken over by members and supporters of the American Indian Movement" in an effort to save it.[11] With rent payments as the only source of income, the housing development struggled to stay afloat. As described in an article from the *Minneapolis Star* in March 1975, "Members of the non-profit housing project [Minnesota Council of Churches] were unable to make mortgage payments for January, February, and March."[12] So "HUD was looking for new management for the two-year old low and moderate-income housing project so the office would not have to foreclose the mortgage," while, at the same time, the complex was also at risk of being condemned. Rather than lose the short-lived investment and evict all tenants, HUD and the Indian Housing Committee board of directors decided "unanimously that the national American Indian Movement office should be recognized as the responsible agent to appoint a new board" in a last-ditch effort to save the housing complex.[13] Subsequently, Dennis Banks (Leech Lake Ojibwe), leader of AIM at the time, was appointed new director of the housing complex.[14] As change and uncertainty at the urban housing complex continued, another turnover of leadership at Little Earth occurred. In his new role as president of the National Congress of American Indians and as a BIA administrator with experience in economic development, Leon Cook (Red Lake Ojibwe) attributed the financial problems of Little Earth to the "altruistic idea" of the Archdiocese and the Minnesota Council of Churches who did not "come to grips with the fact that . . . it had to be run like a business" and instead allowed residents to live there, in certain cases, rent free, including nuns belonging to the Archdiocese.[15]

When planning for the Minneapolis Indian-preference housing program was in its early stages, HUD had only recently become a cabinet-level agency. This coincides with the shift in federal Indian policy more generally toward programs based on need rather than race, specifically programs aimed at poverty rather than programs based on tribal nations'

Figure 13. Aerial view of the Little Earth multitribal housing complex in the Phillips neighborhood of Minneapolis, November 1973. Photograph by Minneapolis Star and Tribune Company. Courtesy of Minnesota Historical Society.

distinct political-legal status and treaty obligations of the federal government.[16] The temporal moment of Little Earth also coincides with the move away from Termination Policy, including the Relocation Program, and the shift toward American Indian self-determination. Yet upon closer analysis, remnants of Termination can be seen in the absence of off-reservation housing programs for Indian people. In many ways, American Indians were thought not to exist once they crossed the reservation boundaries, as if settler colonial boundaries dictate American Indian identity and tribal belonging. As a component of Termination Policy, the Relocation Program provided limited assistance to Indian people who left the reservation to relocate to an urban destination, including one-way transportation to the designated city, short-term housing, and a small stipend for living expenses, as discussed in chapter 3. The overall goal of Termination was to terminate federal obligation, an objective in many ways carried out by moving Indian people to urban areas away from reservations. Little Earth took shape to the backdrop of this recent history.

Temporal Moment of Little Earth

Little Earth, as a local citizen participatory housing program, received Model Cities funds from HUD that were used for its construction, in addition to its FHA mortgage guarantee. But this flow of funding was short-lived; in 1973, the year Little Earth was created, President Richard Nixon imposed a funding moratorium on many HUD programs. At the same time, Little Earth was experiencing its own economic downfall, in large part due to fiscal mismanagement. Then, in 1974 HUD consolidated several programs and funds into the Community Development Block Grant, thereby shifting increased authority to state and local agencies to administer programs and simultaneously creating the Section 8 Program geared toward project-based housing programs. One year later, in 1975, the American Indian Self-Determination and Education Assistance Act, which granted tribes the ability to enter directly into contracts with federal agencies, passed Congress.

The temporal moment of Little Earth's planning, construction, and opening largely overlaps with a dramatic wave of visible American Indian activism from coast to coast. As Little Earth was getting off the ground, the American Indian Movement, which originated in South Minneapolis, gained momentum. Little Earth was, in many ways, born out of the political activism of the 1960s. Founded in 1968 in Minneapolis, AIM grew out of a need to draw attention to and prevent police brutality of the city's growing Native population, largely concentrated in South Minneapolis's Phillips neighborhood. AIM became an activist civil rights organization that worked to tackle racism, promote Indigenous rights and sovereignty, and address unemployment, housing, poverty, health care, and preservation of culture. Though much attention has focused on the militancy of AIM's activism—specifically the Trail of Broken Treaties march to Washington, D.C., and the ensuing occupation of the BIA building (1972), and the highly publicized takeover of Wounded Knee (1973)—less attention has been paid to the local, social service aspects of AIM that sought to improve the daily lives of American Indians in the city.[17]

Despite the intense media scrutiny during the late 1960s and early 1970s, AIM remained a strong supporter of Indian Education Programs and housing for urban Indians. Just ahead of the construction of the South High housing complex that would soon become Little Earth, AIM worked to create two American Indian survival schools in 1972: Heart of the Earth in Minneapolis and the Red School House in Saint Paul. As Julie L. Davis argues, "AIM's origins and its local work in the Twin Cities are much less well understood than its national politics, the schools that AIM people founded have received little attention in either scholarly or popular histories."[18] The same can be said of the role of AIM at Little Earth. Just as Little Earth and Indian survival schools were born out of Native political activism, AIM too was a Native response to Indian policy. This is significant because, though AIM has received a great deal of attention, scholarly and otherwise, its important role at Little Earth has been chronically overlooked. AIM's efforts to guide Little Earth at a time of upheaval challenge and push back against dominant narratives of AIM as predominately militaristic and underscore the organization's community-based problem-solving resolve.

During this same political moment of American Indian activism in the Twin Cities, the American Indian Studies Department at the University of Minnesota was founded just a few short miles away from Little Earth, the first such department in the country. Across Minneapolis and

Saint Paul, a variety of social service, educational, and cultural organizations for American Indians took shape, including the Minneapolis American Indian Center, Heart of the Earth and the Red School House, and the Indian Health Board of Minneapolis, each of which worked to fill a need in the urban Indian community.[19] Like the Little Earth housing complex, these organizations were a direct result of the influx of American Indian people in the Twin Cities. Importantly, these organizations were also a result of American Indian activism, as American Indian community members played key roles in each of these organizations. In many ways, the culturally thriving Indian community at and around Little Earth symbolized and continues to symbolize American Indian rejection of assimilatory efforts imposed by the federal government. At its core, Little Earth remains a strong Native urban community, a multitribal group of Indians who chose to come together, to call a few square blocks in the city home. Minneapolis has remained a sort of mecca for urban Indians, and many of the same social service organizations that first opened their doors in the 1960s and 1970s remain a cornerstone of the Indian community today. In fact, growth continues as new organizations supporting the cultural, educational, social, and health needs of the Indian community continue to open each year, infusing Indian Minneapolis with ongoing culture and community revitalization.

HUD and Indian Housing

Less than a decade prior to the creation of the Little Earth housing complex, President Lyndon B. Johnson signed the Housing and Urban Development Act of 1965 into law, effectively creating HUD. Its primary goal was to build and expand the role of the federal government in housing programs, a component of Johnson's Great Society–era program initiatives that also included the War on Poverty. More specifically, the sweeping Housing and Urban Development Act sought to "assist in the provision of housing for low and moderate-income families, to promote orderly urban development, to improve living environments in urban areas, and to extend and amend laws relating to housing, urban renewal, and community facilities."[20] However, as I demonstrate, the intertwined history of Indian housing and public housing—or, rather, Indian policy and housing policy—goes back much further.

The National Housing Act of 1934 marked the first major intervention of the federal government into the housing sector of American life.[21] The act intervened in the tide of Great Depression–era foreclosures and worked to make homeownership more affordable and accessible. Just three years later, the U.S. Housing Act of 1937 expanded on the previous act and stipulated that decent and affordable housing was a basic necessity for *all* Americans, initiating the public housing movement. Just a decade and a half later, the Housing Act of 1949 reaffirmed the national goal of affordable, safe, sanitary, and decent housing for all citizens. But a gap remained: Who was responsible for the administration of American Indian housing, and where would those funds come from? Despite the pledges of the federal government during the first half of the twentieth century, this question was not answered until 1961, during the Kennedy administration, when Stewart Udall, during his first year as secretary of the interior, created a task force on Indian affairs.

The task force Udall launched recommended the establishment of a branch of Indian housing under the BIA, separate and distinct from HUD's predecessor agency, the Public Housing Administration established in 1937.[22] Moreover, the task force recommended the establishment of a self-help homeownership opportunity program for Indian people on reservations.[23] In 1962, the BIA inquired to the commissioner of public housing as to the ability of the Public Housing Administration to administer Indian housing programs on reservations. The same year, the general counsel to the Public Housing Administration declared there to be "sufficient legislative authority" under the U.S. Housing Act of 1937 for Indian people to in fact be eligible for public housing's low-rent program.[24] To receive funds, tribes were required to establish Indian Housing Authorities (IHAs), similar in operation and structure to Public Housing Authorities, to administer programming and oversee access, distribution of funds, and approval of rental units on reservations. One year later, the BIA and the Public Housing Administration signed a coordination agreement for mutual-help housing programs for Indian people on reservations. Then in 1965, the BIA and the Public Housing Administration signed yet another agreement regarding low-rent programs for Indian people on reservations. That same year, when HUD became a cabinet-level agency, the BIA established the Division of

Housing Assistance, which included the Housing Improvement Program that had the primary goal of rehabilitating individual housing units and a limited amount of new construction for tribal members of federally recognized tribes who lived on reservations.[25] This attention to on-reservation housing remained despite the efforts of the Relocation Program to move Native people off reservation.

Despite all these political efforts, it was not until the Department of Housing and Urban Development Act of 1968 that there was an actual, formal reference to HUD's obligations to low-income families who resided in what were largely undefined "Indian areas." The 1968 act expanded the application of the U.S. Housing Act of 1937 to be inclusive of Indian areas in addition to the more commonly used and described areas of "urban" and "rural nonfarm" locations. At this time, no definition or explanation of an "Indian area" was offered.[26] One year later, two tripartite agreements were signed between HUD, the BIA, and the Indian Health Service (IHS) to ensure housing was safe and sanitary (including access to running water and proper sewage containment and disposal), to construct new and rehabbed Indian homes, and to address the coordination and responsibility of each agency. The BIA revised the Housing Improvement Program for American Indian people in 1970. In 1974, nearly a decade after its creation, the first funds specifically intended for Indian housing were set aside under the HUD umbrella. The same year, HUD and the BIA cooperatively agreed to develop five hundred units of new construction in Alaska as a case study.

One year later, a report titled "Indian Housing in the United States" was prepared and distributed to the Committee on Interior and Insular Affairs. This report pointed to the "special legal relationship" that undergirds Indian housing: "Indian people occupy a somewhat special position by virtue of the Constitution, Executive orders, and various Federal treaties and statutes." Though the report focuses on trust land, it acknowledges the housing needs of American Indians as more "pronounced" than "among non-Indians" due to their geographic and cultural diversity and that both HUD and the BIA are doing a less than satisfactory job administering housing programs. The report called for an "Indian desk" to be established within HUD. Importantly, the report also called on Veterans Affairs and the Farmers Home Administration to do a better job participating in the "Indian housing effort."[27] Later that year, an

Office of Indian Programs was first opened in a HUD office, and in 1976 the first comprehensive HUD handbook on Indian housing regulations was issued. In 1977, the position of special assistant to the secretary of HUD for Indian and Alaska Native programs was created by legislative action.

The same year, the American Indian Policy Review Commission published its "Final Report," which drew attention to Indian housing. Its more than six hundred pages of recommendations included that "Congress reorganize the Indian housing program and give one agency the primary responsibility for coordinating and administering the program."[28] Moreover, the report pointed to the ways "many Native American programs are not adequately defined" so that "they fail to adequately meet the needs of tribes or individual Indians."[29] Here, they provide a specific example from Indian housing:

> HUD is responsible for constructing housing units for Indian people. Program regulations state that HUD will construct the buildings if HEW [U.S. Department of Health, Education, and Welfare] agrees to provide plumbing and sewage facilities. Still another agency, the BIA, is responsible for the construction of roads leading to the home. As a result, HUD cannot begin construction until it has a commitment from HEW to put in the water facilities. HEW cannot agree to put in water until it has the exact location of the house. HUD, in turn, cannot provide the exact location of the home until the BIA stipulates where it will put the roads and driveways.
>
> These problems are compounded by the fact that each of these agencies involved receives separate funding from Congress. As a result, it is possible for HUD to have money available to construct homes but be prevented from doing so because HEW does not have the funds necessary to put in the water systems or because BIA does not have the money to build roads to reach the homes.
>
> This overlap in Indian administration also extends to State and local governments.[30]

Perhaps as a way to recognize and address these calls to improve Indian housing at the federal level, in 1978 a separate Office of Indian Housing was created within HUD, and in 1980 HUD reorganized to establish six regional offices of Indian housing programs.[31] By 1981, an interagency task force on Indian housing was established whose task it was to examine the best way to revise a national Indian housing policy. That same year, a HUD memo titled "Troubled Indian Housing Authorities" worked to address the milieu of problems IHAs faced budgetarily and in terms of management.[32]

Indian housing programs shifted in important ways with the fiscal conservativism of the New Federalism inaugurated under the Reagan administration. In 1982, legislation was proposed to move Indian housing to the BIA and therefore eliminate the existing on-reservation HUD Indian housing programs.[33] This legislation died but was reintroduced a year later, where it failed once again.[34] However, 1983 became a benchmark year for Indian housing. Within HUD, the Secretary's Advisory Committee on American Indian and Alaska Native Housing was created, FHA-insured mortgages were expanded to cover Indian trust lands (i.e., reservations), and HUD proposed Indian-preference regulations. In 1984, HUD appointed the first permanent director of the Office of Indian Housing, John V. Meyers, almost two full decades after HUD was first created. Though a long time in the making, it seemed Indian housing was finally gaining political attention and momentum.

This momentum continued when the Indian Housing Act of 1988 was introduced to Congress in December 1987, before it was signed into law by President Ronald Reagan in June 1988. The Indian Housing Act of 1988 amended the U.S. Housing Act of 1937 as it related to American Indians, placing new so-called responsibilities for the housing needs of American Indians and Alaska Natives squarely under HUD. In doing so, the act created the Office of Native American Programs, which remains charged with administering "housing and community development programs that benefit American Indian and Alaska Native tribal governments, tribal members, the Department of Hawaiian Home Lands, Native Hawaiians, and other Native American organizations."[35] The goal of ONAP is to "increase the supply of safe, decent, and affordable housing available to Native American families," basically the same goal that was described fifty years prior in the U.S. Housing Act of 1937.

Though the Indian Housing Act of 1988 worked to separate Indian housing from other forms of public housing administration, it also promoted mutual-help and self-help homeownership opportunity programs for American Indians and Alaska Natives, including those for non-low-income families. This is significant as it demonstrates a move away from exclusive needs-based funding for Indian people. The act was intended to establish responsibility for American Indian housing needs as separate and distinct from public housing, yet, under the act, Indian Housing Authorities were, by definition, "public housing [agencies]." Moreover, under the Indian Housing Act, only tribes, tribal entities, and IHAs can receive federal funding. HUD policy stipulates "that an [IHA] be established for the Indian tribe to take advantage of" Indian housing programs.[36] Only at this point are tribes, by way of their IHA, able to "take advantage of" available funding and distribute HUD funds as they see fit to on-reservation housing programs and the individual eligible tribal members who participate in these programs. IHAs are created by tribal governments or may be organized by state statute to administer Indian housing programs. In this way, IHAs sort of circumvent tribal governments as they are not necessarily an agency or department of a tribal government; instead, they are legally separate entities. Though this allows for a level of separation between tribal governance and housing administration, it also creates another level of bureaucracy and redirects housing funds to HUD employees (in this case, generally on-reservation tribal members) who administer another level of programming.

Indian housing and public housing continued to remain under the same programmatic umbrella—hence Public and Indian Housing as they exist today. In this way, Indian housing remains inherently linked to public housing as housing based on financial need rather than on treaty guarantees and the trust responsibility of the federal government. It is here that I question the linking of Indian housing and public housing. Why is Indian housing overwhelmingly need-based rather than a program centered on treaties and fiduciary responsibility? Why is the availability of and qualification for Indian housing so heavily tied to an Indian area or reservation, particularly as the federal government has continuously worked to break up tribal land and relocate Indian people? As I address later in this chapter, this would be similarly problematic if Indian Education Programs and funding were only available for those Native students who lived on reservations or who had unmet educational fiscal need.

Moreover, the Indian Housing Act of 1988 offered several key definitions previously ignored or overlooked in legislation. These terms include *Indian, Indian area, Indian Housing Authority,* and *Indian tribe* as follows:

> The term "Indian" means any person recognized as being an Indian or Alaska Native by an Indian tribe, the federal Government, or any State. . . . The term "Indian area" means the area within which an Indian housing authority is . . . authorized to provide lower income housing. . . . The term "Indian housing authority" means any entity that—(A) is authorized to engage . . . in or assist in the development or operation of lower income housing for Indians; and (B) . . . is established—(i) by exercise of the power of self-government of an Indian tribe . . . independent of State law; or (ii) by operation of State law providing specifically for . . . housing authorities for Indians, including regional housing authorities in the State of Alaska. . . . The term "Indian Tribe" means any tribe, band, pueblo, group, community, or nation of . . . Indians or Alaska Natives.[37]

Interestingly, though the Indian Housing Act worked to clarify the distinctions between Indian housing and public housing, it did little to clarify where, geographically, Indian housing programs could be administered by way of "Indian area." The act determined that Indian Housing Authorities were to administer Indian housing programs and distribute funds, but curiously it did not necessarily limit the applicability of these funds exclusively to reservations, though the language used commonly refers to "on-reservation" or "Indian area," suggesting a geographical limit. Similarly, the act left open the interpretation of eligibility based on its own definition of *Indian* and *Indian tribe.* For example, the act does not limit eligibility for funds exclusively to federally recognized tribes but to a "group" or "community" of Indians.[38] Further, the act, nor any previous legislation, does little to limit the ability of IHAs to operate beyond the borders of a reservation. This leaves open the question, or opportunity, of the possibility of an IHA (or multiple IHAs) to administer funds to a housing program or complex, like Little Earth, in an urban area or even to individual Indians.

It is here, I argue, that HUD's public housing policy shifted or, perhaps, was always envisioned to be inclusive of Indian housing, broadly conceived, and I question the federal government's creation and continual use of such a bureaucracy to oversee and administer American Indian housing programs. The bureaucratic gap or dual oversight that exists between the Department of Interior (where the BIA is located and which oversees most American Indian programming) and HUD (where Indian Housing is located) must be made legible and accessible to tribal nations, intertribal agencies, and multitribal entities like Little Earth. In fact, this conundrum of multiple layers of federal administration was specifically acknowledged in 1985 by HUD's Committee on Indian and Alaska Native Housing, which recommended "the separation of the Office of Indian Housing from the Public Housing program, a change based upon the unique and special needs of the Indian constituency," and in the 1977 American Indian Policy Review Commission's "Final Report."[39] Within HUD today, under the Public and Indian Housing umbrella, is the Office of Native American Programs, which administers American Indian housing programs. Today, Indian Housing Authorities must seek approval from HUD, the BIA, and IHS before on-reservation housing construction projects may begin. This contrasts with other Public Housing Authorities who must only work through HUD. It is precisely these layers of federal government oversight and administrative separation that create very real barriers to Indian people's access to off-reservation housing, particularly outside of the public housing sector.

It is revealing and perhaps even startling to see how little attention was paid to urban Indians at the policy level, even though the Relocation Program just one decade prior sought to remove Indian people from their reservation communities and relocate them to urban areas. In a way, this denial of access to services (i.e., Indian housing funds) for urban Indians harkens back to the Termination era, which had only recently ended. By refusing to fund any sort of Indian housing program off reservation, the federal government was (and is) able to covertly eliminate funds to Indian people in urban areas, in this case Minneapolis, by linking resource availability to on-reservation residency. Though Minneapolis was a de facto Relocation destination, urban Indians were virtually ignored in terms of housing once they relocated. As discussed in chapter 3, relocatees were provided short-term living accommodations, often only two weeks, and in many cases the conditions were significantly dilapidated. In this way, the very goal of Termination, to terminate federal funds to Indian people, continued through the effective denial of federal Indian housing funds for urban Indians. The federal government refused to provide funds to urban Indian people for housing, funds and services for which they would be eligible if they had remained on reservations. From this perspective, it is clear the federal government connected its obligation to Indian people to their geographical and residential location—on reservations. Housing for urban Indians, much like during the Relocation era, has remained overlooked. This complicated and problematic scenario clearly demonstrates the ways federal housing policies have worked to limit or manipulate American Indian collective living in urban areas or even suburban neighborhoods, where Native people would instead have enhanced economic opportunities, by continuing to deny federal funds to off-reservation Indians. Moreover, the lack of access to housing funds off reservation is intricately tied to the lack of resources for other Indian programs in urban areas—namely, Indian Health Services.

It is my view that the federal government has the capacity to prevent much-needed funds from reaching individual off-reservation Indians, including those who are enrolled members of federally recognized tribes, considered wards of the government, and in need of housing assistance. In the case of Little Earth in Minneapolis, it has been categorized as a nontribal entity. Indeed, Little Earth is a multitribal entity and thus does not fit easily into the constraints of federal Indian policy or federal housing policy. Little Earth, as an American Indian–preference housing complex run by American Indians for American Indians, remains unable to access federal housing funds specifically earmarked for the tribally enrolled American Indian people who call it home. By historicizing and assessing the temporal moment of the creation of HUD alongside the founding and early years of Little Earth, I show that Little Earth is a remarkable case study to critique federal housing policy and Indian policy as a tool of settler colonialism that affects all Indian people, including urban Indians, precisely due to the lack of federal funds available to off-reservation Indians. This is significant because, as I argue throughout my research, the federal government remains charged with fulfilling its trust relationship to tribes and individual Indian people.

The lack of off-reservation housing funds for American Indian people is further compounded by the fact that the majority of all Indian

people today live off reservation. This amplifies the significance of treaties, which have notoriously gone unfulfilled by the federal government,
as a lasting basis for Indian policy. This also highlights contemporary
challenges about the murky and complex nature of when and where
obligations lie to tribal nations and individual Indians as tribal citizens
and the role of geographical location (i.e., trust land). In this context, I
am thinking particularly of the Snyder Act as a consolidation of earlier
treaties and the ways in which the federal government has carried out its
fiscal responsibility by limiting the direct flow of funds to tribal nations.[40]
Indeed, the federal government has restricted or limited access to Indian
housing funds to a relatively new category of Indian Housing Authorities and tribally designated entities, rather than giving access to individual Indian people. The required establishment of IHAs, necessary to
receive federal funding, can be read as parallel in nature to the role of
the Indian Reorganization Act (IRA) of 1934, which pushed tribal nations
to adopt a specific form of tribal governance. Tribal governments must
adhere to certain qualities to make them legible, and thereby recognizable, to the federal government and therefore also eligible for federal
funds and services. As a previous staff attorney for the Denver Office
of Indian Programs argued in his 1988 legal brief, tribes that create a
housing authority must precisely follow HUD mandates for the structure of an Indian Housing Authority, very similar in nature to "a corpo-
rate set of bylaws[,] . . . and require HUD approval before they can be
amended," eerily similar to the function of IRA constitutions.[41] Moreover, each IHA must also be presented to the secretary of the interior
for review. This level of inspection and scrutiny, perhaps even surveillance, reaffirms the federal government's assumed responsibility for Indian
housing. The artificial levels of bureaucracy do little to strip away federal responsibility; rather, they just mask it.

Today, Little Earth, the only American Indian–run, Native-preference,
Section 8 housing complex in the United States, where over 90 percent of
its residents are Native, remains ineligible for American Indian programs
offered by HUD because it is not a tribal entity or IHA. Each of the
Indian housing programs funded under HUD's Public and Indian Housing umbrella, in particular the Indian Housing Block Grant Program,

requires recipients to be federally recognized tribes or their tribally designated housing entity. In this way, Little Earth, a multitribal housing complex for urban Indians, is precluded from accessing much-needed funds earmarked specifically for Indian people because, unlike a tribal nation, it lacks inherent sovereignty, an IRA-recognized governing structure, and an IHA, never mind the tribal membership of its residents. Similarly, individual Indian residents of Little Earth are ineligible for Indian housing assistance from HUD's Office of Native American Programs because funds are not allocated on an individual basis; instead, they are distributed to tribes via tribally designated housing entities. Therefore, individual Indians and Indian families who choose to live off reservation must apply for public housing resources; they remain ineligible for federal Indian housing funds once they leave the reservation. There are two important caveats to this. One is that the Housing Improvement Program administered by the BIA discussed throughout this chapter requires applicants to be a member of a federally recognized tribe, to live in a designated Indian area, and be at or below 150 percent of the poverty threshold. The second exception is the Section 184 Indian Home Loan Guarantee Program administered by HUD and available to off-reservation Indians in the position to apply for a home loan. This puts into question the limits of tribal enrollment status when Indian people live off reservation and need housing assistance. This also raises questions about what sorts of tribal governments are recognized by the federal government. How may Little Earth situate itself to be legible by the federal government to receive Indian housing funds?

Despite its promises and mission statement, HUD's Office of Native American Programs in crucial ways fails to fulfill its obligations to individual Indian people who choose to live off reservation in urban areas. A conundrum arises about how HUD and the BIA can, or even should, turn over or allow for the funding of multitribal entities like Little Earth when a significant number of residents are members of federally recognized tribes. It also raises the question of resource distribution on a more individual basis rather than at the tribal level. This demonstrates how the federal government only recognizes certain kinds of Indian governments and nationhood as legitimate and therefore as eligible to receive Indian housing funds.

Despite this seemingly clear gap in funding, the problem remains. HUD's Office of Native American Programs administers the Indian Housing Block Grant Program, the Indian Community Development Block Grant Program, and the Title VI Loan Guarantee Program. Begun in 1998, the Indian Housing Block Grant Program provides needs-based funds for Indian housing assistance, including modernization, management, services, and safety, to tribes and tribally designated housing entities. The Indian Community Development Block Grant Program provides funds on a "competitive basis" to tribes "in developing viable Indian and Alaska Native Communities, including decent housing, a suitable living environment, and economic opportunities, primarily for low and moderate income persons."[42] The Title VI Loan Guarantee Program "guarantees repayment of 95 percent of the principal and interest due" on a loan made by "tribes, Alaska Native Villages or [Tribally Designated Housing Entities] (with tribal approval)" for home construction, rehabilitation, infrastructure, land acquisition, community facilities, and financing.[43] Seemingly, Little Earth should be eligible for these programs based on the sheer number of tribal members it houses. However, at present each of these programs is intended to be created and carried out on reservation and must be administered by tribes or tribally designated housing entities. This is a significant drawback and glaring gap in policy, though perhaps intended, because today, as previously stated, the majority of all Indian people live off reservation, a trend that has only gained momentum since World War II and the federally sponsored Relocation Program.

The need for low-income, off-reservation housing continues for Indian people long after the activism of the 1960s and 1970s that witnessed the birth of Little Earth. The programming goals and sheer volume of funds available to the Office of Native American Programs stand in stark contrast to the numerous programs offered under the public housing umbrella. More broadly, housing assistance, though chronically underfunded, is available to non-Native individuals through a slew of public housing programs regardless of where they choose to live. At the agency level, HUD continues to dictate how funds are distributed and requires tribes and tribal members to administer the programs of the federal government, therefore cutting into the actual availability of funds for distribution and application because money is being redirected to pay employees' salaries. The Johnson-O'Malley Program provides an interesting point of comparison here. Established by the Johnson-O'Malley Act in 1934, the program works to subsidize Indian Education Programs in schools across the country, regardless of location, based on the number of tribally enrolled students.[44] These moneys essentially bypass tribes and go directly to the tribally enrolled K-12 students via school districts and Indian Education Programs. Perhaps this could be a model for Indian housing programs off reservation.

Indeed, HUD oversight and administration regulates and limits the ways Indian housing funds can be used, allowing for a gap in federal funding for off-reservation Indian people, rendering urban Indians invisible and therefore allowing them to fall through the cracks. I argue that Little Earth is in fact emblematic of Native self-governance and self-determination in the face of this larger settler colonial structure that refuses to allow for much-needed funds to flow to off-reservation Indians in need of housing programs and assistance. This becomes a way for the federal government to limit, or at least try to limit, Indian peoples' access to housing, property, and visible and vibrant off-reservation communities. Here, Little Earth is an example of the ways off-reservation Indians have been abandoned by the federal government. The urban Indians who call Little Earth home are not eligible for federal moneys for Indian housing due to HUD's stipulation that their moneys may only be directed toward certain types of recognized tribal governments. This sort of funding mechanism and requirement excludes other kinds of Indigenous governance systems and individual Indians, thereby severely limiting federal responsibility and obligation. In fact, creative self-governance did and continues to happen at Little Earth despite the attempts at the federal level to erase and deny responsibility to off-reservation Indians. Questions remain about the limits to on-reservation HUD funding, as well as the federal government's refusal to see Indians as modern, urban residents. Moreover, it must be restated that Indian people remain citizen-members of their tribal governments beyond the borders of the reservation. So, why does it seem that American Indians have been denied access to Indian-specific housing programs and funds off reservation?

The shift from a focus on Indian blood and race toward tribal membership or citizenship to determine who is and is not considered

Indian further complicates the funding of Indian programs—in this case, who is eligible for housing services from the federal government. As enrolled tribal members, tribal citizenship does not stop at the border of the reservation; you are a tribal citizen regardless of where you live. This is a benefit or privilege of dual citizenship in the United States and a tribal nation. As legal scholar Matthew L. M. Fletcher points out, "Tribal membership is the key indicator of whether or not an America Indian qualifies for federal, tribal, and, to a lesser extent, state services such as educational scholarships, preference in employment and housing, and health care."[45] However, HUD grants funds to ONAP, who then distributes those moneys to tribal nations based on their sovereign status and the legibility of their IHA. Though Little Earth is not a sovereign tribal nation, the majority of its residents are enrolled members of federally recognized tribes—specifically those bands of Ojibwe and Dakota scattered across the state of Minnesota. And although there is scant scholarship on federal spending for off-reservation American Indian housing, much has been written about off-reservation American Indian health care, an important point of comparison. As American Indian health-care scholar Caryn Trombino discusses:

> Actions by the BIA ensure that Native Americans suffer not only from inadequate federal funding, but that extant federal funding is not equally accessible to urban Indians, despite the fact that they now make up more than 50 percent of the total American Indian population. For example, the Snyder Act of 1921 provides authorization for federal appropriations to fund social services such as general assistance, health care, child welfare, and employment assistance to a class of eligible beneficiaries defined as "Indians throughout the United States." However, the BIA has generally limited the class of beneficiaries to American Indians living on or near reservations, excluding urban Indians from these assistance programs.[46]

Though Trombino specifically examines the failure in funding administration of the BIA and IHS, the same can be said of HUD, which administers the Indian housing programs. Eligibility for many programs and services available to American Indian people as a direct result of the federal trust responsibility to Indian people, based on the history of treaty-making, is premised on tribal enrollment in a federally recognized tribe.

Similarly, as Trombino notes in her examination of urban Indian health care, although urban American Indians are often eligible for state and federal assistance programs that they must apply for, they are, or rather should be, already eligible for social service and assistance programs based on their legal-political status as tribally enrolled citizens, "special services to which they are entitled by their former treaties, and thus the federal government's continuing trust obligation," regardless of where they live.[47] This is particularly poignant, if not worrisome, as the federally sponsored Relocation Program drove thousands of Indian people to urban areas with no long-term plans for housing. Indeed, the Relocation Program's basis in Termination Policy worked to break ties and obligations of the federal government to Indian people. Here, questions of tribal sovereignty and individual tribal membership come to a head and force us to consider the triangulation of off-reservation Indians, housing or private property ownership, and federal obligations. The disavowal of the housing needs of urban Indians is further highlighted when attention is given to the Section 184 Indian Home Loan Guarantee Program, the only HUD-administered, off-reservation housing program for Indian people that guarantees them federal home loans. At the same time, comparison to the Johnson-O'Malley Act for Indian education off-reservation provisions becomes increasingly relevant or is perhaps a model to look to.

Now, in the twenty-first century, Little Earth remains unique as a housing complex envisioned by and for American Indian people, a place where culture and capitalism intersect. As a Native-preference housing program, Little Earth has continuously offered programs specifically for its American Indian residents. Today, residents can access basic social service programs and, equally as important, culturally relevant support services, including educational programs, elder care, health services, and cultural activities. Little Earth lies in the heart of the south Minneapolis Phillips neighborhood with immediate access to the American Indian Cultural Corridor, where a whole city neighborhood is experiencing Native-centered revitalization. At once, Little Earth is a place where community members work to reclaim a previously lost space and struggle for funding to house American Indian people who have long called Minneapolis home.

5

INDIAN HOMES AND INDIAN LOANS
SUBURBAN INDIANS AND THE SECTION 184 INDIAN HOME LOAN GUARANTEE PROGRAM

I felt persecuted by history, tortured by fate. I wanted it all to be one thing or the other. I hated being half-white and half-Indian. We are the only Comanches in a white suburb, and even the white suburb was unsatisfyingly lame.

—PAUL CHAAT SMITH, *Everything You Know about Indians Is Wrong*

When our fellow Americans are denied the American dream, our own dreams are diminished. . . . While some have prospered . . . middle-class Americans . . . are seeing the American dream slip further and further away. . . .

America is the sum of our dreams. And what binds us together, what makes us one American family, is that we stand up and fight for each other's dreams, that we reaffirm that fundamental belief—I am my brother's keeper, I am my sister's keeper—through our politics, our policies, and in our daily lives. It's time to do that once more. It's time to reclaim the American dream.

—BARACK OBAMA, speech at Bettendorf, Iowa, November 7, 2007

IN THE FALL OF 2013, the Jabs family moved into their long-awaited and newly built home in Elk River, Minnesota.[1] The Jabs family was fully involved in the design, layout, and construction of their forever home—all three bedrooms, two baths, attached three-car garage, and intentionally unfinished basement—in a newly plotted development. The family carefully chose Elk River—a northern suburb of Minneapolis, nestled alongside the Mississippi River, a place of recent redevelopment and population growth—for its easy access to the Twin Cities, affordability, schools, and future marketability, should they eventually decide to sell. The Jabs family is only one of the increasing numbers of American Indian individuals and families who have moved to suburban communities, in Minnesota and nationwide, over the past several decades. In fact, by 2000, over one-quarter of all American Indian people who lived in Minnesota lived in a suburb of Minneapolis or Saint Paul.[2] This is a dramatic increase from 1980 and 1990 when only 14 percent of Minnesota's American Indian people lived in a suburb of the Twin Cities.[3]

The family of four, including two children, appears to be typical or similar to any other suburban family in the Twin Cities. However, the Jabs family is set apart from the vast majority, and certainly all their neighbors, in the suburb that was over 93 percent white at the time of the 2010 Census. The Jabs family built and purchased their home using the Section 184 Indian Home Loan Guarantee Program (IHLGP). The IHLGP, created in 1992, is nestled under the Housing and Community Development Act and administered by the Department of Housing and Urban Development (HUD).[4] The IHLGP is advertised as a way to promote and increase homeownership for American Indians who have historically been viewed as an "underserved" market.[5] Mrs. Jabs and her family are eligible for the program and entitled to its benefits—a low down payment, low interest rates, no requirement for monthly mortgage insurance, "protection from predatory lending," and designated staff of the federal government to work with and administer the loan guarantee program—precisely because she is an enrolled member of a federally recognized tribal nation.

Indeed, suburban Indians are a distinct and significant subgroup of American Indians socioeconomically and in terms of racial identity. These American Indian people, who are suburbanites based on their residential location, are dissimilar from their American Indian counter-parts in urban areas and from those who live on reservations in rural places not only because of their residential location but also because of key socioeconomic indicators and in terms of identity. Further compli-cating issues of identity, suburban Indians must be recognized as sepa-rate from non-Native suburbanites because of their unique and lengthy histories associated with place, including Elk River—places that are simultaneously Indian places, with lengthy Indian histories, and subur-ban spaces.[6] More, American Indian people remain legally and politi-cally distinct from non-Natives because of their history of treaty-making with the federal government, the only racial/ethnic group to do so, cementing the political-legal relationship that exists today, which has been affirmed in the Constitution and in the courts. Similarly, American Indians are citizens of sovereign tribal nations. This is significant, as today many American Indian people have access to education, health care, and housing programs due to land cessions and treaty making processes.

It is also important to recognize the ways suburban Indians dis-rupt the urban–reservation Indian dichotomy. Suburban Indians not only open the door to a supposedly new American Indian geography but offer a chance to consider the significance of geographic residence for American Indians. Similarly, suburban Indians (and all American Indians) force us to reconsider the white–Black binary, particularly in terms of housing. Though most attention to housing programs, both historically and contemporarily, has centered on comparisons between white and nonwhite people, most commonly Black people, American Indians are almost always left out of the conversation and statistics. Amer-ican Indians in suburbs remind us to consider the role of place, identity, and homeland—something that is generally not at stake for other racial-ized groups.

Moving beyond the white–Black binary, and to be inclusive of American Indians, an increasing number of scholars and community members have begun to reconcile histories of colonization, slavery, racial violence, and reparations. For American Indians, similar conversations are beginning to occur in the realm of land acknowledgments and Land Back movements. Taken together, a move beyond these dichotomies and binaries pushes scholars, policy makers, and even local area residents to reconsider what it means to be an American Indian person in a suburb and what it means to live in a suburb today, on land that Native people were disposed of and excluded from. Moreover, suburban Indians offer a new lens from which to think about homeownership and the ways in which American Indian people's access to homeownership has been regulated, the entanglements of land and property and homeownership, the relationship between Indigenous dispossession and homeownership, and the role of mortgages to buy land you have long been dispossessed from.[7] Finally, suburban Indians (and other American Indian homeowners, landowners, and private property owners) force us to reconcile what homeownership can, should, and could mean in terms of culture, consumption, and capitalism.[8] These are topics or questions I pose here, and throughout this chapter, but do not easily wrap up.

With a focus on American Indian homeownership, this chapter centers on the Section 184 Indian Home Loan Guarantee Program as marking a clear shift in federal housing programs available to American Indian people—from those exclusively for on-reservation American Indian people, based on a low-income status, and linked to public housing within HUD, to a housing program that allows for much-needed off-reservation homeownership and accompanying landownership opportunities. Further, I build on the notion that American Indian housing programs, including the IHLGP, originate from the treaty-making processes that occurred between individual tribal nations and the federal government throughout the eighteenth and nineteenth centuries. Therefore, the IHLGP is significant in that it remains the first and only federally administered home loan program for Indian people who live outside of reservation boundaries.

The IHLGP was designed to address the historic and ongoing discrimination and inequality in the housing market that has long prevented American Indian people from attaining homeownership, both on and off reservation. My examination of homeownership between the years 1980 and 2010 across suburban, urban, and rural locations throughout Minnesota reveals that suburban American Indians are increasingly more likely to achieve homeownership than urban or rural/reservation Indians despite factors that often worked against them, including the lack of access to housing assistance programs. Finally, in this chapter I combine policy critique with population and socioeconomic data from the U.S. Census to demonstrate the interconnected nature of improved educational opportunities, steady and better-paying employment, and housing opportunities and the way these forces have influenced and incentivized Indian peoples' move to suburban areas. Each of these components, as part of the federal government's longtime efforts to allegedly civilize and assimilate Indian people, deserves new attention in the twenty-first century as Indian people have made suburbs and homeownership their own, both taking advantage of federal policy and pushing back against it, muddying the waters of settler colonialism, dispossession, identity, and property.

To reveal these tensions around recent experiences of American Indian homeownership, I juxtapose the Section 184 Indian Home Loan Guarantee Program alongside the lead-up to the housing bubble of the early 2000s. I begin with an overview of federal housing policies of the 1990s and into the early 2000s to consider the ways homeownership continued to be promoted and supported by the federal government. This is significant because, on the one hand, homeownership has been long advertised as a symbol of the American Dream, subsidized by the federal government for many; yet, on the other hand, it has continually been out of reach for many people of color, including American Indians. Similarly, homeownership and the long-term costs to furnish and maintain a home have been viewed as a marker of assimilation, as evidenced in the Relocation Program. Yet for American Indian people, who have long been urged and forced to assimilate into dominant culture via policy and practice, this has often taken the shape of close monitoring and regulation by the federal government, including where American Indian people may live. Though we often think of this regulation of space in terms of reservations, it is my intervention that we must also examine housing and homeownership opportunities (or lack thereof) for American Indian people outside of reservation areas. In the second half of this chapter, I offer a basic quantitative overview of recent American Indian demographics in Minnesota that highlights the continuous growth in the suburban Indian population across the state. This contemporary focus paints a picture of the realities for many of today's suburban Indians—a demographic group that has often been ignored in contemporary scholarship in American Indian studies, urban studies, and housing and suburbanization.[9] Importantly, this sort of analysis is not intended to suggest that there is a better or worse place to live for

American Indian people. Rather, this research highlights the ongoing forms of economic colonialism Indian people have encountered across residential locations and underscores the significance of programs like the IHLGP—programs that are crucial to American Indian economic equality and homeownership.

The Jabs family offers a single-family case study from which to think about the lives of other contemporary American Indian people in the suburbs of Minneapolis and Saint Paul. The history and experience of this one American Indian family offer a glimpse into the suburban American Indian experience today. This family story is part narrative, a rhetorical device to tell a more nuanced and accurate history, and part autoethnography, an exploration of my relationship to this research. I have a close, personal connection with the Jabs family, and their story of suburbanization is not unlike my own. Like other scholars who use autoethnography to "interrogate the documentary record," the Jabs family story offers a lens to better understand the creation and intent of the IHLGP and how it has altered and influenced homeownership for Indian people in suburbs, as well as what homeownership can mean for identity and community.[10] The narrative I have woven together in this chapter, an experience inextricably linked to broad historical and contemporary

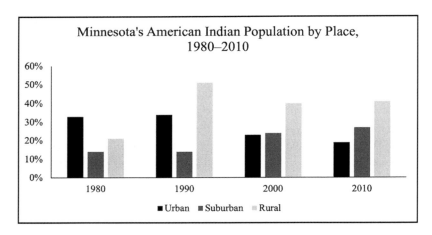

Figure 14. Minnesota's suburban Indian population saw growth between 1980 and 2010, while the urban Indian population gradually declined in the same time period. Since 1990, the rural, including on-reservation, population of American Indians in Minnesota has also declined.

federal Indian policies and federal housing programs, is what defines the importance of this family history to a larger audience. The recentness of suburbanization and suburban Indians helps to explain the lack of research and archival materials on Indian people in suburbs; this includes the ways off-reservation Indian people have experienced housing policies and homeownership. Throughout this chapter I tie the Jabs family story and experience to census data, forming and building an entirely new archive of suburban Indians.

Federal Housing Programs and American Indians

In a 2008 *New York Times* article, the columnist compares the "eerie resemblance" of the economic downturn that was unfolding across the country and that which occurred in the early 1990s after the "boom years" of the 1980s, especially in the housing market. The author declares that "the housing market would suffer more this time because of the reckless lending practices that allowed too many people to buy homes with little or no money down."[11] This *New York Times* piece, and plenty others like it in the months before and after, centered on the vast housing market across the United States. Yet, American Indians had long experienced not only the volatility of the housing market but also varying levels of exclusion due to lack of access to land and loans. In response to both recessions, that of the early 1990s and the one unfolding in 2008, the federal government would pass legislation not only to bolster the housing market but, more specifically, to expand American Indian peoples' participation in and access to it.

Almost two years into his presidency, George H. W. Bush signed into law the Cranston-Gonzalez National Affordable Housing Act on November 28, 1990. This particular piece of legislation had seven clearly stated objectives:

(1) to ensure that every resident of the United States has access to decent shelter or assistance in avoiding homelessness; (2) *to increase the Nation's supply of decent housing that is affordable to low-income and moderate-income families* and accessible to job opportunities; (3) to improve housing opportunities for all residents of the United States, *particularly members of disadvantaged minorities, on a nondiscriminatory basis*; (4) to help make neighborhoods safe

and livable; (5) *to expand opportunities for homeownership*; (6) *to provide every American community with a reliable, readily available supply of mortgage finance at the lowest possible interest rates*; and (7) to encourage tenant empowerment and reduce generational poverty in federally assisted and public housing by improving the means by which self-sufficiency may be achieved.[12]

Only two years later, the National Affordable Housing Act was amended and expanded as the Housing and Community Development Act, signed into law on October 28, 1992. It was these two pieces of legislation that led to the creation of the HOME Investment Partnerships Program and significantly revised Homeownership and Opportunities for People Everywhere programs.[13] In fact, the HOME Program was established in direct response to the 1988 hearing of the National Housing Task Force: "Concerned that existing [housing] programs were not meeting the nation's affordable housing needs, members of the Housing Task Force argued to the committee that the level of federal funding specifically dedicated to affordable housing should be increased in order to fully address affordable housing issues."[14] The Housing and Community Development Act brought renewed attention to the creation of more affordable housing for low-income and very low-income families while allowing states more jurisdiction and authority over their distribution and management.

The 1992 Housing and Community Development Act also ushered in the creation of the IHLGP. As originally introduced by Representative Henry González (D-TX), the IHLGP sought to address the "underserved," on-reservation American Indian community that had long been ignored, discriminated against, or left out of home loan programs. The official and original aims of the IHLGP included the following:

Because of the unique status of Indian lands being held in Trust, Native American homeownership has historically been an underserved market. Working with an expanding network of private sector and tribal partners, the Section 184 Program endeavors to increase access to capital for Native Americans and provide private funding opportunities for tribal housing agencies with the Section 184 Program. To help increase Native access to financing, the Office of Loan Guarantee within HUD's Office of Native American Programs, guarantees the Section 184 home mortgage loans made to

Native Borrowers. By guaranteeing these loans 100 percent, we encourage Lenders to serve the Native Communities. This increases the marketability and value of the Native assets and strengthens the financial standing of Native Communities.[15]

The importance of the IHLGP in the history of housing is significant, as American Indians have faced chronically low levels of homeownership. By working to address the contemporary housing needs of tribal citizens, the IHLGP has become one way the federal government has worked to assume its trust responsibility to American Indian people.

Today, the Jabs family's suburban home is but one of over 44,350 IHLGP loans nationwide, including 558 in Minnesota guaranteed by the program as of August 2019. Nationally, these homes represent over $7.5 billion that the federal government has invested in and guaranteed to American Indian individuals and federally recognized tribes for home purchase, construction, renovation, and refinance, as well as the associated immeasurable opportunities for upward mobility through home equity, tax breaks, resale value, and stable housing. By way of the federal government's 100 percent guarantee of these home loans, the IHLGP encourages private, local banks and lenders to offer home mortgages to American Indian individuals and tribes, both on and off reservation, making it the first federally administered home loan program to do so.[16]

Yet, to understand the need for home loan financing and the low rates of homeownership for American Indian people, we must look to where we have been. Indeed, low rates of homeownership, as faced by a significant number of American Indian communities and individuals over the last seventy years, can be traced to the legal status of trust land on reservations and, of course, to the longer histories of settler colonialism and racism, as discussed in previous chapters. Reservation land, held in trust by the United States government, cannot be used as collateral to secure a mortgage in the event of foreclosure because a bank cannot legally collect on trust land (or assume ownership over it) should the mortgagor default. Nor would it be ethical for a bank to sell a foreclosed property located on trust land within a reservation to a nontribal member to collect on its financial losses. This conundrum has prevented many Indian people who live on reservation from accessing a private mortgage for home construction or purchase, as many banks would not and will not insure a loan without a guaranteed form of substantial collateral (i.e., the land or property). Therefore, the IHLGP has worked to address this sort of catch-22 by guaranteeing home loans for Indian people who meet required loan-approval criteria, including employment verification and income thresholds, as well as being enrolled citizens of a federally recognized tribe. However, it must be pointed out that the supposed problem in lack of access to mortgages is not the legal status of trust land. Rather, the legal status of trust land demonstrates the complicated and interrelated nature of federal–tribal relationships and landowning systems based on capitalism, alongside American Indian land tenure systems. Whereas trust land was theoretically established as a way for the federal government to supposedly protect Indian land from leaving Indian and tribal hands by promising federal oversight and management (hence the guardian–ward relationship), trust status simultaneously and problematically disallows Native peoples who live on trust land to engage in certain forms of capitalism. This is despite the federal government's longtime effort and expectation of American Indians to assimilate and engage with capitalism and thus become full American citizens. Therefore, the notion of trust land and private property draws our attention to the ways land has been monetarized, in many ways alienating land from traditional tribal communities while also excluding many individuals, specifically American Indians, from access to housing as homeownership is almost always premised on the purchase of land. In this way, homeownership on reservation has long been constrained and denied by federal policy for individual American Indians through trust land status.

Perhaps more significant, the expansion of the IHLGP marked an important shift in the federal government's trust responsibility to house Indian people, both on and off reservation. As originally unveiled in 1992 and used by thousands of American Indian individuals and families for over a decade, the IHLGP was limited to use on reservations. But, in 2004 the program was expanded for use by eligible tribal members across the entirety of twenty-four states for new home construction, home purchase, home rehabilitation, and home refinance.[17] Beginning in 2004, the Indian area of the IHLGP was revised to be more expansive and inclusive. In conjunction with the Native American Housing Assistance and Self-Determination Act of 1996, the IHLGP was amended to allow for greater flexibility in its application and eligible areas, allowing individual tribal nations more freedom to designate an Indian area and thus more authority to administer the IHLGP to tribal members who lived outside the borders of the reservation. This was a monumental step forward for American Indians seeking homeownership opportunities off reservation. Additionally, the expansion of the IHLGP can also be read as supportive of and affirming enhanced tribal sovereignty by granting tribes more autonomy over the designation of and claiming of an eligible Indian area.

The IHLGP, then, has become a strategy of the federal government to begin to address the devastation and lasting legacies of over two centuries of federal Indian policies and unequal housing programs and policies. In fact, the IHLGP has helped open the door to homeownership for American Indian people whose ancestors were removed from and dispossessed of their traditional land bases by working to guarantee home loans for eligible tribal members outside of often-isolated reservation communities. This is important because today's reservation communities can be distant from and much smaller than the expansive and traditional tribal land base of many tribal nations. However, despite the expansion to off-reservation areas in 2004, a major caveat to the IHLGP remains and must be scrutinized.

The home to be built, purchased, refinanced, or renovated with the IHLGP must still be within a designated "Indian area." An Indian area is a hard-to-nail-down geographic designation made by a tribal housing authority (also commonly referred to as the Indian Housing Authority of a tribally designated housing entity) and in conjunction with—or with approval from, rather—the federal government. Most basically, an Indian area, for the purposes of the IHLGP, is a geographic region, both entire states and individual counties (both of which problematically rely on imposed colonial boundaries), that has been designated or recognized as the traditional or historic land base of a particular tribal nation. So, any one or more tribal nations may claim a geographic land base as an Indian area where the IHLGP may be administered. As described by the National Congress of American Indians, "tribal service areas often include not only reservation land, but also nearby areas outside the reservation's boundaries."[18] Moreover, the National Congress of American Indians notes that under our current model, it is "customary to think of Native people and Native resources as being counted within a prescribed area. . . . Specific programs serving AI/AN populations rely on different definitions of service areas" or, in the case of the IHLGP, Indian areas.[19] However, it is important to point out that a tribal service area is not contiguous with an Indian area for the purpose of the IHLGP. In the case of Indian housing and other services provided to Indian people by the federal government, Indian areas or service areas are often delineated not by tribal nations but by census definitions of metropolitan statistical areas, which are further defined by the Office of Management and Budget, adding multiple layers of federal oversight and administration. This multilevel, multiagent, multigovernment designation of what an Indian area is has led to much confusion, particularly for American Indian

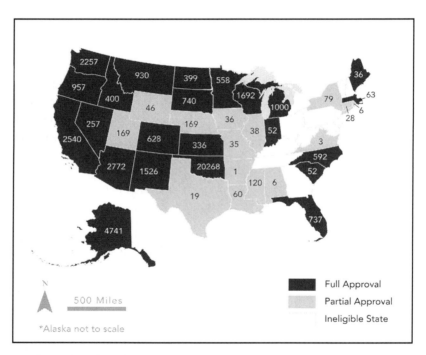

Map 5. Number of Section 184 loans used as of August 2019. In states shaded dark gray, the entire state has been approved for Section 184 loan use. In states shaded light gray, select counties in the state have been approved for Section 184 loan use. States in white remain ineligible for Section 184 loans. Map by Katherine Koehler; adapted from the Loans Guaranteed with Section 184 map by the U.S. Department of Housing and Urban Development.

people interested in accessing the IHLGP who live in an ineligible state or county.

Further complicating the matter of an Indian area, and deserving of more attention, is the fact that an individual American Indian applicant's tribal membership or citizenship does not need to match the corresponding tribal nation whose Indian area the property subject to the IHLGP falls within. Put another way, if we return to the opening narrative of the Jabs family, Mrs. Jabs is an enrolled tribal member of a tribe whose homelands and reservation are in California. She used the IHLGP to purchase a home in Minnesota, where she has no tribal connections or tribal history, yet the entirety of Minnesota is considered the Indian area of other tribes. This can cause confusion for some potential applicants who may erroneously assume they are ineligible for the IHLGP because they live away from their tribal homelands. Further complicating the Indian area designation is determining which individual counties within a state may or may not be eligible for the IHLGP. Take, for example, the state of New York. Within the state of New York, the IHLGP can be used across all counties of the state except Bronx, Kings, New York, Queens, and Richmond. A quick look at a map reveals that these five counties are the counties that immediately surround New York City, including Manhattan, Brooklyn, and Staten Island—areas with arguably some of the most expensive real estate and most competitive housing markets in the country. It is unclear what the guidance is around designating or claiming an Indian area, as well as any incentive for a tribe or the liability to claim the land as such. The role of the county or state in approving land as an Indian area for the IHLGP is also unclear.

Despite these caveats, the IHLGP has the potential to reconcile a certain aspect of land loss by supporting Indian people who choose to purchase a home on or off reservation. As such, the IHLGP works to counteract the debilitating inadequacies in housing metropolitan area American Indians. To do so, the IHLGP supports individual and family homeownership off reservation, thereby allowing an individual or family to choose their residential location—urban, suburban, rural, or reservation—with access to a federally insured home loan. The longevity of the loan program itself, in existence now for three decades, has provided opportunities for homeownership and its accompanying economic benefits for Indian people rather than becoming another temporary fix for Indian Country and Indian people. Though there are certainly critiques of the program, the IHLGP has worked to address many of the historic, race-based, and economic discriminations American Indian people have endured and continue to endure as they seek out mortgages and home loans.

The 1992 Indian Home Loan Guarantee Program was closely followed by expanded efforts to promote homeownership among all racial and ethnic minorities under the HUD leadership of Henry Cisneros. Cisneros, the tenth secretary of HUD, appointed by then President Bill Clinton, has been widely credited with loosening mortgage requirements to allow for expanded homeownership. In partnership, under the leadership of Henry Cisneros and Bill Clinton, HUD presented what has been recognized as the National Homeownership Strategy. In May 1995, President Bill Clinton unveiled the National Homeownership Strategy with the following letter:

> Our nation's greatest promise has always been the chance to build a better life. For millions of America's working families throughout history, owning a home has come to symbolize the realization of the American Dream. Yet sadly, in the 1980s, it became much harder for many young families to buy their first homes, and our national homeownership rate declined for the first time in forty-six years. Our Administration is determined to reverse this trend, and we are committed to ensuring that working families can once again discover the joys of owning a home. . . . Working together, we can add as many as eight million new families to America's homeownership rolls by the year 2000. Expanding homeownership will strengthen our nation's families and communities, strengthen our economy, and expand this country's great middle class.[20]

President Clinton closed his opening remarks with optimism: "Rekindling the dream of homeownership for America's working families can prepare our nation to embrace the rich possibilities of the twenty-first century."[21] Included in the eighty-seven-page report *The National Homeownership Strategy: Partners in the American Dream,* HUD outlined key steps to better realize the American Dream for all Americans. Specific action items to be carried out included "Native American Home

Financing Needs." Here, the document outlined how the National Homeownership Strategy would "empower tribes to design homeownership models that meet their cultural, spiritual, and functional needs."[22] Though there was clear recognition of the limited financing available for on-reservation housing development, there was virtually no mention of the housing needs for off-reservation tribal members. Despite this, "Homeownership Opportunities for Native Americans" stipulated the "need to understand the unique nature of tribal organizations, cultures, and economies; the complexities of land ownership and government status; and the relationship among various Federal, State, and tribal agencies."[23] Yet, once again, the focus remained on on-reservation housing development.

Then in early 1996, another report on American Indian housing needs was published. According to the *Assessment of American Indian Housing Needs and Programs: Final Report,* "housing problems of American Indian and Alaska Natives remain considerably more severe than those of non-Indians in all parts of America" and a significant effort needs to be placed "on attracting private mortgage lending."[24] The major findings of the report also state that "the number of [American Indian and Alaska Native] households at moderate- and higher-income levels is substantial, and homeownership rates for these groups are well below those for non-Indians at the same income levels" and that "emphasis should be on expanding their access to assistance within the framework of Federal housing programs."[25] Though published four years after George H. W. Bush signed the Housing and Community Development Act of 1992 into law, including the IHLGP, not enough time had elapsed for the report to fully consider the actions and benefits of the IHLGP.

Introduced into Congress in March 1996 by Representative Rick Lazio (D-NY), the Native American Housing Assistance and Self-Determination Act (NAHASDA) was "an act to provide Federal assistance for Indian tribes in a manner that recognizes the right of tribal self-governance, and for other purposes."[26] An objective of the NAHASDA was to "assist and promote affordable housing activities to develop, maintain, and operate affordable housing in safe and healthy areas for occupancy by low income Indian families."[27] Exceptions to the purposes of the NAHASDA included tribal assistance for "homeownership activities" or "loan guarantee activities" to "Indian families who are not low-income families . . . because there is a need for housing for such families that cannot reasonably be met without such assistance." The NAHASDA sought to grant greater autonomy to tribal authorities in the administration of housing programs, including the IHLGP. Additionally, the NAHASDA worked to better organize and simplify assistance programs for tribal nations and individual Indian people. By consolidating numerous housing assistance programs available to tribes, the NAHASDA created the Indian Housing Block Grant Program. By allowing for greater tribal authority and self-determination, tribes benefit from the NAHASDA and the Indian Housing Block Grant Program through down payment assistance and rental assistance to tribal members, the construction of new homes and rental units, the purchase of homes for ownership and rental, and the renovation of homes for ownership and rent for tribal members.

Despite the aims and promises of the IHLGP and NAHASDA, neither are without critique from those within and outside of the American Indian community. The 1997 *Native American Housing* report to the Subcommittee on VA, HUD, and Independent Agencies reminds us that "providing housing assistance for Native Americans is challenging and costly."[28] Among the challenges given in the report was the "cultural and geographic" diversity of tribal nations, as "there are over 550 separate Indian nations, with unique cultures and traditions, not all of these conditions are equally prevalent throughout tribal areas, nor do they have a common impact on developing and maintaining housing."[29] The report highlights the diversity of tribal nations, on-reservation conditions, and proximity to metropolitan areas as challenges the federal government faces when creating Indian-specific housing programs and policies. There is not a one size fits all approach that will successfully work. The NAHASDA has been further critiqued as it would "at least initially, cause HUD's oversight workload to increase."[30] Federal assistance to tribal nations and Indian people has also been critiqued more recently because of the economic successes of tribal nations involved in profitable gaming enterprises. However, HUD theoretically cannot take gaming revenue into account when determining a tribe's need for federal housing assistance. A tribe has the ability and authority to use its gaming revenue in a variety of ways, not only for housing.[31] A tribe must demonstrate housing need for its tribal members to be eligible for housing assistance, and generally tribes who have been financially successful in gaming and other enterprises cannot demonstrate the need required for federal assistance.[32]

Despite these efforts and initiatives to bolster the housing market, before the end of the first decade of the twenty-first century we would see not only the boom of the housing market, as promised and envisioned by Clinton and others, we would also see it bust. The failures of the home loan industry, despite federal intervention, oversight, and initiatives to make the housing market more equitable and accessible, led to one of the largest recessions in our nation's history and the first of the twenty-first century.

Indian Loans, Tribal Programs, and Mortgage Lenders

Since at least the mid-nineteenth century, the federal government has been directly involved in the removal, the relocation, and the housing of American Indian people by way of both treaty and federal policies. Attempts by the federal government to provide housing and housing assistance directly to tribes, whether they materialized or not, during the twentieth century include the Snyder Act of 1921, the Indian Housing Program authorized by the U.S. Housing Act of 1937, the Indian Housing Act of 1988, the IHLGP of 1992, and the Native American Housing Assistance and Self-Determination Act of 1996. Despite these initiatives of the federal government, tribes using federally funded resources have been limited in the ways in which funds could be used due to extensive federal regulations and oversight. Often, this has taken the form of a trust relationship, as federal regulations, including restrictions on place, infringe on tribal self-determination. In fact, as previously discussed, nearly all of the funds the federal government has allocated to tribal housing authorities for Indian housing have been exclusively for use on reservation or trust land.[33] The difficulty that surrounds homeownership and housing programs for Native people, particularly those who live off reservation, underscores the tensions that exist among and across the multiple levels of government involved in Indian housing, tribal governments, state governments, and the federal government and the lack of usable funds off reservation.

Despite the inconsistent nature of federal housing policies for Indian people and their broad lack of applicability to all tribal citizens, tribal nations across the country have created their own tribal housing programs for the benefit of tribal citizens. As sovereign nations with economic capital, tribal nations have taken the lead in providing housing resources to tribal members. In fact, many of the efforts of tribal nations to provide financial assistance to tribal members for housing predate the IHLGP of 1992. Now, in the twenty-first century, an increasing number of tribes are able to administer the IHLGP in addition to providing tribal housing resources as a supplement to it. Take, for example, the Minnesota Chippewa Tribe Finance Corporation (MCTFC). The MCTFC offers a home loan program and a loan modification program to tribal members. The Minnesota Chippewa Tribe's home loan program is designed "to promote the advancement and expansion of affordable homeownership programs to Native American member bands of the Minnesota Chippewa Tribe" and "to provide mortgage financing for the purchase, construction, and rehabilitation of single-family homes."[34] The MCTFC has provided direct funding to tribal members through community revitalization funds and administers the tribe's IHLGP. Significantly, the MCTFC home loan and loan modification program (including those it administers as part of the IHLGP) allows for off-reservation housing.

Minnesota's tribal nations are not unique in their desire and ability to assist tribal members in housing pursuits. The 1995 *Assessment of American Indian Housing Needs and Programs* made note of several tribal housing agencies across the country whose work on tribal housing programs predates the implementation of the IHLGP. Included in this list are the Mississippi Choctaw Housing Authority, the Cheyenne River Housing Authority, the Southern Puget Sound Housing Authority, the Zuni Tribe, the Pascua Yaqui, and the Housing Assistance Council/Northwest Area Foundation.[35] With the exception of the Housing Assistance Council/Northwest Area Foundation, each of these housing programs is tribe-specific and includes such housing services for tribal members as placement (rental), general maintenance assistance, drug elimination efforts, advocacy, education, counseling for prospective homeowners, funding, and the maintenance of tribally owned homes.

Many tribe-specific housing programs, including several of those listed above, are applicable on and off reservation land for eligible tribal members. As these programs attest to, tribal nations have long provided assistance to American Indian people, often in ways the federal government has failed to do.

Tribal-based lending programs are significant when it comes to American Indian people's access to home loans and homeownership. Despite the aims of the IHLGP, most lenders across the United States remain ineligible to participate in the program and are therefore not able to provide home loans and mortgages to American Indian people wishing to benefit from the program. A major stipulation of the IHLGP is that lenders complete specialized training on the IHLGP and then apply to HUD to become a designated and approved lender for the program. Under the IHLGP, "lenders must comply with their supervisory agency's requirements concerning net worth, staffing, geographic authorities and industry relationships," including substantial federal oversight and specialized training requirements, to make loans under the program.[36] By May 2020, HUD had authorized just over 120 lenders across the entirety of the United States to administer and service the IHLGP. Many of these lenders and financial institutions are relatively small, existing on a local or regional basis only. This number of eligible lenders significantly pales in comparison to the widespread accessibility of lenders for more traditional home loans, including those administered and regulated by other HUD/FHA programs. Of the list of eligible lenders, many are limited to administering the IHLGP in their state of residence and may not administer loans across state lines. However, there are a small number of lenders, including 1st Tribal Lending and First National Bank & Trust Co. of Shawnee, who have been approved to administer the IHLGP across all states.

Finally, a major unforeseen barrier to the IHLGP lending experience is the required federal oversight of HUD through the manual underwriting process that most traditional borrowers avoid. The Jabs family experienced this firsthand when they were set to close on their own home in late summer 2013. As has become increasingly common, the federal government, including HUD, faces shutdown when the national budget does not receive approval. When a government shutdown occurs,

HUD, which oversees the IHLGP, closes its doors and does not process loans for the IHLGP, including those for individuals and families
with nearing and immediate closing dates. Thus, with a federal government shutdown, which can range from days to weeks, many American
Indian families and individuals who are in the process of using the
IHLGP are caught in a difficult scenario of wait and see. For the Jabs
family, this meant a multiweek delay in closing and moving into their
new home. Fortunately, the Jabs family was in a rental situation that
allowed them the flexibility to remain until they were able to close on
their new home. For other American Indian families, a delay in closing
on a new home can wreak chaos on family budgets and force those who
are hanging in limbo during a government shutdown to find temporary
shelter, further exacerbating the housing crisis that American Indian
families face across Indian Country. This increasingly common conundrum draws attention to the need for improved lending procedures,
better access to local lenders, and a speedier loan process for American Indian community members who already face significant barriers to
homeownership.

Suburbanizing Socioeconomics

During the five years that led up to the Jabs family's move into their
new, suburban home, they had moved a total of four times and lived in
three different states. The father, and sole financial earner of the family,
was laid off from his blue-collar manual labor job during the height of
the Great Recession of 2007–2008, a time when many others were losing their jobs and many families went into home foreclosure. To make
a better life, the Jabs family decided to leave their rental home and move
out of state, which allowed Mr. Jabs, a non-Native, to attend a one-year
training program with promises of steady, reliable, and much-needed
employment. After a second move one year later, the family was still
renting, this time in a third state, traversing the Midwest. Finally, the
family caught a break. Mr. Jabs landed a job at a local company in their
native Minnesota and the family was able to return home. Yet, after their
third move with two young children who required an increasing amount
of space, they were still renting—this time a small, two-room, one-bath,
older home in a northeastern suburb of the Twin Cities.

As the Great Recession continued, the requirements and restrictions for home loan applications and programs became increasingly stringent. It was precisely during this time that the Jabs family took advantage of the little-known IHLGP—an opportunity to make a better life for their family. Though the Jabs family had been living in suburban and rural locations for the last several years, they had always been renters, with homeownership opportunities continuously out of reach. As single-income, first-time homebuyers in their midthirties with less than stellar credit, the Jabs family knew they would have difficulty qualifying for a traditional home loan, especially since they lacked the savings or family resources for a substantial down payment—resources many white, middle-class home buyers rely on. Indeed, it was the benefits of the IHLGP, including guaranteed financing, a low down payment, and a low interest rate, that proved to be a much-needed break for the overworked, tired, yet hopeful Jabs family who had long hoped to purchase a new home with access to good schools for their young children and with convenient access to their place of employment.

The quest to become suburban homeowners for the Jabs family, and other American Indian peoples, is directly tied to real and imagined socioeconomic benefits. In fact, we can and should look to basic quantitative socioeconomic data to better understand contemporary American Indian homeownership. By examining three key measures of socioeconomic status—education, employment, and homeownership, all data that are collected by the U.S. Census—we are better able to assess the access to upward mobility many suburban Indians, as compared to rural, reservation, and urban Indians, have been able to attain. These three socioeconomic indicators are important in this analysis precisely because they are generally linked together over time. For instance, higher levels of education attainment generally translate to higher rates of better-paying employment and lessen the likelihood of unemployment, and more stable employment often translates to higher levels of homeownership. However, each of these socioeconomic markers is also directly tied to the available resources of each location—urban, suburban, or rural—and the quality of those resources, specifically schools, employment, and housing. These socioeconomic markers underscore the inherent connection between residential location and homeownership in a specific location; here I am specifically thinking about how property taxes, based on location and value of property, fund schools. Similarly, employment and income generally dictate locations individuals and families have access to in terms of homeownership due to cost-of-living expenses and average home prices.

Like many suburban Indians across the Twin Cities, Mrs. Jabs is an enrolled tribal citizen of a tribe that is located outside of Minnesota. In 2010, nearly 44 percent of American Indian people in Minnesota who lived in the suburban communities that surround Minneapolis and Saint Paul self-identified as Ojibwe, while 14 percent identified as Dakota. Since Minnesota is the traditional and historic homeland of the Dakota and Ojibwe people, this is somewhat expected, as both tribal groups have retained strong cultural ties to place. Perhaps surprising, though, is that the suburban Indians who reside throughout the Twin Cities are much more tribally diverse compared to Minnesota's urban and rural/reservation Indians. This is significant as it demonstrates a certain level of mobility of suburban Indians in the Twin Cities. At the time of the 2010 Census, Minnesota's suburban Indians variously identified as Alaska Native tribes, including Tlingit, but also came from such diverse tribal backgrounds as Blackfoot, Cherokee, Iroquois, Comanche, Crow, Menominee, Navajo, and Choctaw in addition to "Chippewa" and "Sioux," tribes with traditional land bases in Minnesota. The tribal diversity of suburban Indians encourages us to consider the numerous factors that undergird suburban residency, many of which are directly tied to socioeconomic status, as I discuss later.

Education

For those with the ability and means to move to or across suburban areas, education is generally considered a pull factor. The same holds true for American Indian families. When the Jabs family sought a suburban home, education, along with affordability, was a key factor as they moved from renters in one suburb to homeowners in another. Mrs. Jabs, who grew up in a suburb of Minneapolis, participated in an Indian Education Program as a K–12 student and sought the same educational programming and benefits for her young children. Likewise, Mr. and Mrs. Jabs both desired a quality school system that incorporated new technologies and promised high achievement rates for its students. The Elk River School District, where the Jabs family's children are enrolled, offered both an Indian Education Program and rigorous academic standards.

Elk River Schools are not alone; throughout the seven-county Twin Cities metro area, many of the forty-eight school districts, including Minneapolis Public Schools and Saint Paul Public Schools, operate Indian Education Programs. These K–12 programs, funded by the federal government, are specifically for American Indian students and their families and exist as a direct result of the historic treaty-making process and obligations to Indian people in exchange for their land.[37] These programs, which focus on both academics and culture through enrichment activities and various support systems, can be a major draw for Indian students and families. For Indian families moving out of urban areas or leaving rural or reservation communities, metropolitan Indian Education Programs can provide a vital link to culturally relevant learning opportunities and act as liaisons between the school district's staff, teachers, and parents.

Across Minnesota, graduation rates for all students increased to 83.2 percent in the five years leading up to 2018. For American Indian students in the state, this number increased nearly 3 percent to 51 percent over the same time span. However, despite gains, American Indian graduation rates across the state remained below that of Hispanic, Black, multiracial, Pacific Islander/Hawaiian, Asian, and white students.[38] Nationally, approximately one-third of American Indian students attend schools in metropolitan school districts; this is also the case in Minnesota, where one-third of the state's Native students are enrolled in school districts within the seven-county metro area. Unfortunately, regardless of where an American Indian young person attends school within the state of Minnesota, including Bureau of Indian Affairs and tribally run schools on reservation, statistically speaking, only half will graduate within four years. Minnesota ranks among the lowest in the nation for American Indian graduation rates.[39]

The low education attainment rates for American Indian students, particularly in Minnesota, underscores the significance of educational opportunities and access to a quality and culturally relevant education system. While education attainment has generally been thought of as a

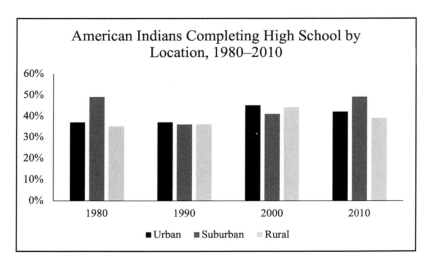

Figure 15. Suburban Indians completed high school at higher rates than urban and rural/reservation Indians in 2010. In 1990 and 2000 graduation rates across all residential locations were comparable.

precursor to success, there are neither clear nor consistent patterns of education attainment for American Indian people in Minnesota based on place or, more specifically, on suburban, urban, or rural/reservation residential location. For instance, despite suburban American Indians' higher rates of high school completion in 1980 (49 percent), these gains were quickly lost by 1990 when suburban, urban, and rural/reservation American Indian people in the state had nearly the same high school completion rates (36 percent, 37 percent, and 36 percent, respectively). Then, in 2000, slightly more urban and rural/reservation American Indian people completed high school than did suburban American Indians. As shown in Figure 15, suburban Indians' high school completion rates surpassed that of other American Indian residential groups across the state in 2010.

Though there have been similar high school completion rates for American Indians regardless of residential location, a slight shift in the percentage of American Indians entering and completing college can be observed by those who reside in suburban locations. Based on census data for the years 1990 and 2000, more suburban Indians in Minnesota "completed some college" than Indian students in urban or rural/reservation areas of the state. The completion of "some college" by a higher percentage of suburban Indians, as displayed in Figure 16, particularly in the years 1990 and 2000, led some suburban Indians to continue their education to four full years of college. In 2010, education attainment for American Indian students from rural/reservation areas nearly reached the levels of suburban Indians' education attainment, and urban Indian students followed closely behind. American Indians who live in suburbs had consistently higher rates of completing four or more years of college than urban or rural/reservation American Indians in Minnesota, despite similar high school graduation rates. These education attainment rates are particularly interesting because the attainment rates for rural/reservation American Indians in Minnesota closely follow, if not match, education rates for urban Indians. This is significant because the majority of colleges and universities within the state are located within the metropolitan area, not in rural/reservation areas. This draws attention to the required mobility and movement of Indian people who live in rural/reservation areas and who desire to attend an institution of higher education.

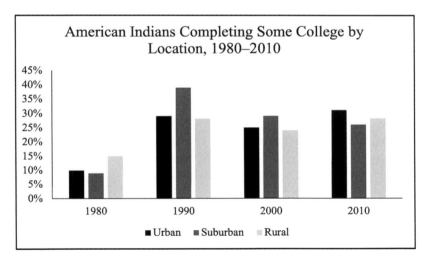

Figure 16. The rate of suburban Indians completing some college has declined since 1990. This drop may be attributed to the number of students completing at least four years of college, as seen in Figure 17.

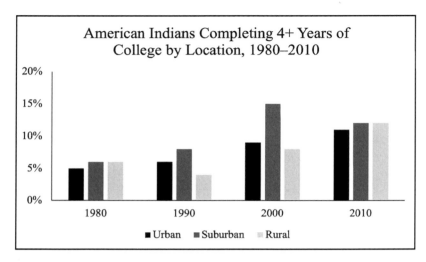

Figure 17. Suburban Indians tend to complete four or more years of college more often than urban or rural/reservation Indians.

Employment

Opportunity for employment is a major push factor propelling Indian people away from often-isolated and economically depressed reservation areas and toward metropolitan areas. A survey conducted in the early 1990s determined that "the primary reason tribal members gave for living off the reservation was the necessity of obtaining employment."[40] This sentiment also rang true for the Jabs family as they sought a suburban home that would provide a comfortable commute for Mr. Jabs, the sole income earner for the family. Though the Jabs family resides in suburban Elk River and Mr. Jabs is employed in another suburb, a quick twenty-minute drive away, residential location played a key role for the family as they sought affordable housing located in a good school district and within close proximity to employment opportunities. For them, like other suburban Indians, rural/reservation and urban housing choices are not always an available or a desirable option.

According to the Bureau of Labor Statistics, the U.S. unemployment rate for individuals aged sixteen and over began steadily increasing in January 2007, which roughly coincides with the beginning of the Great Recession. The national unemployment rate has slowly, yet gradually, improved since peaking at nearly 10 percent unemployment in late 2010.[41] However, Minnesota seems to have been affected by the Great Recession earlier, with the lowest levels of statewide unemployment (3.9 percent) appearing in May and June 2006, then climbing to an 8.3 percent unemployment rate during April, May, and June 2009. Economic recovery, as measured by unemployment levels, also began earlier in Minnesota, as seen by decreasing unemployment levels since mid-2009. While these nationwide and statewide trends reveal much about recent economic outlooks, Minnesota's American Indian population across suburban, urban, and rural/reservation locations provides insight on the linkages between residential location and employment levels for this population subgroup.

Between 1980 and 2010, the unemployment rate for those American Indian people living in the suburbs of the Twin Cities remained consistently and substantially lower than American Indian people living in urban and rural/reservation locations of Minnesota.[42] In contrast, the employment rates for American Indians living in the suburbs of Minneapolis and Saint Paul have also been consistently higher than American Indians living in rural/reservation areas or in Minneapolis or Saint Paul. The statewide employment rate for American Indians in Minnesota was 51 percent in 1980. American Indian people in the state's suburbs

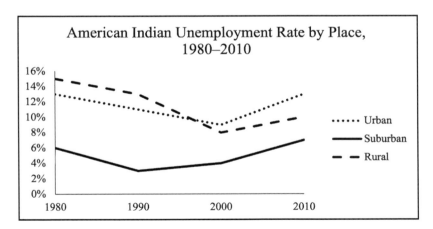

Figure 18. Though showing similar trends over time, the unemployment rate for suburban Indians has remained consistently lower than that for urban and rural/reservation Indians.

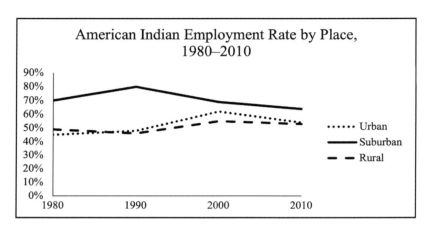

Figure 19. The employment rate of suburban Indians has remained higher than both urban and rural/reservation Indians, though the employment rate across all residential locations became closer to one another between 2000 and 2010.

were the locational group to exhibit higher rates of employment, at 70 percent. In 2010, American Indians in suburbs were again the only locational group with higher employment levels, 64 percent employed, than the American Indian statewide rate of 56 percent.

Interestingly, as employment levels began to decrease for suburban Indians in the early 2000s, the number of individuals "not in the labor force" steadily increased, yet this was only the case for American Indians in suburbs.[43] For both urban and rural/reservation Indians in Minnesota, whose employment levels increased between 1980 and 2000, the "not in the labor force" numbers for each place decreased between 1990 and 2000 but increased for suburban Indians. Generally, as sustained unemployment levels hold steady or increase, there is a rise in the number of individuals considered not in the labor force, as they stop actively looking for work. As the "not in the labor force" rate for suburban Indians increased between 1990 and 2000 and decreased for urban and rural/reservation Indians, we must consider the potential and possible causes of exit from the workforce. In 2010 there were a comparable number of Indian people not in the labor force regardless of location (Figure 20). But when comparing 1990 numbers with 2010, a dramatic change for suburban Indian people can be seen. Additionally, what accounted

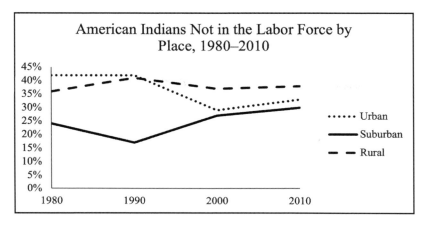

Figure 20. In 1980 and 1990, significantly fewer suburban Indians left the labor force [this includes those no longer looking for jobs and those who have retired] than urban and rural/reservation Indians. The rates for American Indians not in the labor force across all residential locations became more similar in 2010 than in the three decades prior.

for the decline in those suburban Indians not in the labor force between 1980 and 1990? This number remained relatively constant for urban and rural/reservation Indians during the same time span. This opens a series of questions specifically focusing on suburban Indians. Why have their unemployment rates been considerably lower than their urban and rural counterparts, while the percentage considered to be not in the labor force are similar in 2000 and 2010? Does this reflect an increasing number of suburban Indians who are moving into retirement, which is also considered not in the labor force, or something else, like stay-at-home parents? Additionally, where are suburban Indian people working—in urban areas to which they are geographically close or in a suburb?

Homeownership

Despite the efforts of the federal government, many of which have been discussed throughout this book, homeownership among American Indian people, on and off reservation, remains far behind the ownership rates of individuals of other race groups nationwide. According to the U.S.

Census, in 1980 the national rate of homeownership was just over 65 percent, inclusive of all residential locations. In the same year, suburban American Indians in Minnesota faired just slightly better than the overall national average, as 69 percent were homeowners—numbers that have not been achieved since then. In the same year, 73 percent of American Indian people in Minneapolis and Saint Paul (urban Indians) were renters, while only 29 percent of rural/reservation Indians rented. By comparison, in 1980 only 24 percent of suburban Indians in Minnesota rented their home or apartment, marking a stark contrast to their urban and rural/reservation peers. Homeownership versus rental status statistics from 1980 reveal a large discrepancy in rates of homeownership for Indian people across Minnesota. Rates of homeownership for American Indian people living within the urban cities of Minneapolis and Saint Paul have consistently been much lower than Indian people in suburbs and Indian people in rural/reservation communities. Though additional studies are needed to fully understand these discrepancies and inequalities, certainly the lack of access to financing or mortgages and the differing costs of living across geographic locations play a substantial role in access to homeownership.

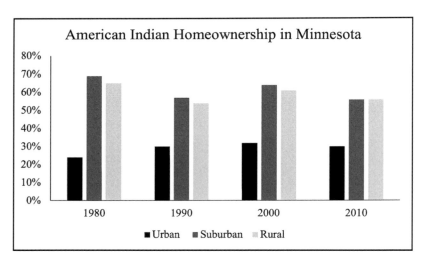

Figure 21. American Indian homeownership has been consistently and significantly lower for American Indians in urban areas than for American Indians in suburban and rural/reservation areas.

Rates of homeownership for rural/reservation Indian people in Minnesota have closely mirrored those of suburban American Indians in the state. Perhaps surprising are the high rates of outright ownership (mortgage paid in full) of homes by Indian people who live in rural/reservation areas compared to the suburban Twin Cities (Figure 22). However, a high rate of outright homeownership for American Indians in rural/reservation areas throughout Minnesota can largely be explained by the location of the state's reservation communities, since all but one of the state's eleven reservations are located in rural areas.[44] In 2000, 76 percent of the state's American Indian people who lived in a rural/reservation area either lived within or directly adjacent to a reservation.[45] Although many American Indian people struggle to build or purchase homes through traditional forms of lending off reservation, as discussed previously, a number of tribal nations are able to offer financial support to tribal members for the purchase or construction of a home on reservation. It is also important to point out that many of these homes owned outright have been in one family and passed down for generations.

High rates of outright homeownership on reservation must also be recognized as a condition of reservation trust land. Since reservation land is held in trust by the federal government, most Indian people who own their homes on reservations do not own the land that the home sits upon, which is generally not the case for non-Natives and off-reservation homeowners, who do own the land their home sits upon.[46] Thus, Indian homes on reservation trust land are theoretically more affordable since only the home, as a physical structure, must be mortgaged or purchased, not also the land beneath it. Moreover, and as discussed previously, as a result of the recent economic success of tribal nations' gaming efforts, other tribes throughout the country are able to put earned gaming revenue back into the tribal community. This often occurs as individual payments to tribal members and as much-needed investments in affordable housing for tribal members. Individual tribal housing organizations, including the Minnesota Chippewa Tribe Finance Corporation, are also often able to offer a limited amount of financial support to tribal members seeking homeownership.[47] As a crucial component of this program, which began in 1977, the MCTFC administers the IHLGP and provides financing and loan services to eligible members of the Minnesota Chippewa Tribe. Each of these factors has directly

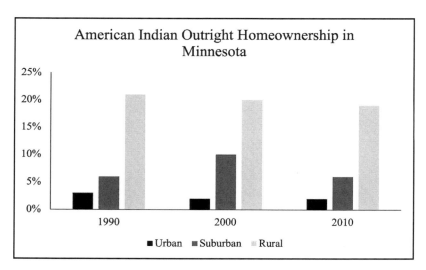

Figure 22. American Indians in rural/reservation areas are significantly more likely to own their home outright [free and clear, without a mortgage] than American Indians who live in suburban and urban areas.

contributed to the higher rates of American Indian homeownership across the rural/reservation communities of Minnesota, though these figures can often be misleading, especially without additional context.

When attention is focused on rates of homeownership via mortgage, homeownership rates shift. American Indians who lived in suburban areas in 2000 and 2010 were, on average, over 10 percent more likely to own their homes than rural/reservation Indians (Figure 23). And both groups were more likely to own their homes than urban Indians across the same time periods. Not only are American Indian people who live in suburbs more likely to be homeowners, they are also much less likely to be renters than urban Indians. The number of rural/reservation American Indian renters in the state has been only marginally higher than suburban Indian renters, likely due to access to affordable housing on reservation and the lack of adequate and affordable rental options on reservation.

When Mrs. Jabs was young and growing up in a suburban community a mere fifteen minutes from where she now resides with her own family,

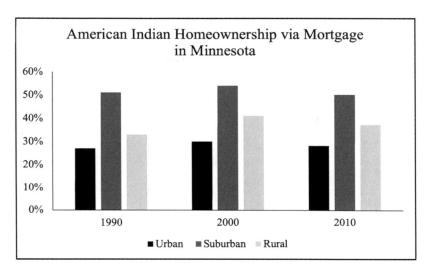

Figure 23. Suburban Indians are more likely to access homeownership through mortgage than American Indians in urban and rural/reservation areas.

she never pondered the implications of being a suburban Indian. Her parents had built the suburban home where she spent much of her youth with financial support of an American Indian homeownership program, prior to the IHLGP. Mrs. Jabs regularly visits her mother, who has since returned to her home reservation out of state, as well as her father, who lives nearby in another suburb of the Twin Cities. The dynamics of the expanded Jabs family, across reservation and suburban residential locations, is at once remarkable, yet not.

The mobility of American Indian people today is as strong and alive as it has ever been. This mobility—or movement between suburban, urban, and rural/reservation areas—has regularly been noted as creating "difficulty" when providing assistance to Indian families seeking homeownership.[48] The mobility of Indian families can be observed in the return to the reservation of many Indian people who left a generation prior under the auspices of the federal government's job training and Relocation Program or two generations ago at the height of the Great Depression. Norman Crooks (now deceased), one-time chairman of the Shakopee Mdewakanton Sioux Community, details his family's migration west to California looking for work before returning to tribal

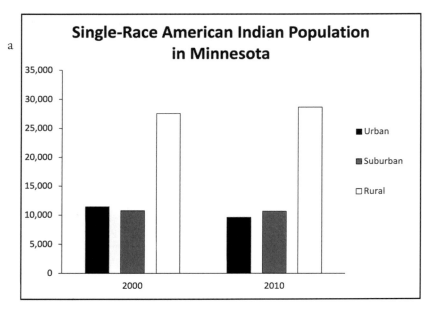

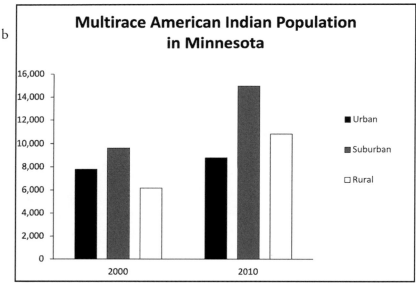

Figures 24a and b. American Indians who identify as American Indian only, as reflected in the U.S. Census, are significantly more likely to live in rural/reservation areas (2000 was the first year the U.S. Census Bureau allowed individuals to identify as more than one racial group). Suburban Indians are much more likely to identify as American Indian in conjunction with another racial group than urban and rural/reservation Indians.

land in Minnesota in 1936. At the time, the land where the Shakopee Mdewakanton Community is now located was considered "relief land," land that was set aside by the government for Indians friendly to whites during the U.S.–Dakota War. Today, the Native residents of this area are recognized as some of the wealthiest Indians in the country; it is simultaneously Indian land and suburban land.[49]

In more recent times, population mobility can often be seen in less dramatic ways. For example, there has been a gradual decrease in the percentage of American Indian people living in Minneapolis and Saint Paul over the last thirty years. Certainly, some of this population has shifted to suburban areas, while others perhaps moved to or returned to their rural or reservation communities. However, since 2000, over 50 percent of the state's American Indian people have resided in the suburbs of Minneapolis and Saint Paul.[50] Interestingly, this shift toward an increasingly suburban American Indian population coincides with the ability of individuals to self-identify with one or more races on census materials. These are astounding demographic shifts; in the years between 1980 and 1990, only 14 percent of American Indian people lived in suburbs throughout Minnesota. American Indian people who exclusively identified as American Indian on census materials are significantly more likely to live in a rural/reservation location than in an urban or suburban area (Figure 24a). Conversely, American Indian people who self-identify as American Indian in combination with one or more races on census material are much more likely than single-race American Indians to live in suburbs, as compared to urban and rural/reservation Indians (Figure 24b).[51]

This shifting movement of American Indian people, while significant, is not a new phenomenon. As I discuss in each of my previous chapters, American Indian people have continuously migrated throughout the twentieth century, both independent from and in response to federal, state, and local policies. As I demonstrate in this chapter, the last several decades have witnessed the movement of Indian people into increasingly suburban areas across Minnesota for both single-race and multirace American Indian peoples. This shift and growth in population has closely followed marked improvements in education, employment, and homeownership for American Indian people, particularly for those who live in suburbs. While historical migrations of Indian people have

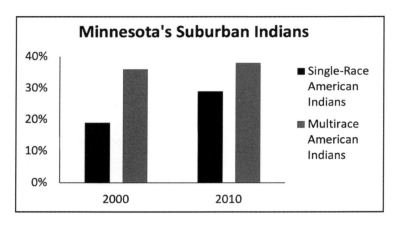

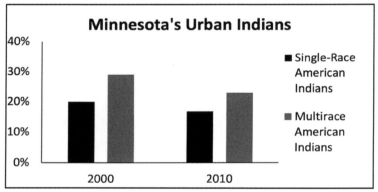

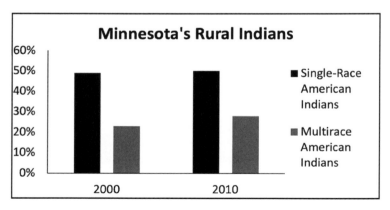

Figure 25. Suburban Indians, urban Indians, and rural/reservation Indians in Minnesota identify as single-race American Indians or as multirace American Indians on census forms.

been well documented, the resources of the late twentieth and early twenty-first centuries—education, jobs, homes—have altered what the migration and movement of Indian people look like.

The data on suburban Indians and off-reservation American Indian homeownership are severely limited. Though what is offered here only scratches the surface, the need for more is abundantly clear. To better meet the needs of today's Indian people, and the needs of tribal nations, a more far-reaching study of on- and off-reservation homeownership is needed—specifically, a study that examines access to lending institutions, the use of the IHLGP, and the use of tribe-specific housing programs. Indian policies, particularly as they unfolded in the 1990s and early 2000s, have asked us, as scholars and community members, to reconcile the need for off-reservation housing and homeownership programs with the dire need for on-reservation housing. We must not overlook the fact that today nearly 70 percent of American Indian people live off reservation and within an "Indian area," across Indian spaces and suburban places.

The need for adequate Indian housing, on reservation and off, remains a constant reminder of the complicated legacies of dispossession and racism.

Conclusion

RACIALIZING PUBLIC SPACE
AMERICAN INDIAN HOMELESSNESS AS HOUSELESSNESS AND EXCLUSION

The histories of dispossession and settler colonialism, including ongoing waves of development and suburbanization, are directly connected to the ongoing and increasingly visible American Indian homelessness crisis unfolding across the United States, both on and off reservation. During the summer of 2018 an encampment of American Indian people who were experiencing houselessness took shape in Minneapolis alongside Hiawatha Avenue. Through the fall and early winter of 2018 this encampment grew and expanded, constantly juxtaposed by the urban highway, its oblivious neighbor and perpetual audience. At its peak, over two hundred tents were perched in this makeshift encampment, home to hundreds of individuals—adults, children, elders, and pets. At the time, this encampment was the largest homeless camp in Minnesota's history. Its size was only reduced, and its residents were only housed, when an imminent and brutal Minnesota winter came knocking on the door. Despite homelessness being a long-entrenched issue in the Twin Cities and across the nation, particularly for Native folks, efforts to address this crisis have significantly lagged.

Then the Red Lake Nation, an Ojibwe nation located in northern Minnesota, led a number of groups—City of Minneapolis and State of Minnesota officials, community members, and local nonprofit organizations, including the numerous Native nonprofits based out of Minneapolis and Saint Paul—to make a plan to house those who called the encampment home; overwhelmingly, these were American Indian people. The Red Lake Nation, who had purchased a parcel of land in the city of Minneapolis in 2016 with hopes of economic development and the construction of affordable housing, offered their parcel for temporary shelter when the city failed to secure an alternative site. Red Lake's parcel of land, located at 2105 Cedar Avenue, had previously been used for industry and had been sitting vacant. Yet, it would take time to clear the site, with winter's chill setting in, and prepare the site for the construction of more suitable, even if temporary, shelter for those without a home to call their own. With snow and subzero temperatures rapidly approaching, a collaborative effort to create temporary shelter and services took shape. Slowly but surely, the Red Lake Nation, the City of Minneapolis, and numerous social service agencies and nonprofits stepped up to aid the residents of the encampment in transitioning to the new, three-structure "navigation center."

Each of the three large, tentlike structures that were constructed at the Cedar Avenue site housed approximately forty individuals while providing sleeping cots, hot showers, indoor restrooms, and three square meals a day. On-site security was hired. Though drug use was not allowed or tolerated at the shelter, no one was turned away for arriving under the influence of drugs or alcohol—it was a housing-first strategy. Family units and couples were allowed to stay together, and pets were allowed to remain with their owners. Social service agencies were a constant presence, providing support and guidance for shelter residents as they sought to place those living in the navigation center with more stable and long-term housing, addiction services, health care, clothing, and other basic human needs. Over the winter months, shelter residents were regularly placed into more long-term housing options, freeing up more space in the navigation center to bring folks in from the cold. The navigation center, born out of the Wall of Forgotten Natives encampment, was a relatively successful, though short-term, collaboration that grew out of dire need, extreme visibility, and freezing temperatures. By the spring of 2019, the temporary shelter the navigation center provided would evaporate almost as quickly as the piles of winter snow.

The Twin Cities of Minneapolis and Saint Paul are home to one of the largest urban American Indian communities in the nation. And, as I discuss in previous chapters, the Twin Cities have always been an

Indian place. The region, known by the Dakota as Bdóte, is their traditional homeland, and Dakota ties and presence remain strong today, despite a history marked by exile and violence. Yet it is precisely the treaties of the nineteenth century that set in motion the severe rates of Native people experiencing houselessness in the twentieth and twenty-first centuries, in Minnesota and beyond. This history of dispossession and Native containment must be accounted for when thinking about who has access to space, land, housing, and homes today. The leadership we saw in the Red Lake Nation, who stepped up to house Native community members in 2018, echoed a similar era in the 1960s and 1970s. In direct response to the lack of housing American Indian people in Minneapolis faced in the 1950s and 1960s, it was Native community members who took the lead to advocate for, provide, and manage affordable housing to Native Minnesotans, regardless of their tribal affiliation.

More recently, the Red Lake Nation has again taken the lead to build affordable housing for tribal citizens and other American Indian community members in Minneapolis. At 2105 Cedar Avenue, the site of the former navigation center, on the property they purchased in 2016, the Red Lake Nation built an affordable housing complex. The name of the 110-unit project is Mino-Bimaadiziwin in Ojibwe, which roughly translates to "the good life" in English, and it opened in early 2021. This mixed-use housing complex offers one-, two-, and three-bedroom apartments, as well as a wellness center and an urban-based Red Lake Embassy for tribal members in the Twin Cities. Mino-Bimaadiziwin was funded by low-income housing tax credits, the City of Minneapolis, Hennepin County, the Federal Home Loan Bank, the Metropolitan Council, the Minnesota Housing Authority, and private donations. A goal of Mino-Bimaadiziwin is to house low-income households within a supportive infrastructure with access to substance abuse and mental health services. This affordable housing development, which is open to all who meet specific income requirements, is the first off-reservation direct housing investment by a tribal nation in Minnesota.

The hypervisible 2018 Wall of Forgotten Natives and the ongoing housing crisis are situated within the multiplicity of the historical and political contexts described throughout this book. Though we have witnessed generations of change and, importantly, Native people rising to and overcoming the challenges they have faced, mounting racial discrimination, racial and police violence, and the stressors of an oppressive capitalistic society came to a head during the summer of 2020 in Minneapolis. On May 25, 2020, forty-six-year-old George Floyd, a Black resident of Minneapolis, stopped at a local grocery store to purchase cigarettes. A daily transaction ended in an all too familiar story—another Black man murdered at the hands of the police. We know the details well, and the memory for many is still overwhelmingly vivid and raw. What has not been as visible and clear is the deep and entwined history of this police violence against Black bodies and the history of colonial violence against American Indian peoples that has similarly morphed into state and police violence and oppression.

George Floyd was murdered less than one mile from the Little Earth housing complex, less than one mile from the 2018 Wall of Forgotten Natives, and less than one mile from today's Mino-Bimaadiziwin. In fact, this entire area has long been a cauldron of police violence and the activism of Black, Brown, and Native survivors in response. It was in this precise neighborhood that we saw the birth of the American Indian Movement, which took root in the late 1960s specifically to address police brutality against Native community members. Perhaps it is no surprise that American Indian community members who call Minneapolis home were among the first allies and supports of the protesters and have continued to play a prominent role in the movement that would unravel across Minneapolis and the nation in the weeks and months following Floyd's murder.

As the city of Minneapolis reeled from the murder of George Floyd at the hands of the police, the coronavirus pandemic rapidly spread across an already devastated community. The tension of this social-political moment cannot be overestimated. It was within this atmosphere that the Wall of Forgotten Natives of 2018 was reimagined, reconstructed, and repopulated during the early summer of 2020. Yet these new encampments could not and would not be bound by Hiawatha Avenue. And the activism of many would ignite a larger movement not only against police brutality but also for affordable housing and the urgent need for the accompanying supports for our most vulnerable—the community members who were experiencing houselessness during the dual crises of police violence and coronavirus.

I am intentional in my use of the term *houseless* rather than *homeless* to underscore, recognize, and remember Minneapolis, and all of the

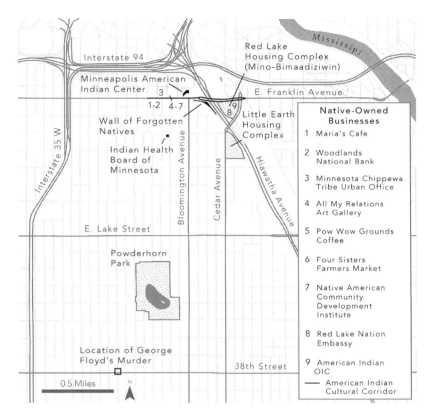

Map 6. Map of Phillips and Powderhorn neighborhoods of South Minneapolis. Map by Katherine Koehler.

Twin Cities region, as the traditional homelands of the Dakota people. Dakota people, Ojibwe people, and all Native people are "home" here, even as visitors to the land. These are Indigenous homelands, home-lands the Dakota have long been dispossessed of and excluded from—just like the many other tribal nations who experienced dispossession from their own homelands that span the United States, coast to coast. To acknowledge and name this dispossession of the past forces us to reconcile history's impact on the present, including the ongoing and deliberate exclusion from certain spaces and places.

To be homeless is to be without a "home." Yet many Native folks in the Twin Cities are home. Rather, Native folks in the Twin Cities have been prevented and obstructed from accessing houses—as a physical structure. This deliberate effort to prevent Native people from accessing houses or housing, a physical residence, is not new, and a careful look at history highlights how engrained the regulation of space has been over time, as I have touched on in previous chapters. To call attention to houselessness, we can center the role of capitalism in the creation and maintenance of a lack of housing for all. Houselessness did not exist in traditional Native communities before the arrival of Europeans, Americans, and capitalism to Native communities. Rather, Native communities, many of which engaged in a subsistence lifestyle, housed those who needed homes as a matter of kinship and tribal responsibility. From the theft of Indian land, to forced treaty negotiations and unfulfilled treaty promises, to exile, to the creation of the reservation system, and through the Relocation Program of the mid-twentieth century, Native people have been repeatedly denied access to their homes and homelands, and today many find themselves houseless within their homelands.

Encampments for those experiencing houselessness are not a new phenomenon. Across the country, folks who have experienced houselessness have long set up encampments or groups and clusters of tent shelters. This can help to create a sense of community and makes sense for logistic reasons, including a sense of safety among neighbors. In warmer climates, like those in Los Angeles and San Diego, these encampments exist on a much more permanent basis where weather is not necessarily a limiting factor. However, large encampments in the Twin Cities have taken more time for the general population, specifically those who are housed, to adjust to. Or perhaps the well-known "Minnesota nice" makes certain individuals that much more uncomfortable with the visibility of houseless encampments, as they offer a visible and ever-present reminder of the failings of our society to protect and house each member, a basic human right. Thus, with the dual crises of coronavirus and police violence that came to a head in Minneapolis during the summer of 2020, perhaps it is no surprise that houseless encampments, where members of our society have been chronically cast and pathologized, would also become enveloped in the movement for social and racial justice.

The encampments created by those experiencing houselessness spread across the city, where the effects of coronavirus and police violence have been particularly acute. The dense living conditions of encampments, with the lack of access to fresh, clean water and restroom facilities, allowed the virus to run rampant. This was further compounded by a lack of access to health care that many folks experiencing houselessness also endure. Folks who have made the encampments their home are also predominantly people of color, with American Indians overrepresented in statistics on homelessness. In fact, though American Indians compose about 1 percent of the state's total population, they represent approximately 15 percent of the state's houseless population. For Black folks, the numbers are equally dire. Though Black people are 14 percent of the state's total population, they represent half of the state's houseless population. It is also important to point out that statistics on houselessness are almost always undercounted, as the mobility of those experiencing houselessness make quantifying their numbers difficult.

Over the summer of 2020, city parks across Minneapolis became a refuge for those experiencing houselessness, and it was not long before it became obvious that the Minneapolis Park and Recreation Board, which oversees the parks administratively, had inherited a crisis. In May 2020, Minnesota Emergency Executive Order 20-55, a "Covid-19 Peacetime Emergency," took effect. This order limited the capacity of homeless shelters and the number of individuals living at outdoor encampments to adhere to the space-based limits imposed by the efforts to contain the contagious and rapidly spreading virus. As such, many folks experiencing houselessness were forced to relocate and find new spaces. Powderhorn Park, located only blocks from where George Floyd was murdered and blocks from the Little Earth housing complex, became the site of a massive encampment, surpassing the size of the 2018 Wall of Forgotten Natives encampment, with over 550 tents set up within the 468-acre park at its peak, taking over the title of the largest houseless encampment in the state's history. In fact, by midsummer 2020, at least forty City of Minneapolis parks were home to encampments of houseless community members.

But it was at Powderhorn Park, with the backdrop of a growing encampment, that many of the members of the Minneapolis City Council gathered on June 7, 2020, pledging to dismantle the Minneapolis Police Department as we have known it. Just ten days after this declaration, the Minneapolis Park and Recreation Board announced that they had approved Resolution 2020-253 and declared their "commitment to provide refuge space to people currently experiencing homelessness while continuing to work with the State, County, City, and non-profit-organizations and other interested parties to identify long term housing solutions for people at the Powderhorn encampment and others throughout the city."[1] Despite the efforts of many on the ground—community members, community organizers, and nonprofit organizations, many of which are led by Indigenous folks and people of color—and the global attention these efforts and encampments received, it would not be long before those who had made encampments across City of Minneapolis parks their home were forced to leave once again.

It is here we must turn to and address the racialization of Black, Brown, and Native bodies. Racialization of specific and othered bodies is not new and has been well documented across such disciplines as American studies, history, geography, sociology, women's and gender studies, ethnic studies, and critical race studies, to name only some. In fact, American Indian people, though long thought of as a racial or ethnic group, are defined politically and legally based on their history of treaty-making with the colonial powers of the seventeenth and eighteenth centuries, and eventually with the newly created United States. Their distinct political-legal identity rests on tribal sovereignty, sovereignty that is inherent and predates the creation of the United States. Despite this, and because race is a social construct, we know American Indian people have long been racialized and marked as other. This is clearly observed in the phenomenon of blood quantum and assumptions about authenticity based on phenotypical markers, including tan or brown skin, dark brown or black hair, dark eyes, and high cheekbones. It is precisely these features that continue to mark Native American people as other.

According to scholars Michael Omi and Howard Winant, racialization is the process that seeks to produce racial meanings in specific time and space as individuals engage with social, economic, and political forces.[2] Moreover, this process is restrictive, imposing literal and figurative boundaries around differently defined groups in a society, largely based on external markers as clues to how we see or read or racialize someone. Racialization is something that occurs when we associate characteristics, practices, or attributes with certain racialized individuals. During the summer of 2020, then, the encampments that spread across Minneapolis, providing a place of refuge for those experiencing houselessness, became racially marked, or racialized, as did the bodies within them. As the encampment at Powderhorn Park grew and temporary tent shelters continued to pop up in place of green grass and baseball fields, neighbors of these parks and encampments grew frustrated.

State and national parks have long been seen as the domain of white Americans—as places of leisure and recreation. A prime example of parks as white places to the exclusion of Native people is Glacier National Park in Montana. Over 1,500 square miles that Glacier National Park encompasses lies squarely on the homelands of the Blackfoot and Flathead Indians. Over time, the tribes have been squeezed out and prohibited from park space as not belonging, and their presence has been seen as a certain detriment to potential white park visitors. Similarly, scholars of geography and race have long studied the proximity of parks to white and nonwhite neighborhoods and the quality and size of these parks.

What has been less studied or examined in recent years is the ways racialized bodies are continuously excluded from park space. Yet on May 25, 2020, just hours before George Floyd was murdered, Amy Cooper, a middle-aged white woman from Manhattan, called the cops on a Black man, Christian Cooper, in New York City's Central Park. Amy Cooper racialized Christian Cooper's Black body as a threat and as not belonging in the park. Later that year, a Native man and U.S. marine veteran became the target of racialized violence in a national park. In late December 2020, Darrell House, who is both Oneida and Navajo, was walking his dog in Petroglyph National Monument in New Mexico. Soon House recognized he was being followed by a park ranger after stepping off a park trail for purposes of social distancing when another group of hikers passed by. Within minutes the park ranger stated verbal commands for House to identify himself, attempted to handcuff House, and eventually tased House multiple times while his sister, who was along for the walk, recorded the brutal encounter on her cell phone.

This racialization of park space—and bodies as belonging in parks or not—is important to consider alongside the regulation of space in terms of housing. We know the historic legacies of exclusionary and racialized housing policies, including the well-entrenched practice of redlining, that the GI Bill was almost always only for white veterans, that race-based covenants limited who could occupy or purchase specific dwellings, that it has been nearly impossible for Native people to secure a mortgage or home loan on reservation, and, more recently, the exclusionary practices of homeowners' associations. In many ways, what has occurred in housing over the last century is now unfolding in park space—the explicit regulation of space by race. The result is that those who are read as other, those who have been most affected by the violence of colonialism, are finding more and more places to be off-limits. We must think of this in terms of homes (who can live where) and in terms of public space (what spaces Native folks and other people of color can safely exist in and occupy). This is, once again, significant to the backdrop of centuries-old and ongoing dispossession of Native lands.

The racialization of nonwhite bodies goes hand in hand with the criminalization of nonwhite bodies. Racial criminalization is the stigmatization of crime as a people of color problem while overlooking or ignoring crimes committed by white people or in white neighborhoods. Racial criminalization specifically links crime to Black and Brown bodies. Racial criminalization has significantly contributed to the constant presence of police in people of color communities and the overrepresentation of people of color in jails and prisons. Thus, as the encampment of folks experiencing houselessness grew and expanded in Powderhorn Park, neighbors drew on the racialization of people and on the criminalization of those who, however temporary, called the park home. This can be understood as an unconscious bias; many of these neighbors welcomed and supported their new neighbors early on and see themselves as progressive and liberal. Many of these housed neighbors understand the need for housing, but frequent police calls, drug use, increased traffic, safety concerns, and late-night noise led to a rapid change in opinion of the encampment.

This growing neighborhood resistance was cemented when, one month after opening parks as a place of refuge, the Minneapolis Park and Recreation Board rescinded its offer. Beginning on Friday, July 18, 2020, the park board began distributing notices to those encamped at east Powderhorn Park to vacate the site within seventy-two hours. On July 31, they gave notices of a looming expectation to remove approximately sixty-five tents in other areas of Powderhorn Park. Then, less than two weeks later, the park board and the Minneapolis Police Department began to remove tent structures and individuals from the encampments.

It is in this space, the regulation of city parks, that I want to end. It is my intention to connect a long history of dispossession and oppression to the events we witnessed as they unfolded during the summer of 2020, and again numerous times since, as those unhoused and living in encampments have become the continuous target of eviction and removal by City of Minneapolis officials. Many policymakers and those who hold the purse strings overlook or have forgotten the history that unfolds in this book. We cannot examine houselessness as a problem that only emerged in the final decades of the twentieth century. Similarly, we, as scholars, activists, policy makers, community members, governing officials, and developers, need to have critical conversations about the regulation of space. So many forms of housing have been off-limits to American Indian people, and their movements across space have been highly surveilled. Today, we frequently witness this same regulation of space in public areas—in parks. Despite the tremendous efforts of Native organizations, nonprofits, and tribes across the Twin Cities to address American Indian houselessness, those with tangible and legible power, those in elected offices, must step up, act, and make change. Until then, we will rely on and we must support those community members on the ground, those who work tirelessly to find houses, provide direct services, and advocate for access to housing for American Indians and for all.

ACKNOWLEDGMENTS

As I sit to write the final words to accompany this book, I am reminded of the journey to get to this point and especially of the many strong women who guided me along the way.

This journey began in the early 2000s when I was completing my bachelor's degree at the University of Wisconsin. Though I majored in political science, it was the two courses I took in American Indian studies during my senior year that really opened my eyes, for the first time ever, to the scholarly field of Native American and Indigenous studies. These classes, taught by two Native women—Theresa Schenck and Denise Wiyaka—were truly a gateway to my future, and I thank them for that.

While working for the Anoka-Hennepin Indian Education Program, I was so fortunate to have the best colleagues and mentors a new employee could ever hope for. Kathy Eisenschenk, Mary Beth Elhardt, Barry Scanlon, and Jennifer Weber were always welcoming and provided the perfect amount of laughter to an often-stressful work environment. They were my first sounding boards as I grappled with American Indian identity and belonging in the suburbs. They have done so much over each of their careers and care so deeply about youth of color, particularly American Indian youth.

My fortunate luck with colleagues continued during my time in the Admissions Office at Concordia University, St. Paul. Briana Eicheldinger,

Tara Humlie, Kelly Macik, Leah Martin, Adrian Perryman, Emily Siegel, and Kristin Vogel are such kind and generous souls. You have each made me a better person and encouraged me to follow my dreams of graduate school. Cheryl Chatman, who has since retired, was also an early beacon of support and encouragement as I navigated the path to graduate school.

During my time at both Anoka-Hennepin and Concordia, I got the itch to expand my horizons by pursuing the American Indian studies degree program at the University of Minnesota while juggling full-time work. During this time, as a first-generation college student, I learned about graduate school, something I knew virtually nothing about up until this point. While taking American Indian studies courses at the University of Minnesota, I was beyond fortunate to enroll in classes taught by David Martinez, Jean O'Brien, and David Wilkins. My time spent in their classrooms was all I needed to take the leap and apply for graduate school. I cannot thank them enough for opening new doors for me and offering the inspiration I needed.

I think I won the lottery as far as graduate school experiences go. My time at the University of Minnesota was full of good friends, great teachers and administrative staff, and amazing mentors, as well as lots of learning, of course. Though American studies was my academic home, my support system spanned multiple departments, institutes, and centers. I am forever indebted to my peers and the faculty who built and have sustained the American Indian and Indigenous Studies Workshop that has morphed and grown into its own highly recognizable and enviable writing group, reproduced across campuses but never duplicated. Katie Phillips, Rose Miron, Jess Arnett, Jimmy Sweet, John Little, Joe Whitson, Amber Annis, Sasha Suarez, Sam Majhor, Marie Balsley Taylor, Akikwe Cornell, Bernadette Pérez, Juliana Hu Pegues, Agleska Cohen-Rencountre, Macey Flood, and Jill Fish—we have traveled together, grown together, celebrated together, and cried together. We have become a family, and I thank you for that. Jess, Katie, and Rose continue to be dear friends and colleagues, and I am so proud to get to work with them professionally across our institutions. My American studies cohort—Karisa Butler-Wall, Eli Vitulli, and our beloved Jesus Estrada-Perez, we will always be each other's biggest fans. You each patiently taught me so much, and I will always hold a special place in my heart for you. My graduate student experience was certainly made better by those who came before me: Jill Doerfler, Heidi Stark, Erik Redix, Kate Beane, Scott Shoemaker, and the late Karissa White; thank you for laying a strong foundation.

Scott Hall, an aging building at the University of Minnesota, quickly became a welcome place of energy and grounding for me. Thank you to the administrative powerhouses of Maria Alexander, Brittany Anderson, and Rodrigo Sanchez-Chavarria, who always knew how to get anything and everything done. American studies and American Indian studies faculty members—Kevin Murphy, Pat Albers, David Wilkins, Bianet Castellanos, Vince Diaz, David Chang, and Kat Hayes—your knowledge and generosity have inspired me in so many ways.

I am tremendously grateful to my dissertation committee members—Carolyn Liebler, Jennifer Pierce, and Coll Thrush. Thank you for reading drafts and revisions along the way and providing such important and critical feedback. Thank you, Carolyn, for your unending efforts to teach me Stata and SPSS. I am so appreciative of the time you spent with me in the Minnesota Population Center, working through census data and quantitative methods. Jennifer, you brought perspective to me as a graduate student and taught me the value of not losing sight of myself. Thank you, Coll, for taking me on as a graduate student and inspiring me with your words and advice. You each made dissertating so smooth and provided a strong base for this manuscript.

To my advisers, Jean O'Brien and Brenda Child, thank you. These two words will never be enough, but I know you both know the love and respect I have for each of you. You both took me under your wings, providing me with the knowledge, skills, and confidence to stand on my own in the often intimidating, competitive, and isolating world of academia. I have spent cherished hours with each of you, whether it was traveling to the archives, going on research trips in northern Minnesota, at happy hours, end-of-semester gatherings, workshops, office hours, or conferences. I hope to be a mentor to my own students the way you were, and continue to be, a mentor to me.

I had the opportunity to spend two years at the University of Virginia as the Native American Studies Postdoctoral Fellow. Here, I was housed in the Department of American Studies and truly grew as a scholar. Anna Brickhouse, thank you for your kindness, gentle humor, and mentorship. Your feedback and support as I developed and revised my book proposal, especially in an area outside your field, were invaluable. David Edmunds, my office neighbor, thank you for your welcoming smile, friendly conversations, great insight, check-ins, and encouragement. Allison Bigelow, Sylvia Chong, Lisa Goff, Adriana Greci Green, Grace Hale, Jack Hamilton, Jeff Hantman, Matt Hedstrom, Jessica Huskey, James Igoe, Carmen Lamas, and Margo Smith, thank you for welcoming me to UVA and Charlottesville and for being such a positive presence, offering your support, and being just truly great all-around friends and colleagues. Katy Mohrman, thank you for being my confidant and my reality TV buddy. Our shared time as postdocs at UVA brought out a beautiful friendship. I think of my time in Charlottesville very fondly, and I learned so much about academia and life during my time there. I will always look forward to visiting.

In many ways, my academic journey came full circle when I joined the University of Wisconsin as an assistant professor. In fact, I now teach in the same American Indian Studies Program that opened the window of opportunity so many years ago. Denise Wiyaka has become a true mentor and a dear friend, always providing a laugh and sound career-minded advice. Larry Nesper, thank you for your commitment to AIS and for your words of wisdom and support. I hope you enjoy the beauty of retirement. Sasha Suarez and Jen Rose Smith, you two are not only strong women but also amazing colleagues and good friends. While I returned to UW and American Indian studies, I am also fortunate to be housed in the School of Human Ecology. Here, the interdisciplinary Department of Civil Society and Community Studies has provided me with a new academic family. Cindy Jasper, Lori Bakken, Lori DiPrete Brown, Connie Flanagan, and Leah Horowitz, thank you for bringing me to your team and supporting me along the way. Jen Gaddis and Carolina Sarmiento, you two have been true friends and wonderful colleagues. I am so thankful to share an office hallway with you both and am excited to grow as a scholar alongside each of you. Carolee Dodge Francis, where would I (or this book) be without you? Thank you for your unending support, your kindness, our lunches, and your unwavering guidance. I know you always have my best interest in mind, something rare to find these days. The dean of the School of Human Ecology, Soyeon Shim, also deserves special mention. She is the unicorn of deans and has been a fierce advocate and supporter of my work;

thank you for your leadership and wisdom. Janean Dilworth-Bart, you have been such an inspiration; thank you for paving the path for those like me and for your gentle words and valuable perspective. We are truly lucky to have you serve as an assistant dean. Steve Kantrowitz and Sarah Carter, thank you for joining my tenure committee, offering valuable feedback, sharing your knowledge, and being such a supporter of AIS at UW.

During my time at UW, I have also had the opportunity to work with amazing graduate students. Jimmy Taitano Camacho, Sarah Lundquist, Morgan Smallwood, Sarah Tate, and Garret Zastoupil—thank you for being the best teaching assistants I could have ever dreamed of. You have eased so many of my worries and have shown such professionalism. A special shout-out to Jimmy, Sarah L., and Garret, who served as teaching assistants during the pandemic. You are rock stars. Ryan Hellenbrand, thank you for joining me in my slightly bizarre obsession with Paul Bunyan and for coauthoring an essay. I am very much looking forward to future writing projects together.

My book and I have benefited from the time, generosity, and expertise of so many others. Thank you to Jessica Cattelino, Daniel Cobb, Larry Nesper, and Steve Kantrowitz for reading a rough, early version of this manuscript. Your feedback and the ensuing discussion through the University of Wisconsin's First Book Program certainly made this a stronger and more well-rounded project. The suggestions offered by the University of Minnesota Press's manuscript reviewers have been tremendously helpful. Chris Andersen, you have always been a supporter of my work, and your gentle and thoughtful critiques and feedback have pushed me to do and be better. Doug Miller, Margaret Huettl, and Ashley Glassburn—thank you for always being such friendly faces at conferences, for sharing your knowledge, and for offering encouragement.

Beyond this book, my scholarship has evolved and been informed by a robust network of scholars, archivists, and editors. J. Kēhaulani Kauanui, Robert Warrior, Brian Hosmer, Lisa Blee, Willy Bauer, and Jody TallBear—thank you for sharing your time and expertise at the University of Virginia symposium I was so fortunate to host. Thank you to the many archivists, including those at the National Archives at Kansas City, Chicago, and College Park, the Newberry Library, and the Minnesota Historical Society, who collected an endless number of books, pamphlets, manuscripts, boxes, and other sources and delivered them to me in my quest to answer this book's guiding questions. Thank you, Jason Weidemann, for answering all of my questions and putting me at ease. This publishing business is no joke, and the seemingly never-ending Covid-19 pandemic threw all schedules and timelines to the wind, so thank you for your patience and gentle reminders. Zenyse Miller, though we have met only via email, your swift replies and guidance have been remarkable. Thank you, too, for your patience and for tolerating my plethora of emails. Ziggy Snow, thank you for your excellent copy-editing skills that make me read like a polished writer.

A special thank you to Katherine Koehler, who took time out of a hectic semester to create the original maps for this book. And to Dawí Huhá Máza for his expertise in the Dakota language and history. His contributions to the Dakota placenames map were invaluable, and his willingness to share his knowledge of the Dakota language certainly made this book much more about Dakota people and Dakota places, particularly in chapter 1.

This manuscript is also the benefactor of a wide variety of funding. While a graduate student, I held American Indian Studies, Institute for Advanced Study, Doctoral Dissertation, and Interdisciplinary Doctoral fellowships that saw me through several years of graduate study and a dissertation, which morphed into this manuscript. The Newberry Library in Chicago also generously provided fellowships that have supported this book project, including the Susan Kelly Power and Helen Hornbeck Tanner Fellowship. Both the University of Virginia and the University of Wisconsin provided research funds that were used to build and expand this project, including participating in numerous conferences and visiting multiple archives.

My close friends and family have continuously shown genuine care, interest, support, and love. To them I am forever grateful. Sarah Langfeld (and Ron and Jan), thank you for always providing an open door and a cold beer over the years (now decades). Now that Wisconsin has become my home, I have gained a beautiful new friend group with Nikki Frank, Liz Hill, and Breanna Taylor, brought together by my dear friend and beautiful soul Kelly Thomsen. Thank you to the larger Thomsen family for the years of love, laughs, Badger football games, and beer (I sense a theme here).

While I have spent the past two years "wrapping this book project up," we have also been living in a global pandemic. As such, I have come to rely on and value my family even more. Thank you. Thank you for always providing a respite from the hecticness of teaching, researching, and writing. Thank you for the calls and texts and pictures and vacations and love. Thank you for providing the structure and the glue for everything I have ever done.

Though 2021 felt like the same recurring and dreaded cycle of Covid case counts and masking, my bright spot was the birth of our baby girl, Violet. She has brought so much pure and innocent joy to our lives. I do not mind the setbacks and the tasks (like manuscript revisions) that are left unfinished when I know my sweet girl is waiting for me. Though Violet may be new, her furry siblings Puffy, Stewart, and our Ruby girl provided constant companionship over the years of writing. Always on my lap or at my side, every writer needs at least one dog.

Finally, this book would never have been complete without my partner and husband, Gabe. Thank you, Gabe, for your love, patience, encouragement, and willingness to go all-in on "daddy daycare." With love and unending gratitude, thank you.

Appendix

TIMELINE
FEDERAL INDIAN AND FEDERAL HOUSING POLICIES, INCLUDING SIGNIFICANT EVENTS AND LEGISLATIVE ACTS

Chapter 1

1862 (MAY 20): President Abraham Lincoln signs Homestead Act

1862 (JULY 1): President Abraham Lincoln signs Pacific Railway Act

1862 (JULY 2): President Abraham Lincoln signs Morrill Act

1862 (AUGUST–SEPTEMBER): U.S.–Dakota War

Chapter 2

1921 (NOVEMBER 2): Congress passes the Snyder Act

1924 (JUNE 2): Congress passes the Indian Citizenship Act

1928 (FEBRUARY 21): Lewis Meriam, director and author of the Meriam Report, releases report to the secretary of the interior

1932 (JULY 22): Congress passes the Federal Home Loan Bank Act

1933 (JUNE 13): Congress passes the Home Owners' Loan Act, creating the Home Owners' Loan Corporation (HOLC)

1933 (JUNE 16): Congress creates the Federal Deposit Insurance Corporation (FDIC)

1934 (APRIL 16): Congress passes the Johnson-O'Malley Act (JOM)

1934 (JUNE 6): Creation of the Securities and Exchange Commission (SEC)

1934 (JUNE 18): Congress passes the Indian Reorganization Act (IRA)

1934 (JUNE 27): Congress passes the National Housing Act of 1934, creating the Federal Housing Administration (FHA) and the Federal Savings and Loan Insurance Corporation (FSLIC)

1937 (SEPTEMBER 1): Congress passes the U.S. Housing Act of 1937 (also known as the Wagner-Steagall Act) for the provision of public housing

Chapter 3

1944 (JUNE 22): President Franklin D. Roosevelt signs into law the Service-men's Readjustment Act of 1944, more commonly known as the GI Bill

1949 (JULY 15): Congress passes the Housing Act of 1949

1953 (AUGUST 1): Congress House Concurrent Resolution 108 announces official start to Termination Policy

1956 (AUGUST 3): President Dwight D. Eisenhower signs Indian Relocation Act into law

Chapter 4

1965: Bureau of Indian Affairs establishes Housing Improvement Program (HIP)

1965 (SEPTEMBER 9): Creation of the Department of Housing and Urban Development (HUD) as a cabinet-level agency

1968: American Indian Movement (AIM) forms in Minneapolis

1968 (APRIL 11): Congress passes the Fair Housing Act

1972: Creation of Indian survival schools in Minneapolis (Heart of the Earth) and Saint Paul (Red School House)

1973: President Richard Nixon announces moratorium on most HUD programs

1973: Founding of Little Earth as an affordable housing complex in Minneapolis

1974 (AUGUST 22): Congress passes the Housing and Community Development Act, which creates the Section 8 program

1975 (JANUARY 4): President Gerald R. Ford signs the Indian Self-Determination and Education Assistance Act into law

1978: Creation of the Office of Indian Housing within HUD

1984: HUD appoints first permanent director of Indian Housing

1988 (JUNE 29): Congress passes the Indian Housing Act (to amend the U.S. Housing Act of 1937)

Chapter 5

1990 (NOVEMBER): President George H. W. Bush signs Cranston-Gonzalez National Affordable Housing Act into law

1992 (OCTOBER): President George H. W. Bush signs Housing and Community Development Act into law

1992: Congress establishes the Indian Home Loan Guarantee Program (IHLGP)

1995 (JUNE): President Bill Clinton unveils the National Homeownership Strategy

1996 (OCTOBER): President Bill Clinton signs the Native American Housing Assistance and Self-Determination Act (NAHASDA) into law

2004: Indian Home Loan Guarantee Program expanded to off-reservation areas

NOTES

Introduction

1. "Purpose of the Indian Education Program," Anoka-Hennepin Schools, accessed December 2022, https://www.ahschools.us/anokahennepin.

2. The official federal definition of *Indian* for education program services states that *Indian* means any individual who is (1) a member (as defined by the Indian tribe or band) of an Indian tribe or band, including those Indian tribes or bands terminated since 1940, and those recognized by the state in which the tribe or band reside; or (2) a descendant in the first or second degree (of a parent or grandparent) as described in (1); or (3) considered by the secretary of the interior to be an Indian for any purpose; or (4) an Inuit or Aleut or other Alaska Native; or (5) a member of an organized Indian group that received a grant under the Indian Education Act of 1988 as it was in effect October 19, 1994.

3. See chapter 2. The Johnson-O'Malley Act (JOM; 25 U.S.C. § 5342 (1934)) provides federal subsidies to schools. JOM funds may be used for culture, language, and academic programs, as well as for dropout prevention. To receive JOM funds, schools must collect enrollment and blood quantum information from American Indian students and families. Students who are one-quarter or more Indian blood of a federally recognized Indian tribe are eligible for JOM services and their school is thus eligible for JOM funding.

4. An exception to this is Owen Toews, *Stolen City: Racial Capitalism and the Making of Winnipeg* (Winnipeg: Arbeiter Ring, 2018). Here, Toews examines the creation of Métis suburbs around Winnipeg in the 1940s and 1950s.

Though in the Canadian context, Toews grapples with state policies and market forces that displaced Indigenous peoples from their land to make way for urban development. In the case of Winnipeg, Métis suburbs were outgrowths of exclusionary urban developments and a direct result of settler colonial dispossession.

5. Toews, *Stolen City,* 107.

6. See Gerald Vizenor, *Survivance: Narratives of Native Presence* (Lincoln: University of Nebraska Press, 2008).

7. I rely on the work of legal scholar Virginia Davis as a framework that informs how I understand and discuss the long history of the federal government's intervention in American Indian housing. See Virginia Davis, "A Discovery of Sorts: Reexamining the Origins of the Federal Indian Housing Obligation," *Harvard BlackLetter Law Journal* 18 (2002): 211–39.

8. For more on imperialism and the city as a Native place, see Nicholas Blomley, *Unsettling the City: Urban Land and the Politics of Property* (New York: Routledge, 2003), 107–9.

9. J. Kēhaulani Kauanui, "'A Structure, Not an Event': Settler Colonialism and Enduring Indigeneity," *Lateral: Journal of the Cultural Studies Association* 5, no. 1 (Spring 2016): https://doi.org/10.24158/L5.1.7. American Indians in this sense were not passive bystanders but individuals and communities who fought to "exist, resist, and persist."

10. This spans the highly visible—for example, the work of Dakota sisters Kate Beane and Carly Bad Heart Bull, who led efforts toward the Bde Maka Ska name change in Minneapolis—to the less visible work of families like mine who established a home in the suburbs and contribute to a vibrant, growing, and supportive Native community.

11. Paige Raibmon, *Authentic Indians: Episodes of Encounter from the Late-Nineteenth-Century Northwest Coast* (Durham, N.C.: Duke University Press, 2005).

12. For more information on seasonal rounds, see Chantal Norrgard, *Seasons of Change: Labor, Treaty Rights, and Ojibwe Nationhood* (Chapel Hill: University of North Carolina Press, 2014); Brenda J. Child, "A New Seasonal Round: Government Boarding Schools, Federal Work Programs, and Ojibwe Family Life during the Great Depression," in *Enduring Nations: Native Americans in the Midwest,* ed. R. David Edmunds, 182–94 (Urbana: University of Illinois Press, 2008); Brenda J. Child, *My Grandfather's Knocking Sticks: Ojibwe Family Life and Labor on the Reservation* (St. Paul: Minnesota Historical Society Press, 2014).

13. Douglas K. Miller, *Indians on the Move: Native American Mobility and Urbanization in the Twentieth Century* (Chapel Hill: University of North Carolina Press, 2019).

14. For more on urban Indian experiences, see Miller, *Indians on the Move*; Susan Lobo and Kurt Peters, eds., *American Indians and the Urban Experience* (New York: Altamira, 2001); Donald Lee Fixico, *The Urban Indian Experience in America* (Albuquerque: University of New Mexico Press, 2000). For more on Indian urbanization in the Twin Cities, see Nancy Shoemaker, "Urban Indians and Ethnic Choices: American Indian Organizations in Minneapolis, 1920–1950," *Western Historical Quarterly* 19, no. 4 (1988): 431–47; Kasey Keeler, "Putting People Where They Belong: American Indian Housing Policy in the Mid-Twentieth Century," *Native American and Indigenous Studies* 3, no. 2 (Fall 2016): 70–104.

15. James Truslow Adams, *The Epic of America* (New York: Blue Ribbon Books, 1931), 411.

16. Matthew B. Anderson, "The Discursive Regime of the 'American Dream' and the New Suburban Frontier: The Case of Kendall County, Illinois," *Urban Geography* 31, no. 8 (2010): 1,081.

17. Kenneth Jackson, *Crabgrass Frontier: The Suburbanization of the United States* (New York: Oxford University Press, 1987), 53.

18. Jackson, *Crabgrass Frontier*, 54.

19. For more on the American Dream and racialized fear, see Anderson, "Discursive Regime of the 'American Dream'"; Jason Hackworth, *The Neoliberal City: Governance, Ideology, and Development in American Urbanization* (Ithaca, N.Y.: Cornell University Press, 2007); David Wilson and Dennis Grammenos, "Gentrification, Discourse, and the Body: Chicago's Humboldt Park," *Environment and Planning D: Society and Space* 23, no. 2 (April 2005): 295–312.

20. Anderson, "Discursive Regime of the 'American Dream,'" 1,081.

21. See Lawrence J. Vale, "The Ideological Origins of Affordable Homeownership Efforts," in *Chasing the American Dream: New Perspectives on Affordable Homeownership*, ed. William M. Rohe and Harry L. Watson, 15–40 (Ithaca, N.Y.: Cornell University Press, 2018); Laurie S. Goodman and Christopher Mayer, "Homeownership and the American Dream," *Journal of Economic Perspectives* 32, no. 1 (Winter 2018): 31–58; Anderson, "Discursive Regime of the 'American Dream.'"

22. Goodman and Mayer, "Homeownership and the American Dream," 42.

23. Anderson, "Discursive Regime of the 'American Dream,'" 1,080.

24. See Dolores Hayden, *Redesigning the American Dream: Gender, Housing, and Family Life* (New York: W. W. Norton, 2002), 210; William M. Rohe and Harry L. Watson, "Introduction: Homeownership in American Culture and Public Policy," in *Chasing the American Dream: New Perspectives on Affordable Homeownership*, ed. William M. Rohe and Harry L. Watson (Ithaca, N.Y.:

Cornell University Press, 2018), 3; Vale, "Ideological Origins of Affordable Homeownership Efforts," 15.

25. Here I am specifically referring to the work of Nicholas Rosenthal, *Reimagining Indian Country: Native American Migration and Identity in Twentieth-Century Los Angeles* (Chapel Hill: University of North Carolina Press, 2012) and James B. LaGrand, *Indian Metropolis: Native Americans in Chicago, 1945–1975* (Champaign: University of Illinois Press, 2005) but also the work of Evelyn Peters and Chris Andersen, eds., *Indigenous in the City: Contemporary Identities and Cultural Innovation* (Vancouver: University of British Columbia Press, 2013), and Renya Ramirez, *Native Hubs: Culture, Community, and Belonging in Silicon Valley and Beyond* (Durham, N.C.: Duke University Press, 2007). Earlier work on Indian urbanization includes Elaine M. Neils, *Reservation to the City: Indian Migration and Federal Relocation* (Chicago: University of Chicago Press, 1971) and Donald Fixico, *Termination and Relocation: Federal Indian Policy, 1945–1960* (Albuquerque: University of New Mexico Press, 1990).

26. Coll Thrush, *Native Seattle: Histories from the Crossing-Over Place* (Seattle: University of Washington Press, 2007).

27. This scholarship has examined suburbia and housing/homeownership as racialized projects. See Jody Vallejo, *Barrios to Burbs: The Making of the Mexican American Middle Class* (Stanford, Calif.: Stanford University Press, 2012); Leonard S. Rubinowitz and James E. Rosenbaum, *Crossing the Class and Color Lines: From Public Housing to White Suburbia* (Chicago: University of Chicago Press, 2000); Thomas J. Sugrue, *The Origins of the Urban Crisis: Race and Inequality in Postwar Detroit* (Princeton, N.J.: Princeton University Press, 2014); Robert O. Self, *American Babylon: Race and the Struggle for Postwar Oakland* (Princeton, N.J.: Princeton University Press, 2005); Andrew Wiese, *Places of Their Own: African American Suburbanization in the Twentieth Century* (Chicago: University of Chicago Press, 2005); Arnold R. Hirsch, "Less than *Plessy*: The Inner City, Suburbs, and State-Sanctioned Residential Segregation in the Age of *Brown*," in *The New Suburban History*, ed. Kevin M. Kruse and Thomas J. Sugrue (Chicago: University of Chicago Press, 2006), 33–56; Matthew Desmond, *Evicted: Poverty and Profit in the American City* (New York: Penguin Random House, 2016); Keeanga-Yamahtta Taylor, *Race for Profit: How Banks and the Real Estate Industry Undermined Black Homeownership* (Chapel Hill: University of North Carolina Press, 2019); Wendy Cheng, *The Changs Next Door to the Diazes: Remapping Race in Suburban California* (Minneapolis: University of Minnesota Press, 2013); Blomley, *Unsettling the City*.

28. For place-based settler colonial histories across the western United States and Canada, see Toews, *Stolen City*; Heather Dorries, Robert Henry, David

Hugill, Tyler McCreary, and Julie Tomiak, eds., *Settler City Limits: Indigenous Resurgence and Colonial Violence in the Urban Prairie West* (East Lansing: Michigan State University Press, 2019).

29. Kauanui, "'A Structure, Not an Event.'" Kauanui questions, "Why have few scholars taken up the question of indigeneity when it is something that implicates most aspects of American culture, politics, and society because the United States is a settler colonial state?" I build on Kauanui's discussion of settler colonialism and settler colonial studies to push back on the lack of engagement with American Indians and Indigeneity across scholarly fields.

30. See Hayden, *Redesigning the American Dream.*

31. Beginning in the late 1880s, the federal government purchased small parcels of land for the Dakota who were living in the state. As Gwen Westerman and Bruce M. White discuss in *Mni Sota Makoce: The Land of the Dakota* (St. Paul: Minnesota Historical Society Press, 2012), this land was purchased in Hastings, Birch Coulee, Prior Lake, and Prairie Island. Dakota communities that had formed at Lower Sioux and Prairie Island worked to organize in the 1930s under the 1934 Indian Reorganization Act "while an informal organization was created at Upper Sioux" by the 1880s, and today's Shakopee community was organized in 1969 at land purchased near Prior Lake (202–3).

32. Ramirez, *Native Hubs.*

33. For example, see Rosalyn R. LaPier and David M. Beck, *City Indian: Native Activism in Chicago, 1893–1934* (Lincoln: University of Nebraska Press, 2020); Rosenthal, *Reimagining Indian Country*; Myla Vicenti Carpio, *Indigenous Albuquerque* (Lubbock: Texas Tech University Press, 2011); Thrush, *Native Seattle*; Ramirez, *Native Hubs*; Bonita Lawrence, *"Real" Indians and Others: Mixed-Blood Urban Native Peoples and Indigenous Nationhood* (Lincoln: University of Nebraska Press, 2004); Toews, *Stolen City.* Importantly, Westerman and White's *Mni Sota Makoce* is an important historical and contemporary Dakota account of the Bdóte region, including the Dakota people's relationship with the land.

34. The Minneapolis–Saint Paul statistical metropolitan area in use today includes sixteen counties, two of which are in Wisconsin. This statistical area is regularly updated based on U.S. Census data on population.

35. For more on my use of space in relation to American Indian people, history, and spatial understandings, see Lisa Brooks, *The Common Pot: The Recovery of Native Space in the Northeast* (Minneapolis: University of Minnesota Press, 2008); Mishauna Goeman, *Mark My Words: Native Women Mapping Our Nations* (Minneapolis: University of Minnesota Press, 2013).

36. I base my use of place on Yi-Fu Tuan, *Space and Place: The Perspective of Experience* (Minneapolis: University of Minnesota Press, 2001).

37. Malinda Maynor Lowery, *Lumbee Indians in the Jim Crow South: Race, Identity, and the Making of a Nation* (Chapel Hill: University of North Carolina Press, 2010), xvi.

38. Established in March 2000, the Minnesota Population Center (MPC) is a University of Minnesota research center established by the vice president for research that houses extensive and diverse demographic data from sources including the U.S. Census and international censes. Steven Ruggles, Sarah Flood, Sophia Foster, Ronald Goeken, Jose Pacas, Megan Schouweiler, and Matthew Sobek, IPUMS USA: Version 11.0, Minneapolis, Minn., 2021, https://doi.org/10.18128/D010.V11.0.

39. The federal government protects individual census data for seventy years to ensure data privacy and to protect identity.

40. Microdata, as defined by the Minnesota Population Center, are composed of individual records containing information collected on persons and households. The unit of observation is the individual. The responses of each person to the different census questions are recorded in separate variables. Microdata stand in contrast to more familiar summary or aggregate data. Aggregate data are compiled statistics, such as a table of marital status by sex for some locality. There are no such tabular or summary statistics in the IPUMS data. Microdata are inherently flexible. One need not depend on published statistics from a census that compiled the data in a certain way, if at all. Users can generate their own statistics from the data in any manner desired, including individual-level multivariate analysis.

41. An Act to Provide for Taking the Tenth and Subsequent Censuses (Census Act), Pub. L. No. 45-195, § 3, 20 Stat. 473 (1879).

42. For more on American Indians in the census and American Indian populations, see Chris Andersen and Maggie Waltner, *Indigenous Statistics: A Quantitative Research Methodology* (New York: Routledge, 2013); Joane Nagel, *American Indian Ethnic Renewal: Red Power and the Resurgence of Identity and Culture* (New York: Oxford University Press, 1997); Nancy Shoemaker, *American Indian Population Recovery in the Twentieth Century* (Albuquerque: University of New Mexico Press, 2000); Carolyn Liebler, "Counting America's First Peoples," *Annals of the American Academy of Political and Social Science* 677, no. 1 (2018): 180–90; Carolyn A. Liebler, "Homelands and Indigenous Identities in a Multiracial Era," *Social Science Research* 34, no. 4 (2010): 596–609; Carolyn A. Liebler and Meghan Zacher, "History, Place, and Racial Self-Representation in 21st Century America," *Social Science Research* 57, no. 11 (2016): 211–32.

43. Miller, *Indians on the Move*.

44. I do not include the Native American Direct Loan, a home loan program begun in 1992, for American Indian veterans here as it is limited to American Indian veterans and the American Indian spouses of veterans.

1. Land of Loss and Survival

A note on Dakota language and translations: I am forever grateful to Dawí Huhá Máza (Iron Limbs) for his knowledge of the Dakota language and for helping me with translations. He is a kind and generous human. I have incorporated Dakota throughout this chapter to remind readers that Mnísota Makhóčhe remains an Indian place. Any errors with the language and translations are mine alone.

1. Gary Clayton Anderson and Alan R. Woolworth, eds., *Through Dakota Eyes: Narrative Accounts of the Minnesota Indian War of 1862* (St. Paul: Minnesota Historical Society Press, 1988), 63. See also, "Preserving Faribault's Past," Faribault Heritage Preservation Commission, accessed August 2021, http://faribaulthpc.org/people-index/; "US Dakota War of 1862," Minnesota Historical Society, accessed March 2020, https://www.usdakotawar.org/history /taopi.

2. For more on the concept of firsting and lasting, see Jean O'Brien, *Firsting and Lasting: Writing Indians Out of Existence in New England* (Minneapolis: University of Minnesota Press, 2010).

3. O'Brien, *Firsting and Lasting.*

4. See Gwen Westerman and Bruce White, *Mni Sota Makoce: The Land of the Dakota* (St. Paul: Minnesota Historical Society Press, 2012).

5. Westerman and White, *Mni Sota Makoce,* 140.

6. For more on Fort Snelling, see Peter DeCarlo, *Fort Snelling at Bdote: A Brief History* (St. Paul: Minnesota Historical Society Press, 2020).

7. For more on these treaties, see Westerman and White, *Mni Sota Makoce.*

8. Westerman and White; Clifford Canku, *The Dakota Prisoner of War Letters: Dakota Kaskapi Okicize Wawapi* (St. Paul: Minnesota Historical Society Press, 2013); Christopher J. Pexa, "Transgressive Adoptions: Dakota Prisoner's Resistances to State Domination Following the 1862 US-Dakota War," *Wicazō Ṡa Review* 30, no. 1 (April 2015): 29–56.

9. An Act to Abrogate and Annul Treaties with the Dakota Nation, ch. 37, 12 Stat. 652 (1863).

10. Winnebago Removal Act, ch. 53, 12 Stat. 658 (1863).

11. Dakota Removal Act, ch. 119, 12 Stat. 819 (1863).

12. Roger D. Billings, "The Homestead Act, the Pacific Railroad Act, and the Morrill Act," *Northern Kentucky Law Review* 39, no. 4 (2012): 700.

13. Mary Ellen Snodgrass, *The Civil War Era and Reconstruction: An Encyclopedia of Social, Political, Cultural, and Economic History* (New York: Routledge, 2015), 467.

14. Billings, "Homestead Act, the Pacific Railroad Act, and the Morrill Act," 706.

15. Morrill Land-Grant Act of 1862, Pub. L. No. 37-108, 12 Stat. 503 (1862) (codified as 7 U.S.C. § 301 et seq).

16. Robert Lee and Tristan Ahtone, "Land Grant Universities: Expropriated Indigenous Land Is the Foundation of the Land-Grant University System," *High Country News,* March 30, 2020, https://www.hcn.org/issues/52.4/indigenous-affairs-education-land-grab-universities.

17. Lee and Ahtone, "Land Grant Universities."

18. Lee and Ahtone.

19. Morrill Land-Grant Act of 1862.

20. In 1994, President Bill Clinton signed the Equity in Educational Land-Grant Status Act (H.R. 4806, 103rd Cong.). This piece of legislation is broadly known as the 1994 Land-Grant Act. This legislation designated tribal colleges and universities across the United States as land-grant institutions. The act set aside a one-time amount of $23 million to fund endowments at the twenty-nine tribal colleges and universities, to be divided among them. This is significant when considered along with the dispossession of Indian land that would fund the 1862 Morrill Act and the role of agriculture across tribal and reservation communities. In addition to the 1862 Morrill Act, a second Morrill Act was passed in 1890 that led to the creation and funding of seventeen colleges and universities for Black people; today these institutions are part of the larger historically Black colleges and universities system in the United States. See Second Morrill Act of 1890, 26 Stat. 417 (1890) (codified as 7 U.S.C. § 321).

21. Harold M. Hyman, *American Singularity: The 1787 Northwest Ordinance, the 1862 Homestead and Morrill Acts, and the 1944 G.I. Bill* (Athens: University of Georgia Press, 2008), 36.

22. Homestead Act, 12 Stat. 392 (1862).

23. Greg Bradsher, "How the West Was Settled: The 150-Year-Old Homestead Act Lured Americans Looking for a New Life and New Opportunities," *Prologue* 44 no. 4 (Winter 2012): 27.

24. Similarly, the General Land Office, who issued the eventual Homestead land patents, also did not collect information on a Homestead applicant's race. Thus, we are left to piece together information on race, largely based on citizenship, from a number of sources. However, significant records exist that remind who was not a citizen of the United States and therefore ineligible for the Homestead Act.

25. "Homesteading by the Numbers," National Park Service, accessed February 2020, https://www.nps.gov/home/learn/historyculture/bynumbers.htm.

26. See chapter 2. For more on American Indian citizenship, see Cathleen Cahill, "'Our Democracy and the American Indian': Citizenship, Sovereignty, and the Native Vote in the 1920s," *Journal of Women's History* 32, no. 1 (2020): 41–51; K. Tsianina Lomawaima, "The Mutuality of Citizenship and Sovereignty: The Society of American Indians and the Battle to Inherit America," *American Indian Quarterly* 37, no. 3 (2013): 331–51.

27. While American Indians were not explicitly excluded from accessing land through the Homestead Act, it was not intended for their use. In recent years, a number of scholars and community members have begun to examine the ways Native people, often "mixed bloods," actively used the Homestead Act to secure land outside of reservations.

28. For more on Allotment and racialized land policies, see David A. Chang, *The Color of the Land: Race, Nation, and the Politics of Landownership in Oklahoma, 1832–1929* (Chapel Hill: University of North Carolina Press, 2010); C. Joseph Genetin-Pilawa, *Crooked Paths to Allotment: The Fight over Federal Indian Policy after the Civil War* (Chapel Hill: University of North Carolina Press, 2012); Rose Stremlau, *Allotment, Jim Crow, and the State: Reconceptualizing the Privatization of Land, the Segregation of Bodies, and the Politicization of Sexuality in the Native South* (Lincoln: University of Nebraska Press, 2017).

29. Aileen Moreton-Robinson, *The White Possessive: Property, Power, and Indigenous Sovereignty* (Minneapolis: University of Minnesota Press, 2015), xix. See also Cheryl Harris, "Whiteness as Property," special issue, *Harvard Law Review* 106, no. 8 (1993).

30. Billings, "Homestead Act, the Pacific Railroad Act, and the Morrill Act," 713.

31. Richard Edwards, Jacob K. Friefeld, and Mikal Brotnov, "Canaan on the Prairie: New Evidence on the Number of African American Homesteaders in the Great Plains," *Great Plains Quarterly* 39, no. 3 (Summer 2019): 224, 236.

32. Homestead Act, § 2.

33. Homestead Act.

34. For more on trust land and access to home loans, see chapter 5. For more on reservation trust status and housing, see Kristen A. Carpenter and Angela R. Riley, "Privatizing the Reservation?" *Stanford Law Review* 71 no. 4 (2019): 791–878; Jessica A. Shoemaker, "Transforming Property: Reclaiming Indigenous Land Tenures," *California Law Review* 107 no. 5 (2019): 1,531–607.

35. These specific terms were used on the 1900 and 1910 U.S. Census "Special Inquiries Relating to Indians" to describe the "dwellings" that Indian people lived in. This information was gathered exclusively on Indian people.

In 1900 the question enumerators were to ask, "Is this Indian living in a fixed or in a moveable dwelling?" In 1910 the question was "Is this Indian living in a civilized or aboriginal dwelling?"

36. Much of Neill's archival collections are accessible at the Minnesota Historical Society and Macalester College, both located in Saint Paul, Minnesota.

37. Edward D. Neill, *History of the Minnesota Valley, Including the Explorers and Pioneers of Minnesota* (Minneapolis: North Star Publishing, 1882).

38. O'Brien, *Firsting and Lasting.*

39. Henry Sibley arrived at Mendota in 1834 to take over management of the regional American Fur Company post, becoming a prominent fur trader and establishing significant ties to the Dakota community. Sibley would go on to serve in Congress, become the first governor of the state of Minnesota in 1858, and serve as a U.S. general during the U.S.–Dakota War in 1862, infamously leading the charge to "quell" the violence.

40. "Mendota: Walking in the Foot Steps of History," City of Mendota, accessed September 2020, http://www.cityofmendota.org/donations.html.

41. Edward Fleming, James Almendinger, Joshua Anderson, Taylor Brehm, Jasmine Koncur, and Jason Ulrich, *An Archaeological Survey of Dakota County, Minnesota* (St. Paul: Department of Anthropology and Saint Croix Watershed Research Station and the Science Museum of Minnesota, 2018), 109.

42. Westerman and White, *Mni Sota Makoce,* 20.

43. Edward D. Neill, *History of Dakota County and the City of Hastings, Including the Explorers and Pioneers of Minnesota* (Minneapolis: North Star Publishing, 1881), 511.

44. Neill, *History of Dakota County and the City of Hastings,* 512.

45. See O'Brien, *Firsting and Lasting.* Like the practice of firsting, the use of language such as *last* deliberately works to terminate an Indian presence and thereby allows for non-Native claims to space. Further, the use of this rhetoric keeps Indian people in the past and does not allow for participation in the present.

46. Westerman and White, *Mni Sota Makoce,* 125.

47. The village of Shakopee withdrew its charter in 1861 due to conflicts with the Dakota in the lead up to the U.S.–Dakota War. The village reincorporated again after the war in 1870.

48. Edward D. Neill, *History of Hennepin County and the City of Minneapolis: Including the Explorers and Pioneers of Minnesota* (Minneapolis: North Star Publishing, 1881), 232, 330.

49. For more information on Indian women's work and gendered labor, see Brenda Child, *Holding Our World Together: Ojibwe Women and the Survival of Community* (New York: Penguin Books, 2013).

50. U.S. Census Bureau, *Scott County, Minnesota, Indian Population, Sha-kopee City* (1900), 21.

51. Here, the term *ration Indian* is used to describe an American Indian person who relied on the federal government food distribution program. In the mid-1880s the federal government began to issue ration tickets to American Indian people, often those who lived on reservation, who would then exchange those tickets for food items. This eventually became more recognizable as the Commodity Supplemental Food Program. U.S. Census Bureau, *Scott County, Minnesota, Indian Population, Shakopee City* (1900), 21.

52. Westerman and White, *Mni Sota Makoce,* 126. Thitháŋka Thaŋnína is recognized as the first Dakota village on the Minnesota River and dates back hundreds of years.

53. Neill, *History of Hennepin County,* 225. Born in Ireland circa 1791, Peter Quinn arrived in Bloomington around 1843. He served as an Indian interpreter at Fort Snelling and married an Ojibwe woman (Angeline Quinn) with whom he had seven children. He died during the U.S.–Dakota War while serving as a Dakota interpreter for Captain Marsh.

54. Neill, *History of Hennepin County,* 231.

55. Neill, 232.

56. Neill, 232.

57. Neill, 232.

58. Neill, 238.

59. Similar to Neill, Albert M. Goodrich was a white man who wrote many place-based histories of the Twin Cities region. See Albert M. Goodrich, *History of Anoka County and the Town of Champlin and Dayton in Hennepin County, Minnesota* (Minneapolis: Hennepin Publishing, 1905).

60. Goodrich, *History of Anoka County,* 52–53.

61. Coll Thrush, *Native Seattle: Histories from the Crossing-Over Place* (Seattle: University of Washington Press, 2007), 76.

2. Pivotal Policies

1. The Pembina Band of Ojibwe historically lived along the Red River of the North and its tributaries, just to the west of the present-day boundary of the White Earth Reservation. Today, descendants of the Pembina Band are tribal members of Ojibwe communities in Minnesota, North Dakota, Montana, and Manitoba because of land cessions, treaties, and removal.

2. The Gruettes' movement away from White Earth and to the metropoli-tan Twin Cities should also be considered part of the longer history of removal from traditional homelands to the White Earth Reservation. Established as a

reservation by an 1867 treaty, White Earth was intended to be the reservation home for Ojibwe peoples from Michigan, Wisconsin, and Minnesota. At the time of the 1920 federal census, Mississippi, Pillager, Pembina, Superior, and Fond du Lac Bands of Ojibwe were present. For a more detailed Ojibwe history, see William Warren, *History of the Ojibway People* (St. Paul: Minnesota Historical Society Press, 2009).

3. See chapter 1.

4. Kenneth Jackson, *Crabgrass Frontier: The Suburbanization of the United States* (New York: Oxford University Press, 1987), 11.

5. See Douglas K. Miller, *Indians on the Move: Native American Mobility and Urbanization in the Twentieth Century* (Chapel Hill: University of North Carolina Press, 2019); Nicholas Rosenthal, *Reimagining Indian Country: Native American Migration and Identity in Twentieth-Century Los Angeles* (Chapel Hill: University of North Carolina Press, 2012).

6. See Brenda J. Child, "A New Seasonal Round: Government Boarding Schools, Federal Work Programs, and Ojibwe Family Life during the Great Depression," in *Enduring Nations: Native Americans in the Midwest,* ed. R. David Edmunds, 182–94 (Urbana: University of Illinois Press, 2008); Brenda J. Child, *My Grandfather's Knocking Sticks: Ojibwe Family Life and Labor on the Reservation* (St. Paul: Minnesota Historical Society Press, 2014); Chantal Norrgard, *Seasons of Change: Labor, Treaty Rights, and Ojibwe Nationhood* (Chapel Hill: University of North Carolina Press, 2014).

7. Louis Gruette Death Certificate, April 23, 1938, Minnesota Historical Society Death Certificate Index; Mary Gruette Death Certificate, January 2, 1976, Minnesota Historical Society Death Certificate Index. The Gull Lake Band of Ojibwe is a sub-band of the Mississippi Chippewa. Prior to moving to White Earth, the Gull Lake Indian Reservation and community was located to the west of Mille Lacs Lake, near present-day Brainerd in north-central Minnesota.

8. Philip J. Deloria, *Indians in Unexpected Places* (Lawrence: University Press of Kansas, 2004), 168.

9. Jodi Larson, Kyle Engelking, and Karen Majewicz, *The Story of the Suburbs in Anoka and Hennepin Counties* (Anoka, Minn.: Anoka County Historical Society, 2011), 16.

10. Deloria, *Indians in Unexpected Places,* 153.

11. Melissa L. Meyer, *The White Earth Tragedy: Ethnicity and Dispossession at a Minnesota Anishinaabe Reservation, 1889–1920* (Lincoln: University of Nebraska Press, 1999).

12. David E. Wilkins and K. Tsianina Lomawaima, *Uneven Ground: American Indian Sovereignty and Federal Law* (Norman: University of Oklahoma

Press, 2002), 71–72; Felix S. Cohen, *Handbook of Federal Indian Law* (1941), 237, Native American Constitution and Law Digitization Project, accessed October 2022, https://thorpe.law.ou.edu/cohen.html.

13. My focus is exclusively on the Snyder Act of 1921. The subsequent 1924 Snyder Act is widely recognized and associated with the Indian Citizenship Act. To distinguish between the two, I exclusively refer to the 1921 Snyder Act as such and the 1924 Indian Citizenship Act as such.

14. Snyder Act, 25 U.S.C. §13 (1921) (emphasis added).

15. Treaty with the Winnebago, art. 3 and 5, February 27, 1855, 10 Stat. 1172 (ratified March 3, 1855, proclaimed March 23, 1855).

16. Treaty with the Winnebago, art. 2, April 15, 1859, 12 Stat. 1101 (ratified March 16, 1861, proclaimed March 23, 1861).

17. Wilkins and Lomawaima, *Uneven Ground,* 71.

18. Wilkins and Lomawaima, 72.

19. U.S. Commission on Civil Rights, *A Quiet Crisis: Federal Funding and Unmet Needs in Indian Country* (Washington, D.C.: July 2003), 18.

20. Cohen, *Handbook of Federal Indian Law,* 237 (emphasis added).

21. Paul C. Luken and Suzanne Vaughan, "'. . . Be a Genuine Homemaker in Your Own Home': Gender and Familial Relations in State Housing Practices, 1917–1922," *Social Forces* 83, no. 4 (June 2005): 1,607.

22. "'Own Your Own Home' Campaign Plans Announced," *American Architect* 115, no. 2,257 (March 26, 1919): 466, https://archive.org/details/americanarchite115newyuoft/page/466/mode/2up.

23. Luken and Vaughan, "'. . . Be a Genuine Homemaker in Your Own Home," 1,607.

24. Indian Citizenship Act, 43 Stat. 253 (1924). Prior to the 1924 Indian Citizenship Act, Indian people were able to access U.S. citizenship on a piecemeal basis. For example, American Indian veterans of World War I were granted U.S. citizenship for their military service; American Indians who had allotments and maintained them for the requisite number of years (often twenty-five) were also granted U.S. citizenship based on their assumed level of assimilation by measurement of financial capability. See Frederick E. Hoxie, *A Final Promise: The Campaign to Assimilate the Indians, 1880–1920* (Lincoln: University of Nebraska Press, 2001); Melissa Nobles, *Shades of Citizenship: Race and the Census in Modern Politics* (Stanford, Calif.: Stanford University Press, 2000); Circe Sturm, *Blood Politics: Race, Culture, and Identity in the Cherokee Nation of Oklahoma* (Los Angeles: University of California Press, 2002).

25. Kevin Bruyneel, "Challenging American Boundaries: Indigenous People and the 'Gift' of US Citizenship," *Studies in American Political Development* 18 (Spring 2004): 32–33.

26. For more on American Indian voting in South Dakota and Arizona, see the following court cases: Rosebud Sioux Tribe v. Barnett (2022) and Brnovich v. Democratic National Committee 594 U.S. (2021).

27. Institute for Government Research, *The Problem of Indian Administration* (Baltimore: Johns Hopkins Press, 1928), 3, https://narf.org/nill/documents/merriam/b_meriam_letter.pdf (hereafter referred to as the Meriam Report).

28. Meriam Report, 4.

29. Meriam Report, 729–32.

30. Meriam Report, 732.

31. Pauline Brunette Danforth, "The Minneapolis Urban Indian Community," *Hennepin County History* 49, no. 1 (Winter 1989–1990): 5.

32. Franklin D. Roosevelt, "Message to Congress on the Objectives and Accomplishments of the Administration," June 8, 1934, American Presidency Project, accessed March 2021, https://www.presidency.ucsb.edu/documents/message-congress-the-objectives-and-accomplishments-the-administration (emphasis added).

33. Roosevelt, "Message to Congress."

34. Alice Kehoe, *A Passion for the True and Just: Felix and Lucy Kramer Cohen and the Indian New Deal* (Tucson: University of Arizona Press, 2014), 30.

35. Johnson-O'Malley Act, 25 U.S.C. § 5342 (1934), 596.

36. Senator Burton Wheeler of Montana and Congressman Edgar Howard of Nebraska were the act's legislative cosponsors and namesakes. Indian Reorganization Act, more formally known as the Howard-Wheeler Act, 48 Stat. 984, 25 U.S.C. (1934).

37. Kehoe, *Passion for the True and Just*, 9, 26.

38. For more on Indian land tenure, see Lisa Brooks, *The Common Pot: The Recovery of Native Space in the Northeast* (Minneapolis: University of Minnesota Press, 2008).

39. Johnson & Graham's Lessee v. McIntosh, 21 U.S. 543 (1823).

40. Also known as "fee to trust" land acquisitions. This process is overseen by the Bureau of Indian Affairs. For more on this process, see Department of the Interior, Bureau of Indian Affairs, Office of Trust Services, "Acquisition of Title to Land Held in Fee or Restricted Fee Status (Fee-to-Trust Handbook)" (version 4, issued June 28, 2016).

41. Carcieri v. Salazar, 555 U.S. 379 (2009). In this court case, the Supreme Court held that the federal government may not place land into trust for tribes who were not federally recognized at the time of the 1934 Indian Reorganization Act. In recent years there have been significant efforts to address this issue, known as the Carcieri fix, including the introduction of federal legislation (which has not been passed as law at the time of this writing).

42. Kehoe, *Passion for the True and Just*, 32.

43. In operation between 1932 and 1957, the Reconstruction Finance Corporation made loans and provided financial support in the wake of the Great Depression. Designed to promote confidence in lending and spending, this agency of the federal government was in operation between the New Deal era through WWII. The Federal Home Loan Bank Act, 48 Stat. 1246 (1934), served to make homeownership more affordable by creating the Federal Home Loan Bank Board and Federal Home Loan Banks that worked to create credit reserves and increase the supply of credit in the housing market.

44. National Housing Act, 48 Stat. 1246 (1934).

45. Jackson, *Crabgrass Frontier*, 203.

46. See the United States Federal Housing Administration, *Underwriting Manual: Underwriting and Valuation Procedure Under Title II of the National Housing Act* (Washington, D.C.: Government Printing Offices, 1936).

47. For more information on FHA lending practices and redlining, see Jackson, *Crabgrass Frontier*; Richard Rothstein, *The Color of the Law* (New York: Liveright Publishing, 2017).

48. James W. Loewen, *Sundown Towns: A Hidden Dimension of American Racism* (New York: Touchstone, 2005), 7, 23, 116. See also Hennepin County Deed Book 1235, page 261, November 21, 1930, Hennepin County Government Center, Minneapolis.

49. Kevin Fox Gotham, "Racialization and the State: The Housing Act of 1934 and the Creation of the Federal Housing Administration," *Sociological Perspectives* 43, no. 2 (Summer 2000): 300.

50. Shelley v. Kraemer, 334 U.S. 1 (1948).

51. Hurd v. Hodge, 334 U.S. 24 (1948).

52. Alison R. Bernstein, *American Indians and World War II: Toward a New Era in Indian Affairs* (Norman: University of Oklahoma Press, 1999), 164. See also Hurd v. Hodge, fn76.

53. Suzanne Mettler, *Soldiers to Citizens: The G.I. Bill and the Making of the Greatest Generation* (New York: Oxford University Press, 2007), cited by Patricia Kelly Hall, "Privileged Moves: Migration, Race, and Veteran Status in Post-World War II America" (PhD diss., University of Minnesota, 2009).

54. For an example of a restrictive covenant, see Hennepin County Deed Book 1235.

55. Institute on Metropolitan Opportunity, "Twin Cities in Crisis: Unequal Treatment of Communities of Color in Mortgage Lending" (Minneapolis: University of Minnesota Law School, 2014).

56. U.S. Housing Act, 50 Stat. 888 (1937).

57. George Lipsitz, *The Possessive Investment in Whiteness: How People Profit from Identity Politics* (Philadelphia: Temple University Press, 2006), 373.

58. Matthew B. Anderson, "The Discursive Regime of the 'American Dream' and the New Suburban Frontier: The Case of Kendall County, Illinois," *Urban Geography* 31, no. 8 (2010): 1,081.

59. Anderson, "Discursive Regime of the 'American Dream,'" 1,090.

3. "We Must Do This Ourselves"

1. This is a pseudonym used to protect the identity of the individuals whose Relocation records I accessed at the National Archives, as the required seventy-five years had not elapsed. I continue to use pseudonyms for each individual whose Relocation records I discuss in this chapter and accessed at the National Archives in Kansas City. According to the Department of Commerce, the median household income for all families in the United States in 1953 was $4,200. If Owens worked the entire year at this pay, his annual income would be $4,680. U.S. Census, *Current Population Reports: Consumer Income* (Washington, D.C.: U.S. Government Publishing Office, 1955), 2.

2. Minneapolis Area Office, Records of the Bureau of Indian Affairs, RG 75, series 5, National Archives at Kansas City.

3. Minneapolis Area Office, Records of the Bureau of Indian Affairs, RG 75.

4. Minneapolis Area Office, RG 75.

5. Minneapolis Area Office, RG 75.

6. Alison R. Bernstein, *American Indians and World War II: Toward a New Era in Indian Affairs* (Norman: University of Oklahoma Press, 1999), 24.

7. Servicemen's Readjustment Act, 58 Stat. 284 (1944).

8. See chapter 2. Housing Act, 63 Stat. 413 (1949).

9. Alexander von Hoffman, "A Study in Contradictions: The Origins and Legacy of the Housing Act of 1949," *Housing Policy Debate* 11, no. 2 (2000): 299.

10. Arnold R. Hirsch, "'Containment' on the Home Front: Race and Federal Housing Policy from the New Deal to the Cold War," *Journal of Urban History* 26 no. 2 (2000): 158.

11. Hirsch, "'Containment' on the Home Front," 163.

12. President Truman established the Hoover Commission, more formally known as the Commission on Organization of the Executive Branch of the Government. The Hoover Commission receives its name from former President Herbert Hoover, whom President Truman appointed to lead it. The commission was one of two bodies in existence between 1947–1949 and 1953–1955

that were charged with reducing and consolidating the number of federal departments while simultaneously increasing their operational capacity post–World War II and post–Korean War. Upon completion, it was estimated that the recommended eliminations and consolidations would save the federal government billions of dollars.

13. Kenneth R. Philp, *Termination Revisited: American Indians on the Trail to Self-Determination, 1933–1953* (Lincoln: University of Nebraska Press, 2002), 68. For a discussion of McCarthy-era emphasis on conformity, see Ned Blackhawk, "I Can Carry On from Here: The Relocation of American Indians to Los Angeles," *Wicazō Ša Review* 11, no. 2 (Fall 1995): 16–30.

14. Philp, *Termination Revisited,* 68; Vine Deloria Jr. and Clifford M. Lytle, *The Nations Within: The Past and Future of American Indian Sovereignty* (Austin: University of Texas Press, 2006), 192.

15. Termination Act, H.R. Con. Res. 108, 67 Stat. (1953); Relocation Act, ch. 930, Pub. L. No. 84-959, 70 Stat. 986 (1956).

16. For more information on Termination Policy, see Philp, *Termination Revisited*; Donald L. Fixico, *Termination and Relocation: Federal Indian Policy, 1945–1960* (Albuquerque: University of New Mexico Press, 1990); Brian Hosmer, ed., *The Native American Legacy of Harry S. Truman* (Kirksville, Mo.: Truman State University Press, 2010); Roberta Ulrich, *American Indian Nations from Termination to Restoration, 1953–2006* (Lincoln: University of Nebraska Press, 2010).

17. Today, more than fifty years after Termination was officially ended, much of this land has yet to be recovered by tribal governments. "Termination," Indian Land Tenure Foundation, accessed March 2019, https://www .iltf.org/land-issues/termination. See also Ulrich, *American Indian Nations from Termination to Restoration.*

18. See Nicholas Peroff, *Menominee Drums: Tribal Termination and Restoration, 1954–1974* (Norman: University of Oklahoma Press, 2006).

19. Blackhawk, "I Can Carry On from Here," 18.

20. Relocation field offices were located in Chicago, Los Angeles, Dallas, San Francisco, Denver, San Jose, Cleveland, Saint Louis, and Cincinnati.

21. Chicago Field Employment Assistance Office, Records on Employment Assistance, 1951–1958, folder 1, Placement Statistical Report, February 1952, National Archives, Chicago.

22. Donald Fixico, *The Urban Indian Experience in America* (Albuquerque: University of New Mexico Press, 2000), 13.

23. Gregory W. Craig, Arthur M. Harkins, and Richard G. Woods, *Indian Housing in Minneapolis and Saint Paul* (Minneapolis: University of Minnesota, 1969).

24. Minnesota Governor's Human Rights Commission, *The Indian in Minnesota: A Report to Governor Luther W. Youngdahl of Minnesota by the Governor's Interracial Commission* (Saint Paul), April 1, 1947.

25. Bernstein, *American Indians and World War II,* 169.

26. Minneapolis Area Office, Records of the Bureau of Indian Affairs, RG 75.

27. Minneapolis Area Office, RG 75.

28. Michael J. Bennett, *When Dreams Came True: The GI Bill and the Making of Modern America* (Dulles, Va.: Potomac Books, 1999), 26.

29. See chapter 2; Shelley v. Kraemer, 334 U.S. 1 (1948).

30. "Helen Lightfoot in the 1940 United States Federal Census," Ancestry, accessed June 2016, http://www.ancestry.com.

31. Hennepin County Deed Book 1235, page 261, November 21, 1930, Hennepin County Government Center, Minneapolis.

32. Hennepin County Deed Book 1235, 261.

33. Association on American Indian Affairs, "The American Indian Relocation Program: A Report Undertaken with the Assistance of the Field Foundation, Inc." (New York, December 1956).

34. Kenneth R. Philp, "Stride toward Freedom: The Relocation of Indians to Cities, 1952–1960," *Western Historical Quarterly* 16, no. 2 (April 1985): 175–90.

35. Association on American Indian Affairs, "American Indian Relocation Program."

36. Minneapolis Area Office, Records of the Bureau of Indian Affairs, RG 75.

37. Minneapolis Area Office, RG 75.

38. Here I am specifically referring to land held in trust on reservation and the inability to use that land as collateral to secure a home loan.

39. Institute on Metropolitan Opportunity, "Twin Cities in Crisis: Unequal Treatment of Communities of Color in Mortgage Lending," (Minneapolis: University of Minnesota Law School, 2014).

40. Cathleen D. Cahill, *Federal Fathers and Mothers: A Social History of the United States Indian Service, 1869–1933* (Chapel Hill: University of North Carolina Press, 2011), 6.

41. Brenda Child, *Boarding School Seasons: American Indian Families, 1900–1940* (Lincoln: University of Nebraska Press, 2000); K. Tsianina Lomawaima, *They Called It Prairie Light: The Story of Chilocco Indian School* (Lincoln: University of Nebraska Press, 1995).

42. For more on the domestic ideals of the Cold War, government surveillance, and McCarthyism, see Elaine Tyler May, *Homeward Bound: American Families in the Cold War Era* (New York: Basic Books, 2008).

43. For more on blood quantum and statistical extermination, see Norbert S. Hill and Kathleen Ratteree, eds., *The Great Vanishing Act: Blood Quantum and the Future of Native Nations* (Wheat Ridge, Colo.: Fulcrum Publishing, 2017); Kim TallBear, *Native American DNA: Tribal Belonging and the False Promise of Genetic Science* (Minneapolis: University of Minnesota Press, 2013).

44. Minneapolis Area Office, Records of the Bureau of Indian Affairs, RG 75.

45. Minneapolis Area Office RG 75.

46. Minneapolis Area Office, RG 75.

47. Minneapolis Area Office, RG 75.

48. Minneapolis Area Office, RG 75.

49. Minneapolis Area Office, RG 75.

50. Minneapolis Area Office, RG 75.

51. Minneapolis Area Office, RG 75.

52. Bennett, *When Dreams Came True,* 24.

53. Kenneth Jackson, *Crabgrass Frontier: The Suburbanization of the United States* (New York: Oxford University Press), 206.

54. Fixico, *Urban Indian Experience in America.*

55. For more about the erasure and replacement of Indian place histories, see Coll Thrush, *Native Seattle: Histories from the Crossing-Over Place* (Seattle: University of Washington Press, 2007).

56. Chicago American Indian Oral History Project Records, 1982–1985, Ayer Modern MS Oral History, Newberry Library, Chicago.

4. Intersections of Responsibility

1. "History of Little Earth," Robert G. Style, accessed July 2020, http://robertgstyle.com/writing/leinside1.pdf.

2. See chapter 3.

3. Governor's Human Rights Commission, *Minnesota's Indian Citizens: Yesterday and Today* (St. Paul: State of Minnesota, 1965).

4. See chapter 1.

5. See K. Tsianina Lomawaima, "The Mutuality of Citizenship and Sovereignty: The Society of American Indians and the Battle to Inherit America," *American Indian Quarterly* 37, no. 3 (Summer 2013): 333–51.

6. "Housing Planned on Old South High Site," *Minneapolis Tribune,* February 3, 1971; "Committee to Develop Site," *Minneapolis Star,* February 3, 1971.

7. The Model Cities program was a component of Lyndon B. Johnson's Great Society and War on Poverty programs of the mid-1960s. Though it was

short-lived (it ended in the early 1970s), the Model Cities program funneled federal HUD housing/antipoverty funds directly to local governments, as a reform of earlier housing programs. The aims of the Model Cities program were citizen participation, rehabilitation, and social service delivery.

8. "Our Community," Little Earth, accessed January 2021, https://little earth.org/.

9. "Community Center Joins Indian-Inspired Project," *Minneapolis Tribune,* December 16, 1973, F13.

10. "Our Community," Little Earth, accessed January 2021, https://little earth.org/.

11. "AIM Group to Run Housing Project," *Minneapolis Star,* March 5, 1975.

12. "AIM Group to Run Housing Project."

13. "AIM Group to Run Housing Project."

14. "AIM Group to Run Housing Project."

15. "New Management Reports Progress at South High Housing Development," *Minneapolis Tribune,* June 2, 1975.

16. Heidi Kiiwetinepinesiik Stark, associate professor of political science at University of Victoria, personal communication, January 2, 2017; Matthew Fletcher, "The Original Understanding of the Political Status of Indian Tribes," *St. John's Law Review* (Winter 2008): 153–81.

17. For more on AIM, see Paul Chaat Smith and Robert Allen Warrior, *Like a Hurricane: The Indian Movement from Alcatraz to Wounded Knee* (New York: New Press, 1997).

18. Julie L. Davis, *Survival Schools: The American Indian Movement and Community Education in the Twin Cities* (Minneapolis: University of Minnesota Press, 2013), 6.

19. See Davis, *Survival Schools.*

20. Housing and Urban Development Act, H.R. 7984, Pub. L. No. 89-117, 79 Stat. 451 (1965).

21. For more on the National Housing Act of 1934, see chapter 2.

22. "Indian Housing in the US—A History," RG 220, "Indian Housing," National Archives and Records Administration, College Park, Maryland.

23. "Indian Housing in the US," RG 220.

24. As amended, the U.S. Housing Act states, "Title II of the United States Housing Act of 1937 established low-income housing programs for Indians and Alaska Natives. Title II was repealed by section 501(a) of the Native American Housing Assistance and Self-Determination Act of 1996 (Public Law 104–330)."

25. A tribally designated housing entity is a tribal housing authority established under the U.S. Housing Act of 1937 or is an entity that is authorized by a tribal government (or governments) to receive grants and to provide housing assistance. The Housing Improvement Program continues to be administered by the BIA.

26. Housing and Urban Development Act, Pub. L. No. 90-448 [S.3497] (1968).

27. Committee on Interior and Insular Affairs, "Indian Housing in the United States: A Staff Report on the Indian Housing Effort in the United States with Selected Appendixes," prepared at the request of Henry M. Jackson, Chairman, United States Senate (February 1975), 17–18.

28. "American Indian Policy Review Commission: Final Report," Washington, D.C., submitted to Congress May 17, 1977, 32.

29. "American Indian Policy Review Commission," 248.

30. "American Indian Policy Review Commission," 248.

31. These regional offices currently include: Alaska Region (Alaska); Northwest Region (Washington, Oregon, Idaho); Southwest Region (California, Nevada, Arizona, New Mexico); Northern Plains Region (Montana, North Dakota, South Dakota, Wyoming, Nevada, Utah, Colorado); Southern Plains Region (Missouri, Kansas, Oklahoma, Arkansas, Texas, Louisiana); and Eastern/Woodlands Region (all states east of the Mississippi River, plus Minnesota and Iowa).

32. "Indian Housing in the US," RG 220.

33. Indian Housing Act, H.R. 5988 (1982) was sponsored by Representative Morris K. Udall (D-AZ) and introduced on March 30, 1982. Under Title IV: Miscellaneous Provisions, the legislation "[directs] the Secretary [of the Interior] to establish in the Bureau of Indian Affairs an Office of Indian Housing Programs with primary responsibility for administering the programs created by this Act."

34. Indian Housing Act, H.R. 1928 (1983) was sponsored by Representative Morris K. Udall (D-AZ).

35. "About ONAP," U.S. Department of Housing and Urban Development, accessed October 2022, https://www.hud.gov/program_offices/public_indian_housing/ih/codetalk/aboutonap.

36. Mark K. Ulmer, "The Legal Origin and Nature of Indian Housing Authorities and the HUD Indian Housing Programs," *American Indian Law Review* 13, no. 2 (1987/1988): 114.

37. Indian Housing Act, H.R. 3927 (1988).

38. State-recognized tribes can create Indian housing authorities. For example, the North Carolina Indian Housing Authority was established in 1977 by

the state legislature. The North Carolina Indian Housing Authority oversees the following North Carolina state-recognized tribes: Haliwa-Saponi, Coharie, Waccamaw Siouan, Meherrin, Sappony, and Lumbee tribes. The authority additionally administers housing programs for the following state-recognized urban Indian associations within the state of North Carolina: Cumberland County Association for Indian People, Guilford Native American Association, Metrolina Native American Association, and the Triangle Native American Society.

39. See "Indian Housing in the US," RG 220; "American Indian Policy Review Commission: Final Report," Submitted to Congress May 17, 1977, 248.

40. The Snyder Act (1921) authorized appropriations and expenditures on behalf of the federal government, via the Bureau of Indian Affairs, for the administration of American Indian affairs, including "the benefit, care, and assistance of the Indians throughout the United States." The Snyder Act is most invoked as the impetus that created the Indian Health Service and Indian Education Program. For more on the Snyder Act as it relates to Indian housing and federal Indian policy, see chapter 2.

41. Ulmer, "Legal Origin and Nature of Indian Housing Authorities," 120.

42. U.S. Housing and Urban Development, Indian Community Development Block Grant Program, accessed October 2022, https://www.hud.gov/program_offices/public_indian_housing/ih/grants/icdbg.

43. U.S. Housing and Urban Development, Tribal Housing Activities Loan Guarantee Program (Title VI), accessed October 2022, https://www.hud.gov/program_offices/public_indian_housing/ih/homeownership/titlevi.

44. Passed on April 16, 1934, the Johnson-O'Malley Act, as part of the New Deal, authorized federal spending to subsidize education, medical care, and other state-specific services to American Indians through negotiated contracts. This act remains distinct because it was largely meant to address the social service needs of off-reservation Indian people. Today the act is predominantly recognized in terms of Indian education. The act continues to mandate that funds be directed toward Indian students in public schools.

45. Matthew L. M. Fletcher, "Race and American Indian Tribal Nationhood," *Wyoming Law Review* 11, no. 2 (2011): 302.

46. Caryn Trombino, "Changing the Borders of the Federal Trust Obligation: The Urban Indian Health Care Crisis," *Legislation and Public Policy* 8, no. 123 (Fall 2005): 130.

47. Trombino, "Changing the Borders of the Federal Trust Obligation," 132.

5. Indian Homes and Indian Loans

1. Jabs is a pseudonym used to protect the identity of this family.

2. At 27 percent, this number includes American Indian people who identified on census materials both exclusively as American Indian and those who identified as American Indian in combination with one or more races. While 19 percent of individuals who identified as American Indian alone lived in a suburb, 36 percent of those who identified as American Indian in combination with one or more races lived in suburbs in Minnesota.

3. This represents individuals who identified as exclusively American Indian on census forms. Prior to 2000, individuals were only able to record one race on census materials.

4. Throughout this chapter, I use *IHLGP* and *Section 184 Program* interchangeably.

5. In addition to individual members of federally recognized American Indian tribes, Native Alaskans, Alaskan villages, tribes, or tribally designated housing entities are also eligible for the Section 184 Indian Home Loan Guarantee Program. See "Section 184 Indian Home Loan Guarantee Program," Department of Housing and Human Development, accessed March 2020, https://www.hud.gov/section184.

6. See introduction and chapter 1.

7. For more on American Indians and property, see Aileen Morten Robinson, *The White Possessive: Property, Power, and Indigenous Sovereignty* (Minneapolis: University of Minnesota Press, 2015); Breanna Bhandar, *Colonial Lives of Property: Law, Land, and Racial Regimes of Ownership* (Chapel Hill, N.C.: Duke University Press, 2018); Robert Nichols, *Theft Is Property! Dispossession and Critical Theory* (Chapel Hill, N.C.: Duke University Press, 2019).

8. See Alexandra Harmon, *Rich Indians: Native People and the Problem of Wealth in American History* (Chapel Hill: University of North Carolina Press, 2013).

9. Recent quantitative studies of American Indians include Maggie Walter and Chris Andersen, *Indigenous Statistics: A Quantitative Research Methodology* (New York: Routledge, 2013); Carolyn Liebler, "Counting America's First Peoples," *Annals of the American Academy of Political and Social Science* 677, no. 1 (2018): 180–90; Carolyn Liebler, "Homelands and Indigenous Identities in a Multiracial Era," *Social Science Research* 34, no. 4 (2010): 596–609; Carolyn Liebler and Meghan Zacher, "History, Place, and Racial Self-Representation in 21st Century America," *Social Science Research* 57, no. 11 (2016): 211–32.

10. Malinda Maynor Lowery, *Lumbee Indians in the Jim Crow South: Race, Identity, and the Making of a Nation* (Chapel Hill: University of North Carolina Press, 2010), xvi.

11. Patrick McGeehan, "Home Prices Start to Dip, Recalling '90s Slump," *New York Times,* February 3, 2008.

12. Cranston-Gonzalez National Affordable Housing Act, Pub. L. 101-625, 104 Stat. 4097 (1990), as amended (emphasis added).

13. HOME programs were centered on rehabbing owner-occupied housing, providing assistance to low-income home buyers, the creation of new rental housing, and providing financial assistance to low-income renters. The Homeownership and Opportunity for People Everywhere I program (1990–1994) was more squarely centered on homeownership opportunities for low-income families.

14. Katie Jones, Cong. Research Serv., R40118, An Overview of the HOME Investment Partnerships Program (2014), 2.

15. "Section 184 Indian Home Loan Guarantee Program."

16. "Section 184 Indian Home Loan Guarantee Program."

17. "Section 184 Indian Home Loan Guarantee Program." These areas are determined by "participating tribes." The IHLGP may be used anywhere in Alaska, Arizona, California, Colorado, Florida, Idaho, Indiana, Kansas, Maine, Massachusetts, Michigan, Minnesota, Montana, Nevada, New Mexico, North Carolina, North Dakota, Oklahoma, Oregon, South Carolina, South Dakota, Utah, Washington, and Wisconsin. It may be used in select counties in Alabama, Arkansas, Connecticut, Illinois, Iowa, Louisiana, Mississippi, Missouri, Nebraska, New York, Rhode Island, Texas, Virginia, and Wyoming. Ineligible states include Delaware, Georgia, Kentucky, Maryland, New Hampshire, New Jersey, Ohio, Pennsylvania, Tennessee, Vermont, and West Virginia, as well as Washington, D.C.

18. National Congress of American Indians, "The Geospatial Dimensions of Tribal Data," October 2017, https://www.ncai.org/policy-research-center/initiatives/Tribal_Data_Capacity_Geospatial_Data__10_31_2017_FINAL.pdf.

19. NCAI, "Geospatial Dimensions of Tribal Data."

20. U.S. Department of Housing and Urban Development, *The National Homeownership Strategy: Partners in the American Dream* (Washington, D.C., 1995), 3.

21. HUD, *National Homeownership Strategy,* 3.

22. HUD, 50.

23. HUD, 62.

24. Urban Institute Center for Public Finance and Housing, *Assessment of American Indian Housing Needs and Programs: Final Report,* prepared for U.S. Department of Housing and Urban Development (Washington, D.C., 1996), xii–xiii.

25. Urban Institute Center for Public Finance and Housing, *Assessment of American Indian Housing Needs and Programs,* xiii.

26. Native American Housing Assistance and Self-Determination Act, Pub. L. 104-330, 110 Stat. 4016 (1996).

27. Native American Housing Assistance and Self-Determination Act.

28. Report to the Subcommittee on VA, HUD, and Independent Agencies, Committee on Appropriations, House of Representatives, *Native American Housing: Information on HUD's Housing Programs for Native Americans* (Washington, D.C., 1997), 9.

29. Report to the Subcommittee, *Native American Housing,* 9.

30. Report to the Subcommittee, 18.

31. Tribes are also limited in their use of gaming revenue. The Indian Gaming Regulatory Act stipulates that tribes may use gaming revenues for the following: to fund tribal government operations or programs; to provide for the general welfare of the Indian tribe and its members; to promote tribal economic development; to donate to charitable organizations; and to help fund operations of local government agencies. Indian Gaming Regulatory Act, Pub. L. 100-497, 102 Stat. 2467 (1988).

32. For more on the perceived linkages between tribal financial need and recognition of tribal sovereignty, see Jessica Cattelino, "The Double Bind of American Indian Needs-Based Sovereignty," *Cultural Anthropology* 25, no. 2 (May 2010): 235–62.

33. See chapter 4.

34. "Minnesota Chippewa Tribe Finance Corporation," Minnesota Chippewa Tribe, accessed January 2018, www.mctfc.org.

35. Urban Institute Center for Public Finance, *Assessment of American Indian Housing Needs and Programs,* 181–86.

36. "Office of Native American Programs Lender Qualifications," U.S. Department of Housing and Urban Development, accessed October 2022, https://www.hud.gov/program_offices/public_indian_housing/ih/homeownership/184/lender_qual.

37. See introduction and chapter 2 for more on Indian Education Programs, as well as the Snyder Act and the Johnson-O'Malley Act.

38. Graduation rates for Hispanic students increased to 70 percent, rates for Black students increased to 70 percent, rates for multiracial students increased to 72 percent, rates for Pacific Islander/Hawaiian students dropped to 61 percent, rates for Asian students increased to 88 percent, and rates for white students increased to 89 percent. Mary Lynn Smith and Natalie Rademacher, "Minnesota High School Graduation Rates Rise Slightly: Nearly 84 Percent of Minnesota Seniors Graduated in 2019," *Star Tribune,* March 5, 2020, https://

www.startribune.com/minnesota-high-school-graduation-rate-hits-all-time
-high-state-says/568518622/; "Minnesota's Graduation Rates Continue to Rise:
Rates Up for All Student Groups; Gaps between Student Groups Reduced But
Remain," Minnesota Department of Education, accessed March 2021, https://
content.govdelivery.com/accounts/MNMDE/bulletins/2403562.

39. "Common Core of Data: America's Public School," National Center
for Educational Statistics, accessed October 2022, https://nces.ed.gov/ccd/.

40. Urban Institute Center for Public Finance, *Assessment of American
Indian Housing Needs and Programs,* iv.

41. "Economy at a Glance," U.S. Bureau of Labor Statistics, accessed February 2019, http://www.bls.gov/eag/eag.us.htm.

42. American Indians aged twenty and over. In this chapter, *urban* is
defined as Minneapolis and Saint Paul only.

43. The U.S. Census uses the category "not in the labor force" to describe
individuals aged sixteen and over who are not classified as members of the labor
force. This category includes students, homemakers, retirees, seasonal workers
not looking for work, institutionalized persons, and those doing unpaid family work. Please see United States Census Bureau (www.census.gov) for more
information.

44. The Shakopee Mdewakanton Community is widely viewed as being a
suburban geography/community.

45. I analyzed this data using the "homeland" variable at the smallest
geographic unit available for Public Use Microdata Area (PUMA) in IPUMS.
PUMAs generally follow county lines and are broken up into areas of one hundred thousand peoples. Due to the low population density, and to protecting
identity/identifying characteristics, PUMAs are the lowest level of geographic
breakdown available in these more rural regions.

46. This, of course, is complicated when you consider the ownership of
condos or smaller apartment-style units in the city. Generally speaking, when
persons on reservation own their home, they only own the home itself, sometimes passed down from family member to family member, which is much
more affordable than off-reservation housing because ownership is construed
differently.

47. "Minnesota Chippewa Tribe Finance Corporation," Minnesota Chippewa Tribe, accessed January 2018, www.mctfc.org.

48. Urban Institute Center for Public Finance, *Assessment of American
Indian Housing Needs and Programs.*

49. Alvin M. Josephy Jr. Sioux Indian Interview Cassettes, Tape 26, Ayer
Modern MS, Newberry Library, Chicago.

50. This total reflects the total combined percent of single-race and multi-racial American Indian people. This number also includes the Shakopee Mdewakanton Dakota Community.

51. Using the IPUMS "homeland" variable, I determined that in 2000, 61 percent of rural Indian people lived either on or directly adjacent to a reservation.

Conclusion

1. Minneapolis Park and Recreation Board, Resolution 2020-253, 1, accessed October 2022, https://minnesotareformer.com/wp-content/uploads/2020/06/park-board-refuge-resolution.pdf.

2. Michael Omi and Howard Winant, *Racial Formation in the United States* (New York: Routledge, 2014).

INDEX

Housing and Urban Development
Act of 1965, 128
Housing and Urban Development
Act of 1968, 130
Housing Assistance Council /
Northwest Area Foundation, 119,
152
Housing Improvement Program
(BIA), 130, 138, 223n25. *See also*
Bureau of Indian Affairs
Hurd v. Hodge (1948), 86. *See also*
race-based covenants

Ickes, Harold, 79, 82
identity: embedded in place and
property, 7, 46, 66; interconnected with race and citizenship,
22, 47, 90. *See also* American
Indians: identity of; race: racial
self-identification
immigrants, 12, 14, 43, 45, 46–47
Indian: use of term, 19–20, 134,
203n2. *See also* Alaska Natives;
American Indians; Indigenous
peoples
Indian areas, 153–55; use of term,
134. *See also* Indian Home Loan
Guarantee Program; Indian
Housing Authorities
Indian Citizenship Act of 1924
(ICA), 45, 64, 74–76, 215n13,
215n24. *See also* citizenship
Indian Civilization Act of 1819, 71
Indian Community Development
Block Grant Program, 139
Indian Education Programs, 127,
133, 140, 224n40; Anoka-
Hennepin school district, 4; Elk
River, 165; Twin Cities–area,
164–65. *See also* education

Indian Gaming Regulatory Act of
1988, 227n31
Indian Health Board, 128; Minne-
apolis clinic, 1–2
Indian Health Service (IHS), 119,
128, 135, 136, 141–42, 224n40
Indian Home Loan Guarantee
Program (IHLGP), 138, 142,
143–63, *154,* 175–79, 225n5
Indian Housing Act of 1982, 223n33
Indian Housing Act of 1988, 123,
132–33, 134, 159
Indian Housing Authorities (IHAs),
129, 132–33, 135, 137–38, 139,
141, 153, 223n38; use of term,
134. *See also* Tribal Housing
Authority
Indian Housing Block Grant
Program, 137–38, 139, 158
Indian Housing Committee, 123,
124
Indian New Deal, 78–80. *See also*
Indian Reorganization Act of
1934; Johnson-O'Malley Act of
1934
Indian places: use of term, 17–18,
19. *See also* placemaking; places
Indian policies, federal, 14, 32, 34,
48, 78; assimilation objectives, 41,
44–45; creating exclusion, 66–67;
as tool of settler colonialism, 21,
136. *See also* housing, federal
policies, federal Indian policies
entangled with; treaties/treaty-
making; tribes: sovereignty of;
trust responsibility/relationship;
and individual laws and policies
Indian Relocation Act of 1956, 99
Indian Relocation Program. *See*
Relocation Program

Kasey R. Keeler, an enrolled member of the Tuolumne Band of Me-Wuk Indians and direct descendant of the Citizen Band of Potawatomi, is assistant professor in the Department of Civil Society and Community Studies and the American Indian Studies Program at the University of Wisconsin.